D0959561

# EDGEWORK

# EDGEWORK

## EXPLORING THE PSYCHOLOGY
## OF DISEASE

*A Manual for Healing
Beyond Diet & Fitness*

RONALD L. PETERS, MD, MPH

Blue Dolphin Publishing

Copyright © 2003 Ronald L. Peters
All rights reserved.

Published by Blue Dolphin Publishing, Inc.
P.O. Box 8, Nevada City, CA 95959
Orders: 1-800-643-0765
Web: www.bluedolphinpublishing.com

ISBN: 1-57733-116-8


Library of Congress Cataloging-in-Publication Data

Peters, Ronald L., 1944-
    Edgework : exploring the psychology of disease : a manual for healing
beyond diet & fitness / Ronald L. Peters.
        p. cm.
Includes index.
    ISBN 1-57733-116-8 (pbk. : alk. paper)
    1. Medicine, Psychosomatic. 2. Mind and body therapies. 3. Sick—
Psychology. I. Title.

RC49.P45 2003
616.08—dc21
                                                                    200300316


Cover design: Jeff Case

Printed in the United States of America

10    9    8    7    6    5    4    3    2    1

# CONTENTS

# ACKNOWLEDGMENTS

The evolution of this book parallels my own psychological and spiritual growth and is based on the proverbial wisdom, "Physician, Heal Thyself." I have learned to use the perplexing truth that "consciousness creates reality" as a tool to see myself reflected in the thousands of patients that have come to me over the past thirty years. I have listened to them uncover the psychological wounds that contribute to their physical ones. They have shown me that disease is the body's way of healing itself. And it is to each of them that I offer my love and deepest gratitude.

My beloved wife Kathie is a profound teacher and companion for me who has not only encouraged my writing over the years but has also shown me to honor my emotions as well as my intellect. Our relationship is the fertile ground for the growth of love for each other and ourselves. I am also grateful to the artistic insight of Rita and the playful ways of Lucio who have shown me the wonderful side of parenting.

I want to thank Alan Reder for contributing substantial writing, re-writing and editing for this project. Alan is a superb writer whose words reflect a stirring balance between intellect and heart. Carolyne Ruck also provided insight, commentary and editing to parts of this book and I thank her too.

I am deeply grateful to Paul Clemens, publisher at Blue Dolphin Publishing, for his encouragement and support in bringing this book to press. His dedication to helping people grow and heal through literature is an inspiration.

I also want to acknowledge my appreciation to my friends Richard James, Chris Townson, Caroline Rollinson, Leslie James,

Terrance Camilleri, Nancy Arthur, Val and Jeannette Logan, Phil Nerone, Dragomir Vukovich, Lori Gilmore, William Terrien, Betty Toohey, Raquel Morgan, Raleigh Pinskey, Hatjey and Jed Cossonay, Carley and Ken Henius, Renee Hubbs, Dean McComber, Clara McComber, Doug and Dorothy Turner, Dr. Franklin Ross, and Linda Neuwerth, who have shown me day to day personal growth amidst the laughter and tears of living life fully.

Above all I am grateful to God for my life and the opportunity to do His work. I have been blessed by many spiritual teachers, including my patients, for I have learned that God is everywhere and always ready to love and guide me in my life. I am especially thankful for the timeless guidance of Maya and Mafu.

Lastly, I want to acknowledge the many doctors and health practitioners who intuitively know that healing is ultimately an act of consciousness based on love of self and love of others.

# INTRODUCTION

*Come to the edge Life said.*
*They said: We are afraid.*
*Come to the edge Life said.*
*They came. It pushed them . . .*
*And they flew.*
                    Guillaume Apollinaire (1870-1918)

**The mind controls the body.** We have heard about this paradigm-shifting notion time and time again in the last half of the
twentieth century. Research in immunology has contributed to
dozens of books telling us about improved immunity based on
positive states of mind and, conversely, reduced immune function
due to negative states of consciousness. Physicians and psychologists
have told us about the hostile aspects of Type A behavior and the
epidemic of heart disease that plagues our society. Many other
researchers have spoken, a bit more cautiously, about features of the
cancer prone personality. Anxiety and depression contribute to
numerous other illnesses, and continue to afflict up to one-quarter of
the American population. Books have been written on the psychosomatic aspects of common diseases like asthma, hypertension, ulcerative colitis, peptic ulcers, diabetes, just to mention a few. Yet none
have stated the essence of the mind/body issue as succinctly as the
great psychoanalyst Dr. Franz Alexander, when he wrote: "The fact
that the mind rules the body is, in spite of its neglect by biology and
medicine, the most fundamental fact which we know about the
process of life. . . ."

1

But in spite of this outpouring of information on the mind/body relationship, little has changed in the doctor's office to reflect this new understanding. Doctors still devote most of their time trying to find out what is wrong with the body, and patients still try to get rid of their symptoms with the latest offerings from the drug industry. Many of us take vitamins and minerals, try to exercise and relax more, perhaps meditate occasionally, but really little has changed, and the problems in health care continue on. Indeed, paradigms shift slowly as they bear the weight of institutional, social and personal belief systems.

Based on my twenty years of holistic family practice, I too have learned that the origins of most physical disease are within conscious-ness—the body is the messenger of the conflicts, sustained fears, suppressed emotional traumas, disturbed patterns of thinking, and other imbalances that lie within the conscious and unconscious mind. I have learned this by listening to thousands of patients tell the stories that preceded the onset of their illness. I have heard again and again of childhood patterns of neglect, smothering control, abandon-ment, and emotional, physical and sexual abuse. I have heard of the failed relationships, years of marital conflict, and the pain of loneli-ness. I have heard about decades of unfulfilling employment, foiled personal creativity and the quiet desperation of a slowly dying spirit. I have heard about relentless anxiety, depression, denied emotions, destructive beliefs, hopelessness, helplessness, "giving up," and an endless variety of recurrent stresses.

Most importantly, I have seen patient after patient backtrack into consciousness and find the dis-ease within the mind that precipitated the dis-ease in the body. The answers may not come quickly as many issues are hidden in the shadow, or unconscious mind, but they do come and the results of such personal in-depth healing are transfor-mational. I have seen cancer, multiple sclerosis, colitis, hepatitis, high blood pressure, heart disease, depression, and all types of chronic and often "incurable" diseases go into remission or quiescence. These are the reasons I have written *Edgework*.

*Edgework* refers to the edge between what you know about yourself and what you do not know. Dis-ease of any kind is the body's way of getting your attention and inviting this self-exploration, thereby offering true healing. The path may be scary, as change itself is scary for most of us. It is easy to understand what the noted English poet, W. H. Auden, meant when he wrote: "We would rather be ruined than changed; we would rather die in our dread than climb the cross of the moment and let our illusions die."

The idea of *Edgework* came to me during technical rock climbing when I discovered the exhilaration of moving past my fears and expanding my self-confidence and self-understanding. I realized that fear was my friend, not my enemy, as it prepared me for the pulse of adventure, both on the mountain and within myself. Later on, as I listened to my patients, year after year, I realized that they were thrust to the edge by their illness. As fear gripped them, they too felt powerless, but as they began to understand the immense resources and wisdom of the mind/body, they would begin the journey toward healing. Illness had become their mountain, and climbing required courage of the highest order.

In this book, I have reviewed the research and concepts of mind/body healing with an eye towards the practical and personal application of this revolutionary shift in medicine. I present the power of thought as it coalesces into attitude and belief. I also introduce the concept of **emotional wound healing**, a process as natural and essential to health, as physical wound healing. Using this concept, the emotional challenges and stresses that we all encounter in life can be seen as the earliest opportunities for psychological healing, and they become markers on the path toward health, or illness. Therefore, by using the principles of *Edgework* you can prevent disease as well as help to reverse it.

Stress management can become a new experience as the numerous mental and physical signs of stress are redefined as signals for self-exploration. Using the tools of *Edgework,* you can find the deeper reasons for the fears and angers that clutter your pathway, before they become symptoms or medical diagnoses.

Most importantly, you will learn about, or reaffirm, the fundamental principles of self-responsibility for your experience. Self-responsibility is another paradigm shift and potentially society disruptive concept for this New Millennium. This approach will move you from the hapless victim of dis-ease to an explorer within the frontiers of your own consciousness—within the awesome, natural power and wisdom of the mind/body.

This book is for everyone who has dis-ease of any kind. It is especially for those who have serious or "incurable" illness, which creates a powerful motivation to learn about self and make much needed changes if they so choose. I present numerous stories of patients who have used these tools successfully. This book is also for busy doctors who want to use the principles of mind/body healing to complement other therapies for their patients.

Certainly we do not have all the answers about the complex nature of the body/mind, but we do know enough to get started on the right track. *Edgework* explains the essential features of maintaining or restoring health within consciousness, and it offers step-by-step exercises that are designed to make the concepts of health a personal reality.

With Love,
Ronald Peters, M.D.

# 1

# THRUST

# TO THE EDGE

*To the ordinary man, everything that happens to him is either
a curse or a blessing. To a warrior, each thing is a challenge.*

Carlos Castaneda

*Security is mostly a superstition. It does not exist in nature, nor
do the children of men as a whole experience it. Avoiding
danger is no safer in the long run than outright exposure.
Life is either a daring adventure or nothing.*

Helen Keller

"I'm sorry, but your tests show that you have cancer." Solemn
words like these echo in our country's medical offices and hospitals
thousands of times each day. They vibrate in patients' hearts and
minds with shuddering intensity. For most, these words are a death
sentence. In nearly everyone, they awaken the greatest fear of all, the
fear of dying. They are words that thrust a person to the edge, the
edge between life and death.

The first question patients usually ask after getting this bad news
is "Why me?" Experts can only offer the vaguest answers to this
question. Cigarette smoking, diet, some unfortunate genes—all may
be factors, but most often the doctor has to admit, "we don't know."

"What can I do?" patients wonder next. And the doctor usually
responds with chemotherapy, radiation, surgery, or some combination of the same, options that make people shiver with fear and

5

uncertainty. They remember friends or relatives who received these aggressive, painful, and often unsuccessful therapies. They feel shorn of hope, not only of surviving their disease but even of having another "normal" day.

Cancer is perhaps the most dramatic push to the edge. But many other medical diagnoses are received with gloom, and for good reason. Like cancer, heart disease and diabetes can signal the edge between a healthy life and one wrought with pain and suffering. Migraine headaches, ulcers, chronic fatigue, arthritis, depression, multiple sclerosis, Parkinson's disease, and colitis may also siphon life of its freedom and vitality and fill it with discomfort and limitation. Medications may partially relieve some symptoms, but rarely do they restore full health.

The specter of chronic and terminal disease looms over us all. Although our culture does a better job than it used to of stressing preventive measures such as improved diet and exercise, the health-care system still emphasizes the production of new drug and surgical therapies to treat diseases after they appear. But on both the preventive and treatment fronts, medicine is still missing the boat, in my opinion. After twenty years of carefully listening to and observing patients in my practice of holistic medicine, I can say without doubt that some of the most important factors in both preventing and treating disease are some of the most overlooked, even by my holistic colleagues. I am speaking of our thoughts and, even more importantly, our emotions. In conventional medicine, these powerful aspects of consciousness are all but ignored. In holistic medicine, we give lip service to the holy trinity of mind, body, and spirit, but it is the rare practitioner who practices the full implications of that philosophy.

It's not as if doctors are unaware that thoughts and emotions play an important part in healing. Clinicians with any experience on the job at all know that patients with a better attitude are more likely to heal, and most doctors have seen that the so-called "will to live" can extend life in patients with even the most dire long-term prognoses. Considerable research indicates that emotional factors can play a critical role in the onset of disease and may be the missing link explaining some "miraculous" cures; we'll examine some of this evidence later in the book. But few in the healthcare system have followed these leads to their logical conclusion: the integration of psychological *healing* into bodily healing.

In the following pages, we'll explore how this integration can be accomplished with a series of recommendations and exercises. I call this approach Edgework because it pushes us to the edge of our psyche, the boundary between the known and unknown parts of ourselves. Through Edgework, we get to know ourselves better, by examining the emotional feelings and memories we find uncomfortable, the challenges we have resisted, the career and relationship hurdles that seem too high to hurdle, the spiritual emptiness that makes our troubles so hard to comprehend.

Another reason that Edgework is such an apt name for the psychological side of healing is that it deals with our *growing edge*— the barriers we have to push through to become more capable, satisfied, and fulfilled. Invariably, I find that patients with serious illness are flat up against pressing personal challenges in their lives or have deep emotional wounds that they are failing to confront. Does this prove anything about the source of their illness? Of course not. From the moment they take their first breath, all human beings have a growing edge and few take on their issues without at least the occasional retreat. There are personality profiles that do seem to be associated with serious illness, but let's put that matter aside for the moment. Many people who are relatively healthy can identify with the same kinds of psychological issues that the seriously ill face.

But what is different for the seriously ill is the urgency. They are running out of time to deal with their issues. In some cases, the survival value of doing the work is obvious. For instance, the heart patient who is leading a stressful life needs to create at least some islands of serenity in his existence or he may hurry himself to death. In other cases, the disease makes very clear that when it comes to personal growth, there is no time like the present. For the cancer patient with a poor prognosis, why keep putting off the challenge of improving your personal relationships? Why not strip your life down to the things you like and then go for even more of what makes you happy?

The interesting thing is that some patients who take charge of their lives and begin taking the emotional risks they've avoided up to now do in fact appear to defeat their diseases. Others survive much longer than any medical expert would expect. Medical literature abounds with such cases. I am not saying that Edgework cures diseases normally thought to be incurable. But I am saying that these tools, when used in a dedicated manner, can substantially increase the chances for healing. Furthermore, I will say that psychological and personal growth always enhances the life of those who do it, whether their physical lives are extended or not. And sometimes, the life is so enhanced that the body and the person inhabiting it seem to forget that they are sick, *in other words, they become well.* We will revisit this topic again when we examine the difference between curing and healing.

## The Beginnings of Disease—
## Where Thoughts and Emotions Fit

The way that most chronic diseases such as heart disease and cancer begin is not well understood. We do understand that certain behaviors and conditions are risk factors, but those only predict the *likelihood* of someone becoming ill. They are not sole causes. Take lung cancer, for example. Smoking is an obvious risk factor. But not everyone who smokes gets lung cancer. Indeed, most smokers do not, and some smokers outlive most people with so-called healthy lifestyles. So what makes the critical difference? Genes? Other environmental factors such as air pollution? Diet? Exercise habits?

Medical researchers currently feel that people become ill with serious diseases through a complex interaction of factors such as genes, lifestyle choices, environmental conditions, and so forth. But thoughts and emotions are rarely considered in this equation. My clinical experience suggests that thoughts and emotions may be the most underrated factor in the causation of disease and may also be that elusive factor that tips the balance. In a 1979 study, researchers assessed the childhood, marriage, and job stability of subjects as well as their plans for the future and recent losses of significant others. They found that this information was one to two times as important as the subject's smoking history in predicting whether they had lung disease. This doesn't mean that smoking is innocent in lung cancer. But it does indicate that emotional factors may lay the foundation for smoking to do its greatest harm. This is a critical insight. It means that to ignore the mental/emotional factors is to not only misunderstand illness but also to deny ourselves some of the most powerful and readily available tools for treating it.

Emphasizing mental/emotional factors is a radical point of view in modern medicine, but if we consider the history of doctoring worldwide, it is far more radical to ignore the role of thoughts and emotions. In many other cultures around the world, psychological, social, and spiritual traditions have long been integrated with health practices. In non-literate cultures since the beginning of human history, healing of serious illness is normally the job of a shaman, who is also the spiritual leader of the community. Shamans earn their position because of their ability to communicate with the spiritual world on behalf of their people. In these cultures, disease is always seen as some sort of disharmony with the cosmic order. Common diagnoses include relationship troubles, social isolation from the community, violations of community ethics, ill feelings such as jealousy or greed, or insufficient contact with the spirits. In shamanistic cultures, "patients" are less important as individuals than they are as part of larger social and spiritual consciousness. Still, the shaman treats them with methods not unlike modern psychotherapy such as group sharing, dream analysis, hypnosis, guided imagery, and psychodrama. These techniques are designed to uncover unconscious conflicts and raise them to the surface so they can be resolved and released. In that way, they aren't much different from the exercises you'll encounter at the end of this book. The idea of seeing a person's illness as merely a symptom of a tear in the community's social fabric may be foreign to us. However, consider the case of a person in an unhappy marriage who becomes seriously ill. It is easier for us to understand that a problem that begins in the dynamic of the relationship could manifest in the illness of one partner.

In Western terms, traditional Chinese medicine is considered a much more highly evolved medical system than shamanistic healing. But like shamans, traditional Chinese doctors also see disease as disharmony in the patient's universe in all its dimensions, including thoughts and emotions. Chinese medical books catalog unbalanced emotional states and associate them with various physical disorders.

It is true that if you were to go to a traditional Chinese doctor today, you would be treated primarily with physical methods such as herbs, diet, and acupuncture. But it's also true that much of the richness of original Chinese medicine has been lost over the centuries.

Ayurveda, the traditional medical system of India, may be even older than Chinese medicine. It is considered to be the first healthcare philosophy to approach diseases as natural, observable phenomena rather than the work of demons and other supernatural forces. Like Chinese medicine, which it influenced, Ayurveda sees ill thoughts and emotions as leading to physical illness; unlike traditional Chinese doctors, Ayurvedic physicians commonly prescribe methods for mental/emotional healing along with dietary and other lifestyle changes.

Interestingly, our own medical ideas have their roots in Ayurveda, which influenced Persian and then Greek thinking about health. The Hippocratic writings (probably written by several authors although they are attributed to a famous physician named Hippocrates who lived around 400 BC) represented the height of Greek medical philosophy; like Ayurveda, they asserted that disease was caused by natural phenomena that could be studied scientifically and treated rationally with natural therapies and healthy living. The Hippocratic books emphasized that health was determined by an interaction of mind, body, and the environment, the latter including personal lifestyle, air and water quality, diet, and topography of the land. Modern Western medicine grew from these ideas, but somehow became focused almost entirely on physical causes and cures and complete, passive reliance of the patient on the physician. Such concepts as prevention, patients' responsibility for their own health, and the natural healing intelligence of the body—common to Hippocratic, Ayurveda, and traditional Chinese medicine—still have almost no place in modern Western medicine despite its recent efforts to incorporate them. But I believe this will soon change, because ever since the holistic revolution of the 1960s and '70s, our culture has been actively relearning the health wisdom of the ancients.

## Not Just a Therapy But an Adventure

To me, Edgework is more than a promising new approach to healing, more than an adjunct to body-oriented healthcare, more than a way of accessing the inner wisdom of our bodies. It is also the greatest adventure we can pursue—the adventure of self-discovery and, eventually, self-realization. Edgework will challenge you to expand your sense of responsibility, not only for your health, but also for all of what you experience in your life. As a direct consequence of expanding that sense of responsibility, you will begin to assume the personal power that is your birthright. You will also grow in your spiritual understanding because explorations into the inner world of the mind inevitably converge with the realm of the spirit.

The inner adventure is greater than any challenge presented by the physical world. However, the biggest physical challenges do present an apt metaphor for Edgework. In my case, I draw many of my insights from my experiences with mountaineering and technical rock climbing. Shortly after medical school, I met a unique man by the name of Doug Robinson, an elite rock climber who had been featured in a cover story in *National Geographic* and who had made first ascents on the majestic granite walls of Yosemite. I was impressed both by Doug's climbing skills and his passion to push past the limits of his own experience. He lived in the rugged splendor of the high Sierra Nevada Mountains, sleeping on the rock at night and then forging routes on previously unclimbed rock faces the next day. I would come to learn that as he inched his way up a vertical rock face, he was simultaneously inching into the unknown realms of his inner self.

On my first climbing trip with Doug, we hiked into a pristine area of the Eastern Sierra known as Palisades Glacier. We made the day-long hike to a small lake, arriving at about sunset. I could see the glacier nestled at the feet of a half-circle of vertical granite peaks standing like sentinels to the timeless beauty of nature. As we set up our base camp, we began to talk about the next day's climbing. I had no experience with rock climbing and my mind was filled with disturbing images of tiny climbers clinging to one of those huge granite faces thousands of feet above the ground. Sitting around the campfire later that evening, Doug oriented me to the various tools and techniques of climbing. As I listened, I felt fearful and inadequate. Would I have the guts to make a difficult move on the rock? Would I have to turn back because of my fear? Would I be strong enough to climb a series of pitches (a pitch is the amount of climbing that can be done with one full length of rope tied between climbers)? As these thoughts and feelings welled up within me, I tried to suppress them, because I didn't want Doug to see my weaknesses.

Doug's explanations were meant to reassure me about the many safety features of rock climbing. The rope is secured to a nylon strap that is tied around the climbers' waists. The knots are carefully selected and secure. The leader, in this case Doug himself, climbs first, placing special nuts securely into cracks and crevasses in the rock. (Doug's techniques relied on the use of removable "nuts" instead of the traditional bolts that are left behind, permanently defacing the rock.) He then attaches a carribiner (a hinged, metal, oval-shaped device) to each nut through which he threads his climbing rope. The second climber holds the rope from below (holding the rope for the other climber is called "belaying"); if the leader falls, he only drops a short distance from the last nut. For the second climber, it is even safer. If I should fall, I wouldn't drop any distance at all, Doug told me; instead, I would dangle at the same spot until I could secure my footing to try again. But Doug's patient assurances didn't allay my fears. Regardless of how safe climbing was designed to be, scary thoughts continued to pop into my mind and I continued to push them back down.

I still remember my experience on our first pitch the next day as if it had just happened. With me on belay from below, Doug climbed an eighty-foot vertical face with the ease of a squirrel scampering up a tree. As I started up the wall, he sat on the top, protecting me from falling with the rope secured around his waist on belay. The first sixty feet went well; I felt strong and confident as I made move after move up the granite. My mind was alert and my body properly tensed as I surveyed the minute architecture of the rock for places to grab a hold. Of course, I did my best to avoid a direct look back down.

But then, near the top, I reached an area that seemed to me smooth in all directions. I was standing on a ledge about one half inch wide and there wasn't an obvious handhold above me for the final move to where Doug sat. In the language of rock climbing, I was facing a "5.7" move (degrees of difficulty are measured numerically, with a 5.14 considered the most difficult). Fear and doubt began to consume me. With my knees shaking, I broke out in a sweat; my body seemed paralyzed. A memory flashed through my mind of a time I had fallen from a tree. I feared I would fall and injure myself, or have to be hauled up the last ten feet.

Finally, after a moment that seemed like hours, I focused on Doug, who was calling down guidance from above. He told me to take some deep breaths and then center my full attention on a small rocky prominence a few feet above me. As I redirected my mind from my fear to the moment at hand, it cleared and the fear dissipated. The adrenaline flowing in my veins heightened my senses and I saw with sharpened clarity the chiseled details of the black and white speckled granite. I noticed two small handholds, the closest just slightly beyond my reach. Suddenly, I was ready to move, my body pulsing with new energy. As I concentrated my attention further, my knees stopped shaking. And then I went for it, grabbing the small ledge and pulling myself to the top, where I joined Doug with a huge sigh of relief. I was exhilarated. Moments before, I had felt helpless and weak. Now, I felt capable and strong, and knew that this feeling was closer to the real me, the person I could be always if I confronted all my challenges with the same intent to overcome them.

I pondered that episode for the rest of that day and for a long time afterwards. I realized I had reached a boundary within myself, marked by doubt and fear in my abilities. The granite edge on the cliff had forced me to confront this boundary with an urgency not found in ordinary life. Spurred by Doug's directions, I had crossed that boundary and replaced fear with simple awareness and careful intention. I had seen how stress grips and controls the body, and how refocusing can release it. I had faced risk and summoned courage. In short, I had grown that morning and become more of my true self.

## Mary's Story

Although I was a novice that day on the granite walls of the Sierra Nevada, my experience turned out to be a perfect initiation into the "rites" of mountaineering. I have read many books written by mountain climbers. Woven into every account of the delicate maneuvering between cracks and crevasses, the ice falls and rock walls, the storms and freezing weather is the parallel account of inner mountaineering. For every challenge and danger thrown into the climber's path by nature, there are analogues in the cracks and crevasses of the mind—fears, doubts, anger, frustration, grueling fatigue, and disappointments. Illness must be endured on the stark slopes, and sometimes death.

As dramatic as the emotional demands of mountaineering are, I began to notice similar demands played out every day in my medical office. I listened to my patients talking about the fears, doubts, frustrations, and disappointments that preceded the diagnosis of their illness. I saw them paralyzed by fear, doubt, and apathy. But I also saw many of them summon the courage to stop seeing themselves as weak, powerless victims and gradually accept the challenge of their illness as if it was a mountain calling to be climbed. And, I saw them climb the mountain, facing the dangers and discovering the personal power required for the work.

One such patient—we'll call her Mary—came to my office about two months after having had a bilateral mastectomy for cancer of the breast. Mary was complaining of persistent fatigue that prevented her from resuming her work in her insurance agency. Her doctor couldn't find any reason for her malaise and assured her everything was okay, but the problem continued.

I began my consultation by asking Mary about her history with cancer. Fifty years old at the time, she told me she had observed a lump in her left armpit for many years prior to her diagnosis, but thought it was only a hair follicle. One day, she noticed that it had gotten larger. Her doctors first gave her antibiotics for the lump, thinking that it was probably an infected lymph gland. When the lump failed to respond, they scheduled her for excision and biopsy. The excised node showed adenocarcinoma and she was immediately scheduled for surgery to remove her left breast. The right breast also had a lump, presumed to be cancer as well, and so it too was removed, along with lymph nodes from both armpits. Post-surgical tests confirmed that the left breast and axilla (armpit) nodes were cancerous. Surprisingly, the right breast showed only a benign tumor, so it had been taken unnecessarily; the nodes in the right axilla also tested normal. However, because the cancer in the left breast had spread to her nodes, Mary was treated with six months of chemotherapy and also a course of radiation therapy.

I asked Mary about her emotions regarding her ordeal with cancer. She said she had been a little apprehensive about the diagnosis and treatment of her disease, but felt there was no other option. After all, her mother had had breast cancer and she felt it was "probably hereditary." She said all of this with a matter-of-fact tone, like a newscaster. She said she did worry that her cancer would recur in some other part of her body, as it had for her mother, but related this too with little emotion. I noted to myself how unlikely was this tone for a life-threatening situation, but continued my interview without commenting on it.

Mary also had rheumatoid arthritis, a diagnosis made some ten years earlier. Her joint pain was confined mainly to her hands, and in the past few months it had intensified considerably. In my experience, rheumatoid arthritis often occurs in people who have suppressed anger over a number of years. I also noted this to myself without mentioning it to Mary at the time.

As I always do towards the end of my interview, I asked Mary about the stressful experiences in her life, beginning in her childhood. Without hesitation, she mentioned that her mother was "strict" and that they didn't get along. Her mother "didn't love me" and they "never hugged." She was made to work at any early age and remembered picking ferns for local florists at the age of five. She said her father was a "turkey," had a drinking problem, and was generally "hard to live with." As a child, she "had no friends." She admitted at this point that it was hard for her to express her feelings.

After she married, at the age of 21, Mary began raising a family while teaching at the local state college and then working at an insurance agency. She said she struggled for two years after her mother died in 1984. Her arthritis pain intensified during this time, to the extent that she had to stop her work. She acknowledged feeling an inner emotional uneasiness, and occasional turmoil, during this period that she couldn't define very well.

I then asked Mary about stresses during the years preceding her cancer diagnosis, because emotional patterns and clues often make themselves obvious in the pre-diagnosis phase. Sure enough, Mary stated that the demands in her life had steadily intensified in that period. She had been continuing her insurance work from home, feeling "a constant push" in her business. At the same time, her family demands were competing for her attention. In particular, her daughter was making arrangements to marry and establish her own family. Mary said she was driven by "high goals" during this time and worked 12 to 14 hours daily for over two years straight!

As I finished my session with Mary, I listed her diagnoses in her chart notes. I then reviewed with her the patterns I saw in her life, emphasizing how her mind can weaken her immune system, thereby permitting cancer to develop (we'll examine the research that points in this direction later in the book). Carefully, I suggested to her the following issues:

- Lack of self-esteem and self-worth arising from a mother and father who were incapable of showing her love.
- Tremendous repressed anger and pain resulting from a childhood in which the love and nurturing she was entitled to were denied.
- The development of a personality that suppressed all emotions later in life because of intense early childhood pain.
- A workaholic personality that avoided emotional pains by working very hard and sought acceptance/love by what she produced in life.
- Extreme self-judgment—i.e. feeling that she was never "good enough."
- An intensifying of emotional stress prior to her cancer such that she recurrently felt "I can't take it any more." (Cancer patients consistently say something similar, in my experience.)

In sum, I suggested to Mary, her immune system had acquiesced to the pressure of her stresses, both conscious and unconscious, and offered her a way out of her pain—death. My evaluation clearly struck a chord in Mary. As I was offering it, I could feel the emotions welling up in her and soon tears began to flow. Mary knew on a deep, inner level the truth of what I had said. The message was much more convincing than what she had thought about her illness in the past. "I want to heal my pain and live again," she sobbed.

After designing a program of dietary changes and nutritional supplements to boost her immune system, I referred Mary to a good friend of mine who is a psychotherapist and focuses mainly on inner child work (see Chapter 9). Eager to move through her emotional issues now, Mary was attentive, cooperative, and participatory in therapy, which always bodes well for the patient. She did her homework, involved her husband and family as the therapist urged, and made great progress. At one point, she rented sexy movies to watch with her delighted husband. Eventually she quit her insurance job—she had admitted in therapy that her work bored her silly—and she and her husband toured the USA on new motorcycles.

As of this writing, five years have passed without Mary's cancer recurring. But regardless of her medical condition, she is living more joyfully than ever before. Life is no longer a list of tedious things to do. She listens to the soft voice of her feelings and honors it. Her illness moved her to the edge and she accepted the challenge. She uncovered inner tools she had never used before, and expanded her personal power as a result. In effect, she allowed her illness to become her teacher, and it taught her how to love life.

Throughout this book, we will examine many other cases where patients have expressed long-denied emotional pain, looked carefully at their beliefs about themselves and others, sought greater satisfaction in their work and relationship lives, or made other courageous life changes, and then recovered from life-threatening illnesses. Once again, I want to make clear that I do not promise, or even believe, that emotional changes will automatically cure serious diseases. There are many variables in the healing process. But anecdotes such as these occur frequently in medicine, not just in my practice. Clearly, thoughts and emotions, both conscious and unconscious, are powerful forces in the body that can be either harmful or helpful depending on how those forces are directed.

Mary's recovery, as with other such cases, is the product of many factors, just like the origins of her disease. It did not result from psychological healing alone. The surgery, chemotherapy, and radiation helped, buying her time to do the inner work that her illness "offered" her. The diet and food supplement program built up her bodily defenses, helping to keep the cancer at bay and preparing the ground for the psychotherapy to be as successful as possible. And more important than any particular form of psychological therapy was Mary's courage and willingness to make changes. She braved the hurtful memories that stood in the way of her learning more about herself. She allowed herself to feel the pain that she had stored away for most of her life. Most importantly, she took hold of her life instead of allowing herself to be passively pulled through it. She decided to do what brought her joy, and amazingly enough, it did.

The work I did with Mary, and the work I recommended she do with the psychotherapist, is not accepted practice in modern medicine. Although most experts recognize that the "mind" can affect the "body" (this is actually a false dichotomy that I will correct later in the book), this has not been integrated into conventional medicine. As a result, our illnesses are given no meaning within the context of our lives. We feel victimized by them, as if stricken by some accidental quirk of fate. Whatever its tentative recognition of mental/emotional factors, medicine is a long ways from considering disease as a personally crafted opportunity for healing emotional pain and setting life on a different, more fulfilling course.

This is not something for which I blame my colleagues. Physicians are trained to focus on the physical body exclusively and even in that realm, they are only trained in the use of chemical medications and surgery. They are not taught in medical school how to help patients improve their nutritional status and they learn nothing about herbal medicines that are safer and cheaper than drugs. They receive very little psychotherapy training as well (although wise medical professors will mention the importance of a healing "bedside manner.")

I take comfort, though, in the evidence that is mounting on behalf of a new, more holistic approach. In the course of this book, we will look at many studies whose results seem to support my statements about the medical importance of emotions, thoughts, and positive life changes. None of these studies constitute absolute proof although they are compelling and clearly point the way for additional research. But as a physician, my duty is to treat. My patients can't wait until all the results are in. In my clinical experience, treating my patients' psychological and spiritual selves along with their bodies has been extremely fruitful. In addition, unlike most conventional medical approaches, it follows the Hippocratic oath: it does no harm.

# 2

# THE STRESS
# SYSTEM—FROM
# LIABILITY TO ASSET

*The reason worry kills more people than work is that more
people worry than work.*

Robert Frost

The huge impact that consciousness makes on health became
clear to me while studying medicine at UCLA Medical School from
1966-70, but not as a result of anything I was studying in class.
During my junior year, I lived in a small apartment above a carpet
store in Westwood Village, the business community located at the
edge of the UCLA medical campus. Each morning as I walked to
class, I passed by a storefront operated by the Maharishi Mahesh
Yogi's Transcendental Meditation (TM) organization. Plastered all
over the windows were posters with charts and graphs showing the
effects of TM on the body. Everything seemed to improve with
meditation. Blood pressure dropped. Correct body weight was easier
to maintain. Meditators had less muscle tension, fewer diseases, less
stress, better memory.

In my medical classes, I was learning to treat the same problems
the charts and graphs addressed with drugs and surgery. But the TM
claims spoke to something I had been musing about for some time—

that there was more to human consciousness than what my society's educational system had showed me so far, and that this "more" probably affected physical well-being, too. Although the human mind was still largely unexplored territory to Western scientists, books I read by spiritual "researchers" spoke of spiritual and mystical realms inside us. These realms, the authors wrote, offered those who explored them awareness of a cosmic unity and deep understanding of the human experience. These ideas matched my own intuitive sense about life. Somewhere in these higher levels of human nature, I felt, there was much to be learned about the meaning of both health and disease.

The pull for me to study human consciousness was so strong that I began to feel that my medical studies included two curricula. The one taught by my professors at UCLA covered biochemistry, physiology, and the like. It focused on how to repair the body if it should break down, not on how to keep it whole in the first place. It was extremely organized, rigid, and serious, and you couldn't be late for class.

The other curriculum seemed to be authored by a voice I heard inside my own mind. This inner professor didn't care much about outlines and logical presentations, and whenever I showed up was right on time. The next lesson often popped into my mind quite unexpectedly, spurred perhaps by something I was reading or even a random thought. But the lessons did seem to follow a highly organized plan in that they came one right after another, just like any course in a "real" school. Clearly, this teacher wanted me to get the message about the awesome power of our consciousness, power that could enhance health or destroy it depending upon our mental, emotional and spiritual states. One more thing: this unseen professor was one of those rare teachers who always sparked my enthusiasm. I have to admit that I couldn't always say the same about my UCLA classes.

Driven to learn as much as I could about human consciousness, I devoured book after book by people like Meister Eckhardt, Carl Jung, G. I. Gurdjieff, Abraham Maslow, and Chogyam Trungpa. After I completed my medical training, I began practicing in pretty much the conventional way, just as my medical professors had taught me to do. It worked fairly well, but not great. There were many problems for which I could only offer symptom relief with little possibility of a cure. There were also a lot of diseases that were incurable, like cancer and multiple sclerosis. And, my other inner curriculum kept me wondering if I was really using the right tools. I felt a longing to do more for my patients than simply offer symptom-relieving drugs.

I continued to be pulled to classes on meditation and psychology. I attended EST, went to India to study with gurus, and read more books. Then in 1986, everything I had been learning came together while studying with a spiritual teacher here in the U.S. This teacher felt that releasing the emotional pains from childhood was just as important for a person's spiritual growth as meditation. He also explained the process of personal growth in a way that was so compact, lucid, and, to me, intuitively sensible that it has been my operating principle in my own life and my work with patients ever since.

In a nutshell, the explanation goes like this: As you know, the human mind is partly conscious and partly unconscious. The conscious part offers us the familiar mix of thoughts, plans, worries, emotions, expectations, contemplations, and the like, that we experience day to day. The unconscious part, on the other hand, is unknown to us consciously but contains a tremendous amount of personal experiences that have been stored there since birth (possibly since prenatal life, but more on this later). Most of the material stored in the unconscious mind is emotions that were not fully felt and released at the time of the original experience. For example, the child that is abused in some way but not permitted to express the natural anger and pain of the experience, unknowingly seeds the "unfelt" emotions into his/her unconscious mind, where they become emotional wounds. And, just as physical wounds heal automatically without you having to think about it, emotional wounds also have a natural healing mechanism. The stored emotions will unconsciously influence your choices in life in order to set up circumstances, which will permit the unowned emotions to come up, be felt and released. Basically the past will return to us again and again until we allow the emotions to surface into consciousness. Carl Jung addresses this issue when he said: "Emotion is the chief source of all becoming conscious. There can be no transforming of darkness into light and of apathy into movement without emotion." Carl Jung referred to the unconscious mind as the shadow, and its relentless efforts to discharge its contents as shadow projection.

But, as we saw with Mary in Chapter 1, the human ego tries to protect us from the pain by keeping it deeply hidden within the shadow of the unconscious mind. Most of us cede control of our lives to our egos. Consequently, we live our lives controlled by the ego and present to the world, and ourselves, a limited façade rather than our full selves.

The essence of self-realization is to accept all that we are with self-love. Love is the energy of healing, not only for those around us but also for ourselves. The rejected parts of our psyche are also a part of us, and they are a powerful part. We can accept and release the contents of the shadow by allowing ourselves to fully experience emotions as they arise in the course of our lives, as they will in particular when we are faced with intimidating challenges such as relationship difficulties, career hurdles, and physical illness. Thus, this healing process depends on accepting challenges, and the emotional pain they entail, as our own creation instead of blaming them on others around us. In this manner, the shadow within becomes a little lighter, and we know, and own, more of who we really are.

Conversely, if we follow the lead of the ego and keep the "unacceptable" parts of consciousness locked in the shadow, then we are thwarting the natural self-healing mechanisms of the human mind. This self-denial can intensify and become neurosis, which Carl Jung called "a substitute for legitimate suffering." If the feelings that arise from shadow projection are denied again and again, the repressed energy can affect the body, creating physical illness, which in turn presents yet another opportunity for healing the unconscious burden of past denial.

My teacher's model seemed correct to me not only intuitively but also because it fit with other things I had been reading and studying. I contemplated this expanded concept of self-love for many years and then began to use it in my medical practice by inquiring more deeply into the patterns of suppressed pain in my patients. When I did that,

I saw that just as the model suggests, my patients' painful emotions that they had suppressed since childhood would keep reappearing later in life, attached to new circumstances. For example, as psychologists have long recognized, abused children find themselves in abusive relationships as adults with surprising frequency. Similarly, abandoned children often recreate abandonment in adult relationships and children of alcoholics tend to develop relationships with alcoholics later in life. Logically, you would think that the grown-up child of an alcoholic would have learned long before that alcoholics can be abusive and unpredictable and thus they would avoid relationships with them whenever possible. But the power of the shadow to influence conscious decisions in life is formidable, and the need for shadow healing is relentless, so all of us recreate painful incidents in life until we take the risks to own the emotions and grow from the experience.

As I continued my study of the connection between mind and disease, I took particular interest in the intriguing scientific evidence of this connection. Throughout the rest of this book, we will be examining various aspects of this link. We begin that examination in this chapter with one of the most widely accepted aspects of it, the effects of emotional stress on the body.

### The Human Stress System— What It's Designed For and What It's Not

The role of stress in helping to cause disease became apparent to me early in my medical career. I had begun to notice that all of my patients seemed to be experiencing stress of some type. Patients were streaming in with high blood pressure, heart attacks, ulcers, anxiety, depression, headaches—all stress-related medical disorders. The high degree of stress in my practice puzzled me. What was I supposed to do, give tranquilizers to everyone?

In school, I had learned of the remarkable and powerful human fight-or-flight system and its ability to protect us from danger. But it seemed to me that the stress system was more of a liability to my patients than an asset. My effort to resolve this conflict helped inspire the idea of Edgework. I now believe that the potent stress system can regain its proper position as protector to our health and well-being instead of enabler of disease, even in the stress-filled circumstances of contemporary life.

We're going to turn modern stresses on their troublesome head in this chapter, but before we do, it's helpful to understand the human stress system in its original function. The power and beauty of the system is graphically illustrated in the wonderful 1981 film about prehistoric mankind, *Quest for Fire.* In one gripping scene, a tribe of cave people is attacked by a hostile neighboring tribe. A violent battle ensues and one of the attacked tribesmen escapes into the forest; he then finds a cave in which to hide. As he enters, he finds a baby bear huddled in the darkness. A deafening roar—from the cub's huge mother who has just entered the cave behind him—brings his momentary refuge to a shocking halt. He tries to escape but the mother bear grabs him with her teeth, mauling him and eventually ripping off his entire right arm. The caveman finally scrambles far enough away from the mother bear for her to lose interest and she returns to her baby. The man falls onto the forest floor, bleeding from his many wounds including the stump at his right shoulder. But he survives, both because of his will to live and the awesome efficiency of his stress physiology. Had his right arm been torn off in his sleep, he would most likely have bled to death. But the so-called fight-or-flight response mobilized his sympathetic nervous system, which con-stricted his blood vessels, enhanced blood clotting, and triggered his immune system to fight infection.

You and I have exactly the same stress response ability as did our prehistoric ancestors. In fact, dangers would have wiped out the human species without this built-in red alert system. The stress system comes into play far more than you might imagine—in fact, too often in modern circumstances for it to be solely a protective mechanism. Understanding how it works will help you see how it contributes to modern lifestyle diseases such as cancer and heart disease.

The human body has been ingeniously equipped with two nervous systems. The first, the voluntary nervous system, allows us to move our muscles at will. When we choose to walk, talk, eat, run, jump, and so on, voluntary nerves carry that message like telephone wires to the associated muscles in our bodies, which are then mobilized to carry out our wishes. The second part of our neurological "wiring," the involuntary or autonomic nervous system, governs the complex array of internal processes that operate largely beneath the level of our conscious awareness and intentions. Many of these processes are necessary for life and we could never manage them consciously. For example, the autonomic nervous system controls the pumping of blood by the heart, which beats fast or slow depending on the demands of the moment without us having to think about it. The autonomic nervous system also adjusts and coordinates blood pressure, digestion, body temperature, and even many of the ways our emotions are expressed bodily.

The autonomic nervous system is divided into two parts, the parasympathetic and sympathetic. The parasympathetic branch has the job of conserving and restoring the body's energy stores. It does this by causing the voluntary and involuntary muscles to relax. When the parasympathetic branch is activated, the digestive system is stimulated in order to increase nutrient intake and the cardiovascular system quiets down to rest and repair.

In contrast to the parasympathetic system's functions, the sympathetic system prepares us for physical action, which expends our energy. It is most dramatically on display when the body mobilizes under extreme stress and activates what is called the fight-or-flight response. Whenever we perceive something to be dangerous, or in some way stressful, our perception ignites the fight/flight system to prepare us to meet the challenge. The powerful hormone adrenaline courses through our bodies and within seconds we are ready for action with tight muscles, rapid heartbeat, elevated blood pressure, and slower digestion. Blood is diverted from our gut to our brains, and our hands become cool and clammy. Breathing becomes rapid and shallow to increase oxygen levels in the body. Our liver pours glucose, i.e. sugar, into the blood to provide the necessary fuel for active muscles. White blood cells increase in the blood, equipping the immune system to combat any potential infection. Blood-clotting factors are released in case of injury. Our senses are heightened and we begin to perspire.

So far so good—except for one thing. The stress system is designed to prepare us for *physical* action that our life may depend upon, such as fighting or escaping (thus the name "fight-or-flight.") For primitive people, this worked really well since they faced frequent physical challenges that were resolved one way or the other fairly quickly. But few of us today need to evade lions in African savannas, hunt buffalo on the plains, or raid neighboring villages for food. Our modern society largely protects us from the dangers of the outside world. Our stresses are mostly inner challenges that usually can't be resolved with physical action. In these cases, the physical arousal of the fight-flight system does us little good.

**When Dangers Are Within**

Let's expand on this distinction between primitive and modern stresses and how our body responds to them because it's a crucial one. Few would argue that contemporary life is easy just because the lions and tigers are out of the picture. In fact, most people seem to feel that life today is getting more and more stressful all the time. We don't have to hunt for our food, but we do have to pay for it at the supermarket. We also have other bills to pay including house payments or rent, utilities, car payments, furniture, college educations for our kids, cable TV, Internet providers—the list seems to grow every year because there's more and more that we supposedly can't do without. It is imperative that we succeed at work just to make ends meet, yet the ever more flexible, fast-changing, global economy makes our jobs insecure even when our performance is exemplary. It doesn't help that we have to drive to those insecure jobs every day on congested roads and freeways. And that all that traffic just eats up more hours in a day that was already woefully short for all that we had to crowd into it.

When we get home from work, we turn on the television newscast and hear about various crises—global warming, collapsing economies in other countries that are linked to our own, rogue nations with dangerous weapons—that threaten us in some vague way but are too massive and complex for us ever to resolve even if we dedicate our lives to it. For many of us, the delicate state of our personal relationships seem, to our minds anyway, to threaten our survival, too. Yet, we can no more solve those problems in any final way than we can end tensions in the Middle East.

There is no doubt as to the proper course of action for a caveman facing a saber-tooth tiger—he flees or he dies. His stress system serves him well. It prepares him to run away, and if he is fortunate enough to escape, he will then rest while his parasympathetic system returns his aroused system to normal.

But in the absence of tigers and other physical threats, the stress system backfires. Consider financial or relationship worries, for example. Even if we take action steps from the beginning, the problem will probably persist for some time. Yet the fight/flight stress system is the same as it was for cave dwellers millions of years ago. It readies our bodies for physical action—our muscles tense, we get red as our blood pressure rises, our stomach churns, our heart pounds, and our hands become sweaty. If there's no appropriate physical action for the situation, it may take hours or even days for the body to dissipate the aroused state. In the meantime, we sort of stew in our own juices.

In the short term, emotional stresses can cause a headache, upset stomach, or heart palpitations. If similar stresses recur regularly, they can lead to chronic diseases like high blood pressure, ulcers, and heart disease. Hypertension, alcoholism, drug abuse, fatigue, and depression are just a few of the other common ailments attributed in part to chronic stress. Medical textbooks state that 60 to 80 percent of all illnesses are due to stress or other mind/body factors. Evidence that we will examine in Chapter 5 clearly suggests that chronic stress is a strong contributor to the development of cancer.

In short then, our magnificent stress system seems to have become obsolete. Instead of helping us succeed in the face of danger, it now interferes because our challenges have become so vague and complex. Chronic stress in the body is like constantly revving the engine of a Ferrari in the driveway without ever taking it out on the highway. Unable to mechanically "let go," the car begins to break down. Similarly, chronic stress that is not released wears down the body, and can lead to psychosomatic disease. ("Psychosomatic" does not mean "imagined" or "not real." It simply signifies medicine's acknowledgment that many bodily illnesses have origins in psychological states.) It's intriguing to note that primitive people who live much as prehistoric humans did—for instance, the inhabitants of the African Kalahari or the Australian aborigines living in the outback—

don't suffer stress-related diseases. They don't have high blood pressure, heart attacks, ulcers or cancer.

So, what can we do about this profound evolutionary paradox? To explore this important issue, let's look again at the mind/body anatomy of the fight-or-flight system.

The "on-switch" for the stress system is a tiny patch of brain tissue called the hypothalamus, located in the center of the brain. The hypothalamus controls and regulates the entire autonomic nervous system including, of course, the sympathetic branch. The hypothalamus, as the name implies, sits just below the thalamus, a small and mysterious organ that in turn sits just beneath the cerebral cortex, the thinking center of the brain. The thalamus receives information— other than smells—from the body's sensory organs. It then relays this input to the cerebral cortex. This sensory information constitutes our awareness of the world around us. We use it in thinking and in responding to the sensory input.

The hypothalamus is the command center for many primary body functions including hormonal balance, appetite and food intake, and sexual function as well as complex motivational states such as fatigue, hunger, anger, and placidity. Effectively, it is the emotional headquarters of the brain, and also harmonizes the behaviors associated with emotional states.

"Wired" to the hypothalamus, the brain stem and spinal cord below it extend into the body like the trunk of an inverted tree, with branches reaching downward into every part of the human system. Emotions spark the hypothalamus to "electrify" our feelings through the autonomic nervous system into the familiar bodily sensations of emotional arousal. Emotions may be the most obvious proof that mind and body are one because while we think of emotions as occurring in our minds, they are in fact total body experiences.

Emotions have many variations and names. But if we distill them down, they all relate to the primary, and polar, emotions of love and fear. Love encompasses the experiences of compassion, fondness, happiness, and joy, among many other positive states. The derivatives of fear include anger, resentment, frustration, worry, and anxiety, among many others. When received from someone or given to others, love has the power to heal the body. It is also a lifeblood emotion—an infant denied love may fail to thrive or even die. We'll have more to say about love's bodily effects when we look at the healing ability of satisfying relationships in Chapter 11.

To understand how emotions do harm means understanding fear and its derivatives, and in particular the fears that are common in contemporary life. Fears trip the fight-or-flight switch in the hypothalamus. That's fine for a cave person or a modern rock climber. One way or another, that fear will soon be expressed and released and in the meantime it can heighten awareness, prepare the person for quicker responses, and otherwise help ensure survival. But modern stresses, as we've seen, aren't so easily resolved, so they just build up in us as a background condition of our lives. What makes matters worse is that our society hasn't prepared us to deal with emotional issues in a way that could lighten this stress load. Society teaches us intellectual skills but not emotional ones, so few of us have ever learned how to allow our emotions to express themselves in a way that would lighten this background stress load. Indeed, we've been told that the answer is Tylenol for our stress-related headaches, Tums for our emotionally upset stomachs, or prescription drugs for our emotionally caused high blood pressure.

To prevent stress-related illness—and because chronic stress compromises the immune system, we may be talking about most illness to some degree or another—we have to get that fight/flight switch turned off for stresses not connected to our immediate survival. How do we that? We start by properly interpreting stress.

### Using Stress as Your Guide and Teacher

The proper interpretation of danger, or stress, for the individual personality is one of the most crucial features of Edgework. In fact, Edgework completely redefines stress so that the physical signs of stress that you feel as you experience a challenging or threatening situation become signals for inner exploration and increased self-understanding. Instead of just living with stress in the body and then seeking to reduce its troublesome symptoms later, you can turn it to your advantage by learning from it.

In essence, the secret is to embrace stress as an opportunity to understand how you create it for yourself. It becomes the marker for personal psychological exploration and a building block in the most rewarding educational endeavor you'll ever undertake—the pursuit of self-knowledge. Now, your stress system is no longer obsolete. More importantly, it's no longer the relentless generator of stress-related illness. Instead, it is your internal ally, reminding you to inquire within and understand yourself better.

You have probably heard the advice, "Listen to your body." What I'm suggesting here is an aspect of that. Our bodies are constantly sending us messages. Some are strictly physical—for instance, a stiff neck after sitting in front of the computer for a long time can be read as your body telling you to take a break or to align your body more consciously when you sit. But many of the body's messages to us contain non-physical instructions. A tug in your gut when you are hedging in a conversation with your spouse may be the body's way of urging you to be more straightforward in your communication. In fact, stress is usually a message about a change you need to make in your approach to life if you want to have less stress in the future.

Note that stresses often result from persistent, nagging problems such as job dissatisfaction, marital conflict, financial worries, and family problems that we have failed to confront head-on. Rather than listen to the stress signals as the body's friendly guide to self-exploration, we have turned away from the issue at hand, feeling weak and bothered.

It is quite natural, of course, for us to turn away at times. While the human mind finds its greatest fulfillment in expanding knowledge, it also has a need to take at least occasional comfort in the safety of known and charted waters. If we were always venturing into unknown territory, our chances of encountering danger would be pretty high and our chances of long-term survival slim. The ego helps ensure our survival with a reflexive withdrawal from the unknown.

The ego also defends itself fiercely against any attack, and attacks, in the ego's view, include new information that threatens old, cherished concepts (including our concepts about who we are). This too has survival value. If we take in too much new information without integrating it into what we already know, we can be overwhelmed. More importantly, if we can't first test the new information for validity, we risk staking our survival on shaky foundations. (Note how people with weak egos tend to be gullible.)

But like an overcautious parent, the ego wants to hold us back far more than necessary. If we stay too long within the boundaries of ego-defined safety, we invite boredom, unhappiness, depression, and neurosis. "To venture causes anxiety," writes Kierkegaard, "but not to venture is to lose one's self."

We've looked at how the stress response works against us, biologically speaking. But if we take our stresses as cues for growth, we put ourselves in position to take advantage of one of stress' potential benefits. Research has shown that the stress response not only prepares the body for action, but *up to a point*, also enhances the mind. To understand the importance of that point, we need to understand the difference between acute and chronic stress.

Acute stress occurs when we have a fear or anger about something that we perceive in our immediate situation. We immediately feel the effects of the stress response in our bodies. The tight muscles and pounding heart rate we experience are due to the effects of the acute stress hormone, adrenaline. Adrenaline prepares us for quick action by mobilizing and concentrating our physical energies. Most of us are familiar with this sudden stress arousal, whether from a real threat to our physical survival such as an erratic driver near us on the freeway or a psychological stress such as the stage fright we feel before speaking to a large audience.

Chronic stress, on the other hand, is subtler, producing changes in the body designed for sustained action. For example, the hunter who is tracking his prey is producing cortisol, the hormone of chronic stress. The cortisol is helping his body maintain a state of readiness for the duration of the hunt. His blood sugar is rising to feed his muscles and his blood pressure also increases a little for the eventual chase. Once he spots his target, adrenaline suddenly cascades into his body, producing the immediate physical power for the final attack. Again, while you and I don't have to hunt for our food, most of us lead our lives in ways that abound in chronic stresses. And unlike the hunter, who will discharge his stress if he succeeds in landing his game, our worries and frustrations tend to be ongoing, seldom concluded in any decisive way with the action that our stress system is preparing us for.

Now, back to the potential mental advantages produced by the stress response. Acute or mild stress activates the pituitary gland, centered in the brain, which releases a substance called adrenocorti-cotropic hormone, or ACTH. ACTH activates the adrenal glands, which sit on top of each kidney. The adrenal glands, in turn, release the adrenal hormones. As confirmed in experiments, these hormones sharpen the mind and enhance learning.

For example, scientists have injected rats with ACTH and then observed the changes that occur in their bodies. The experiments show that the rats immediately produce large quantities of new proteins in their livers and brains. These complex proteins seem to assist the animals in learning and increasing memory. When the ACTH is injected directly into the rats' brains, the brains immedi-ately begin to grow large numbers of new connecting links between their neurons. Tests of injected rats confirm that, with all these new neural pathways, the animals indeed become more intelligent. They learn faster and solve problems better; interestingly, they also outlive their non-injected companions.

Attractive as the idea may sound when we're feeling "brain-dead," you and I don't need ACTH injections. We get plenty of ACTH when we are under stress. A rock climber gets an internal "shot" of ACTH when faced with a difficult move. With its help, he expands his knowledge of his climbing abilities in the process of completing the move. Similarly, when you approach a new and challenging experience—say, a challenging new assignment at work—the stress you feel in your body is spurring a release of hormones, including ACTH. Thus, not only are you better prepared to meet the challenge physically, but you're also primed to expand your knowledge about the world around you—and perhaps, the world within. As one indication of stress' ability to improve mental functioning, studies with students have demonstrated that a state of mild stress facilitates recall.

But here's the catch, and it's a big one. Notice that I've been careful to qualify beneficial stress as acute or mild. At low levels, stress does indeed increase alertness and preparedness. But at higher and chronic levels, it can have the opposite effect, deteriorating physical and mental performance. High or chronic stress decreases the effec-tiveness of the immune system and, again, can contribute to most of the common ailments seen in our society, including high blood pressure, ulcers, indigestion, heartburn, heart disease, joint pain, low back pain, tension headaches, and migraines. For some, the chronic stress is felt psychologically, producing anxiety, depression, sleep disturbance, or panic attack.

Fortunately, though, we possess a lot of control over the degree of stress we experience. Some stresses are entirely of our own creation—we worry about things that in actuality are no threat to us whatsoever. And even the most real of threats have an internal as well as an external side to them. That is, rather than allow the stressful situation to disable us, we can choose to relate to it as constructively as possible and even welcome its presence in our lives as a spur to grow.

In fact, stress is a necessary part of life so we might as well welcome it. Although we may often fantasize about a stressless life, taking risks, overcoming challenges, and growing is what life is really about. The only way we can experience how magnificent we really are is by testing our abilities to the maximum.

From the standpoint of our bodies and their health, stress should be embraced, too. By reading the message in our stress and committing ourselves to grow from it, we are preventing it from becoming chronic because we are experiencing it consciously rather than allowing it to accumulate unconsciously.

### Emotions and Health: Beyond Stress

Before we leave this chapter, it's important to note that stress is a big part of the picture of emotions and health but hardly the whole picture. The ability of intense life stress to suppress the immune system has been well-established in research, as we'll see later in the book. Many scientists now suspect high stress as a key factor in cancer and other serious diseases. But in my experience, it is not the stress alone that causes the problem. Disease is also caused by the inability to express, and thereby release, the intense emotions associated with the stressful experiences, as well as the emotional pain stored in the unconscious mind from previous life stresses, often occurring very early in life. Medical research is now pointing in this direction, too, as we'll see. Neuroscientist Candice Pert, Ph.D., who discovered many of the biochemical processes involved with emotions, puts it well. Although she's careful to state that her own research is on the molecular level and doesn't really concern emotions per se, she feels that "repressing emotion can only be causative of disease." She notes that many native cultures use emotional release as a key part of their healing practices.

There's a third force, besides stress and emotional release, to keep in mind when thinking about the psychological beginnings of disease, too. Question seriously ill people and you'll often find that they've never found a way to direct their life energies in a manner that engages their creativity and enthusiasm. This too has to do with emotions—having a creative outlet for emotional pain and a passionate pursuit that gives life a sense of purpose, that makes living worthwhile, literally. We'll be saying more about emotional release and passionate pursuits later in the book, but for now consider that optimal health rests on using all of the emotional effects on our bodies to their fullest, most positive potential.

# THE NATURAL INTELLIGENCE OF THE BODYMIND

*This body is a mirror of heaven;*
*Its energies make angels jealous.*

Rumi, *Love's Fire*

*The natural healing force within each one of us is the greatest*
*force in getting well.*

Hippocrates

*Men go forth to wonder at the heights of mountains, the huge*
*waves of the sea, the broad flow of the rivers, the vast compass*
*of the ocean, the courses of the stars; and they pass by them-*
*selves without wondering.*

St. Augustine, "Confessions," *Book X*, chapter 8

Few physicians would argue with the notion that the mind can affect the body, although it is the rare doctor, even in so-called holistic medicine, who really uses this idea in his practice or even has pondered what the full implications of this idea are. Where does the mind leave off and the body begin? It is no longer even useful to ask that question because it implies that mind and body are two separate entities. Those on the cutting edge of studying the interaction

36

between health and psychology have concluded that mind and body are one. There is no boundary between them, which is why they speak of the "bodymind."

In this chapter, we're going to focus in on some human systems that demonstrate the unity of the bodymind most clearly.

We are also going to consider the natural wisdom and built-in healing power of the human body. There is a creative intelligence within the body that some say is connected to the Divine. It organizes and directs the millions of cellular and biochemical processes that have kept you alive since conception. Healing is more likely to occur when we remove the interference to this natural, guiding intelligence. Some of the interference has to do with your lifestyle: diet, habits, exercise and the like. But a lot of it has to do with issues of consciousness and are based on dysfunctional beliefs and emotional blockages. It is important for you to realize that you can rely on this creative intelligence to keep you healthy, or, to restore your health. Our high-tech medical world often obscures the fact that all healing is ultimately self-healing. Doctors simply assist the body's innate healing abilities.

## Supercomputer and Sage—
## The Bodymind's Incredible Knowledge and Abilities

You live in a body as magnificent and wondrous as the universe you gaze into on a clear, starry night. In fact, the body that you take for granted has its own near boundless universe within it, comprised of approximately 100 trillion cells. Within each cell, millions of biochemical reactions take place every moment to orchestrate the experience that you call life. The unfathomable complexity and wonder of the human system sparks the imagination of scientists, poets, and mystics alike as they contemplate the genius that organizes and directs it all. It has been termed the wisdom of the body, and that is probably the most modest term we can apply. Imagine a super-computer that also had the insights of a great sage and you'd be closer to it.

Most of us don't give this wisdom much thought. We let it go about its business as we go about ours. But to do that is to neglect an immensely powerful resource that can not only help us manage our illness but also lead us to the heights of self-knowledge. In fact, because emotions and thoughts play such an important role in our physical health, it is only when we support the body's wisdom to the fullest extent that we get the health results we want. Our bodies give us cues about the condition of our psychological and emotional lives. It is only when we pay attention to those cues and commit to the personal growth that they point towards that our bodies' defenses are fully mobilized in our behalf.

I began thinking about the body's wisdom early in my studies of medicine while reading, appropriately enough, *The Wisdom of the Body* by the well-known Harvard physiologist, Walter B. Cannon. Dr. Cannon described the complex systems that keep the body in internal balance, or homeostasis. His book marked a turning point in my approach to medicine because it helped me realize that the body was incredibly well designed and that medical scientists had only scratched the surface in understanding its complexity. It seemed to me then that the best approach in treating disease would be to cooperate with and support the natural internal intelligence that manages the body's systems. By identifying how we interfere with the creative intelligence that gives us life we can remove the interference and, instead, do things to support this ancient internal healing power. In other words, promoting health seemed to be the best "treatment" for disease, and it required the patient to take responsibility for the process.

My new perspective contrasted sharply with the approach that I had been taught in medical school. My professors asserted that it was the doctor's responsibility to diagnose what is wrong with the patient and then to prescribe a medication or surgery to correct the problem, even though many of those medications and operations only relieved symptoms and did not cure or even affect the problem at its source. My medical classes said very little about patients' responsibility for their health—and not because the patient's role was overlooked but because the medical model is based on the notion that the body is inherently flawed and that we need to hover near the medical system, getting regular check-ups, in order to stay healthy. Basically, the model says, we should depend on the doctor to stay healthy—a rather disempowering notion considering the body's awesome self-correcting and healing potential.

None of what I'm saying about the medical model and my reaction to it is much of a revelation these days. Keep in mind, however, that this was the late 1960s when such ideas were just beginning to percolate in the society. And while a holistic health movement ensued that is only growing larger today, that movement still focuses mostly on the physical aspects of patients' responsibility for their health—eating better, getting more exercise, becoming more knowledgeable about natural remedies such as herbs, and so on. These are important contributions, to be sure, but the movement still undervalues the impact that psychological states have on the bodymind.

To get a closer look at just how thoughts and emotions affect health, it helps to understand how your immune system functions. The immune system is your primary defense against disease and thus plays a vital role in optimal health. Virtually every holistic health system you can name that promotes optimal health, including traditional Chinese medicine, Ayurveda, homeopathy, osteopathy, and naturopathy, takes a strong stand on supporting the immune system's effectiveness. Many of these systems—Ayurveda in particular—emphasize that thoughts and emotions as well as physical conditions can influence the immune system, for better or worse. Also, a number of studies clearly indicate ways that psychological states can powerfully affect the immune system's capabilities. Those studies provide strong clues as to just how those states can lead to disease or health, depending on whether they are negative or positive. Before looking at the research, let's get to know our immune system just a little better.

### Keeper of the Peace—The Immune System Revealed

Of all the many remarkable pieces of standard equipment you came with when you entered this life, none is more ingenious than your immune system. The immune system is thought to be as sophisticated and complicated as the brain. Unlike the brain or other organs, however, it is "de-localized"—that is, not concentrated in one place in your body. Instead, the cells of the immune system are found in every recess and corner of your inner anatomy.

It's helpful to think of your immune system as a massive, highly trained military/police force 100 percent dedicated to defending your health. This force "employs" about one trillion cells in various rings of protection so that if one unit is violated or in over its head, it can immediately summon reinforcements or heavier artillery. The first line of defense is the phagocytes, a group of immune cells that ingest and destroy bacteria and other cellular debris. Neutrophils are the most abundant of these internal defenders and garbage collectors. There are about 100 billion of these cells produced in the bone marrow every day and they account for about 70% of the white blood cells circulating in your body. Neutrophils are produced in such large numbers because they live for only four or five days before they undergo apoptosis, or internally programmed cell death. Macrophages (Latin for big-eaters) are another type of phagocyte that patrol the inner recesses and organs of your body like the police patrolling a dangerous neighborhood. They are more sophisticated than neutrophils and live for months in your body. Just like a police officer who pulls over a speeding driver and asks for some form of identification, the macrophages will encounter a suspicious cell in your body and "ask" for ID through a complex system of cellular recognition. If the cell turns out to be a bacterium, parasite, virus infected cell, or foreign protein that your immune system hasn't "seen" before, the macrophage will attack by trying to eat or engulf the foreign cell and then digest it. The pus that you see around a cut finger as it heals is the residual debris of dead neutrophils and macrophages that gave their lives protecting you from infection.

If the neutrophils and macrophages cannot eat the foreign cells on the spot, the macrophages "radio" the helper T cells, a certain type of lymphocyte (white blood cell formed in lymphoid tissue) considered to be the supreme commander of the immune system. The helper T cell identifies the enemy and then rushes to the spleen and lymph nodes where it stimulates the production of other cells to fight the infection. For instance, the B cells are the air force of our internal defense. If the macrophages can't win the fight with one-on-one combat, the helper T cells order the B cells into action. The B cells produce "missiles" called antibodies, complex protein molecules that target the invader, attaching to it and either killing it or tagging it for other immune cells to finish the job later.

Finally, the immune system forces include some elite forces called natural killer cells. Their fearsome name is well-earned because these cells specialize in killing cells in the body that have been invaded by foreign bacteria or viruses, as well as cells that have turned cancerous. Natural killer cells wield "guns" reminiscent of the laser guns used by the officers in *Star Trek*. These cells approach an invaded or diseased cell and then release a bolt of enzymes, which bores a hole in the targeted cell, which then spills its guts, so to speak, and dies.

Thus, you've been curing cancer in your body every day of your life, without chemotherapy or radiation. This internal cancer prevention system is called the "immune surveillance theory." Your body wisdom knows that on occasion, some of the constantly reproducing cells in your body will go haywire, dividing without control and becoming cancer cells. Fortunately, via the immune system, it has the capacity to grow and deploy natural killers to hunt down these aberrant cells and destroy them.

Are you proud of yourself yet?

The need to understand and support your immune system has never been as important as it is today. The metaphor of war against bacteria, viruses and other microbial organisms is entrenched in our medical system. Since the discovery of penicillin in the 1930s, the pharmaceutical industry has been constantly looking for ever more powerful antibiotics as weapons for the war. However, our microbial adversaries are no easy foes, as it appears that we may be losing the war. Infectious germs are becoming resistant to each new drug faster than we can find a stronger one. And, strange new "enemies" are appearing, like AIDS, Ebola, hepatitis and hanta virus. At this time there is only one antibiotic that kills resistant forms of Staphylococcus aureus, and there are resistant forms of Streptococcus, malaria, and salmonella emerging, causing tremendous worry for doctors, researchers and public health officials alike.

The latest research on microbes suggests they have a "decision making intelligence" that enables them to survive antibiotics much faster than by simple random mutations alone. Germs are the oldest life form on the earth, and they form the base of the food chain for every other life form on the planet, including us. For these and other reasons, many researchers are looking to replace the "us against them" metaphor with one of cooperation or co-evolution. For you and I this means keeping our immune systems strong as they are originally designed to be, and, as we shall see, the most powerful support for strong immunity lies within your mind.

### Consciousness and Immunity—The Mounting Evidence

We may think of our immune system as operating beneath the level of our conscious awareness, but the fact is that our consciousness is constantly intersecting with our immunity, sometimes enhancing it, sometimes inhibiting it. Common sense tells us that people who are satisfied with their personal lives, enthusiastic about their work, and inspired spiritually will probably fight off disease more effectively than people who are depressed. Studies confirm our intuition about this. They also yield some results about "negative" emotions that may surprise you but are consistent with the themes of Edgework.

One well-known experiment used method-trained actors because they are skilled at using their memories and physical sensations to generate intense emotional states so they can act convincingly on stage. The principal investigator of the study, Dr. Ann Futterman, asked the actors to imagine different situations that would make them either happy or sad. For instance, to generate sadness, the actors would be asked to imagine that they had just been rejected for a part they really wanted. To create happy emotions, the actors would be told to imagine that they got the part they wanted and went on to have a fabulously successful opening night. As expected, the researchers discovered that when the actors were extremely happy, their immune systems produced more natural killer cells in their bloodstreams and that the cells functioned more efficiently than when the subjects were feeling emotionally neutral. But interestingly, the same thing happened when the actors were feeling intense sadness.

Another study, this time with students at Southern Methodist University as subjects, obtained a similar result. The researcher asked the students to write about traumatic events and then focus on the negative feelings that arose from the exercise. As with the actors, immune system activity picked up in the dimension the researcher was measuring when the students were in the midst of their emotional experience.

These studies suggest two conclusions. First, short-term emotions do significantly affect the immune system. Second, the distinctions we make between so-called positive and negative emotions may matter far less than fully *experiencing* emotions of all types. It is healthy to experience emotions, the study implies. It is not healthy to suppress them.

Studies of depressed people indicate at least some of the bodily problems with suppressed emotions. We think of depression as being made up of sadness and other related negative emotions. But in fact, depression is a relatively emotionless, withdrawn response to what's going on in the sufferer's life. Depressed people often feel a sense of hopelessness and helplessness, and occasionally some feel suicidal. That's not, however, the same thing as actively experiencing emotions as they arise. People who experience their emotions freely pass through the emotion of the moment and on to another one rather quickly. They can also tell you what they are feeling at any particular time. In contrast, some depressed people are at such a low state of emotional response that they are unable to cry. Others are so out of touch with their emotions that they have no idea they are withdrawing from their normal life until others point it out to them. Given what we've just seen with the research on actors and students, we'd expect that depressed people have less-effective immune systems, and that's just what several studies show.

In 1977, researchers in Sydney, Australia noticed that 29 subjects whose spouses had died several weeks before had suppressed immune system responses. A 1983 study of the spouses of 15 women who were dying of breast cancer turned up similar results, with the effects lasting up to 14 months. It is as if the surviving spouses wished to die and their bodies began to cooperate by lowering their defense against disease. In fact, loneliness in general is associated with compromised immunity in several studies. Interestingly, shamans in many traditional cultures regard illness as a sign of poor social relations and treat patients in part by trying to reintegrate them in the community.

Not surprisingly, chronic stress also leads to impaired immunity. A 1962 study of 16 families found more streptococcal infections in the families with chronic stress. Studies of college students under academic pressure show less natural killer cell activity. Another study showed that military cadets feeling academic stress were more likely to get mononucleosis.

Thinking patterns affect the immune system, too. One longitudinal study (meaning measurements were taken at two different points in time) of 280 men and women showed that the subjects who saw their setbacks in negative terms—in other words, who saw their glasses as half-empty instead of half-full—had significantly less effective immune system function with respect to both helper T cells and natural killer cells. In a study at the University of Pittsburgh, psychologists followed a group of 40 seriously ill cancer patients who had undergone chemotherapy and radiation therapy. Half the group had also gone through a 12-week course that taught them to improve their attitudes by modifying their thoughts. When the researchers checked in several months later, they found that the patients who had taken the course had much higher levels of natural killer cells. Those who had taken the course also lived several months longer, on average, than those who hadn't been through the training.

None of this would matter much if all it meant was that depressed, lonely, stressed, and negative people got a few more colds than the rest of us. But considerably more is at stake. Remember that the immune system works to keep us cancer-free by destroying out-of-control cells on a daily basis. As we've seen in our look at the immune system's anatomy, if natural killer cells aren't doing their job, cancer that would normally be suppressed by the daily "sweep" of these forces can begin to take hold and grow. And that's exactly why scientists who ponder the relationship between emotions and cancer look first at the kind of evidence we just examined. This certainly isn't to say that everyone who goes through hard times is doomed to suffer a horrible disease. But it does point to preventive measures we can take on the emotional level, as I describe later in the book.

### The Mysterious Guiding Force of DNA

Let's head deeper now into the body, and into a deeper bodily mystery—the wondrous world of deoxyribonucleic acid, or DNA. As you learned in your biology classes in school, DNA is the molecule that contains your genetic blueprint, the instructions for making the unique physical and psychological being that you are. You know that you originally received one strand of DNA from your mother and one strand from your father. You were probably also taught in school that your genetic destiny couldn't change, except by accidental mutation. That is, you had no control over what your genes "formatted" you to become, with the exception of random physical changes in the DNA itself. But what if that isn't quite so? What if you could influence from moment to moment the way you turn out? Might that not have profound implications for your health?

Well, it so happens that some research does suggest that you may be able to alter your own DNA. Before we examine that, let's review some basic facts about DNA and about the culture war over who holds the truth about human genetics.

DNA resides in the nucleus of each of your 100 trillion cells. Each cell also contains the biochemical building blocks of the body, floating in an amazing matrix of intracellular fluids. When cells divide, the DNA molecule unzips itself into two parts, attracting the proper chemicals to form two new strands of DNA. Thus, the two cells resulting from the division carry the same genetic instructions as the original cell. It is this marvelous process that insures that newly created cells and tissues in your body are the right ones for you—that is, that fit your unique pattern. This same process enables you to pass on your "immortal" genes to your children.

There are few questions that the above information is true. But considerable debate exists over whether this is the whole story of why we are the way we are, physically and otherwise. On one side of the debate sit the so-called genetic determinists, who maintain essentially that genes are destiny—in other words, we unfold exactly as our genetic instructions determine that we will. The determinists have some powerful evidence in hand, including the obvious fact that we tend to physically resemble our parents. But determinists want to carry the argument further, maintaining that nearly everything that is fundamentally "us," including our behavior, is fated by our genetic heritage. That is, the way our parents raise us and other factors related to our environment have little or no impact on our development.

Genetic determinism also means that we have little personal control in changing our behavioral patterns. For example, some researchers who hold these views have searched for "fat genes" that cause people to be overweight, as if their life circumstances and personal choices have little influence on why they overeat. In one of the more repugnant forms of genetic determinism, some scientists have maintained that the fact that African-Americans as a group tend to underperform the rest of the U.S. population on standardized scholastic tests means that they are genetically inferior.

On the other side of the debate are those who believe that environment is the most powerful influence on a person. In other words, no matter what genetic heritage we bring into the world with us, it can be overcome by the way our parents raise us, life stresses, positive factors in our environment, and so on. People who hold this view believe that the attention, emotional care, and amount of love that a child receives from its parents, even *in utero,* play a major role in its development and subsequent behavior. In fact, the quality of the child's nurturing and family environment early in life shape the child's entire consciousness. Another tenet of this viewpoint asserts that if there is something we don't like about our psychological make-up, we can change it with personal growth work, psychotherapy, and the like. This widely appealing and optimistic view stands in stark contrast to the fatalism of the determinists and is the foundation of many New Age, holistic, and humanistic philosophies.

Of course, as is the case in most such polarized debates, the truth probably lies somewhere in between. For example, in the 1960s and '70s, many humanistic psychologists believed that schizophrenia in children occurred because the children's families were seriously dysfunctional. Since then, strong evidence has emerged of a genetic component in schizophrenia. But genetics don't completely explain this mental illness either, and environmental factors such as family and social stresses do appear to partly account for some cases. So while the final cause of schizophrenia is still unknown, the most widely held theories propose that genes and environment are both impor-tant. That is, only people with "schizophrenia genes" can become schizophrenic, but it takes environmental stresses (for example, unhappy family circumstances or internal environmental changes such as an infection) to cause the genetic potential to express itself. In other words, people with the gene who aren't stressed aren't likely to develop the disease.

I bring all this up because, while I strongly disagree with genetic determinists about the cause of disease, I don't want you to think that

I slight the effect of genes. Of course, genes make a difference, a powerful one. But it is simplistic to suggest that genes explain everything. It is equally simplistic to suggest that genes don't matter, but I'm more concerned with the former position because it is the one that holds most sway in this society, particularly when it comes to diseases and other physical disorders. We are a materialist culture, meaning we put more faith in ideas based on material things we can see, touch, or measure (for example, genes) than we do in things that can't be seen or touched and aren't easily measured (for example, the effect of being loved). This creates two major problems in the health area. One, ideas about subtle influences on our health such as the effect of thoughts and emotions get short shrift, especially from the scientific community. Second, because beliefs have real health consequences (see following chapter), believing that you have a genetic tendency towards a disease that your parents had can itself make it more likely that you will get that disease!

And here's where DNA comes in, because some pioneering work by cellular biologist Bruce Lipton, Ph.D., suggests that even genes themselves may not be the simple switches that the genetic determinists regard them to be. Lipton, formerly on the faculty of the University of Wisconsin School of Medicine and before that Pathology Fellow at Stanford University, has long pursued an interest in the molecular nature of human consciousness. In Lipton's view, genes are not capable of turning themselves on and off on their own. He wrote the following in an unpublished paper titled "Nature, Nurture and the Power of Love":

> ... if a gene can not regulate its own expression, then genes can not be invoked as the "controllers" of organismal expression. Rather than being "self-emergent," gene programs are controlled by "environmental" signals. The dogma of genetic determinism is giving way to a concept that recognizes living organisms as "dynamical systems," ones that are capable of actively reprogramming gene behaviors to accommodate environmental changes.

If DNA is not the primary controlling factor we once thought it to be, how does it receive influential information from the environment? It does so via the cell membrane, the outer covering that all cells have. The membrane is composed mainly of fats and proteins. Among those proteins are special proteins called integral membrane proteins, or IMPs, that are dispersed at frequent intervals on the membrane. Some of the IMPs serve as "receptors" and others as "effectors." The receptors act as the sense organs of the cell, much like our own eyes, ears, and nose. These receptor IMPs respond both to chemical messages from other parts of the body, such as the stress hormone adrenaline, and energy, such as electromagnetic forces. Once they have received these influences from the outside world, they interact with effector IMPs, which then carry out the appropriate cellular behavior.

According to Lipton, virtually every cell function—including DNA synthesis, cell division and reproduction, and hormone release, to mention a few—can be regulated by pulsed electromagnetic energy received by the receptor IMPs. Among other things, Lipton notes, these findings show that biological behavior can be profoundly affected by invisible energy forces, including thought. Now I am not suggesting that the cells in your body are responding to your every thought. But the cells do "listen" to what goes on in the body, so perhaps it is possible that sustained thoughts, or beliefs, can have an impact on cellular functions, including DNA activity.

Lipton also discusses how stress affects cell activity. Broadly speaking, cells respond in two ways to signals from the environment. If the signals are positive and supportive, cells grow. If the signals are stressful, cells retreat or contract from growth activities to protect themselves. Cells cannot grow and protect themselves at the same time. Thus, too much protection leads to poor tissue function and, eventually, disease.

For some people, the stressful experiences almost never stop, thereby bombarding the cells with messages that cue them to withdraw into protective mode. This will happen, of course, whether the stress is real or imaginary because either situation will generate the stress hormones to which the cell responds. As Lipton notes, it is now recognized that cells can rewrite existing gene programs to combat the stressful situation. In other words, a person's belief about the stresses in his or her life may lead to adaptive genetic changes at the cellular level.

Might this process contribute to serious illness such as cancer? It certainly seems to me to be a real possibility. Yes, this is speculation but there are studies beyond Dr. Lipton's that point in this direction as well as the clinical experience of many physicians open to new thinking about illness. We explore cancer in relationship to consciousness in more detail in Chapter 5.

# 4

# THE UNSEEN ANATOMY: THE POWER OF THOUGHT AND EMOTION

*The material body is a river of atoms, the mind is a river of thought, and what holds them together is a river of intelligence.*

Deepak Chopra, MD

The wisdom built into your immune system, DNA, and other parts of your physical anatomy is almost unfathomable. But the wonders of the body don't end there. Although invisible to most people, your true anatomy extends well outside the physical perimeter of your body; it also encompasses invisible entities and connective pathways inside your body. Unlike your organs, blood vessels, nerves, and so on, this anatomy has no physical presence in the ordinary sense. It is composed, like light, of pure energy and can't be apprehended by the senses, at least in the usual way that you see, hear, smell, taste, and feel other things. But it is no less real and no less important to your well-being. Some call this your "energy body." I call it your unseen anatomy.

In actuality, the term "unseen" is a bit of a misnomer. "Hidden" might be more accurate. Some gifted individuals are able to see the emanations of energy, called auras, which extend outside the body. Auras can also be captured by special photographic techniques. In addition, some alternative healers are trained to feel auras (which vibrate as well as glow) and manipulate them. For instance, the healer will rotate his hand in specific ways to "stir" the aura above a wound; this is said to speed healing.

The ancient art of acupuncture, which goes back thousands of years, also involves feeling and working with the unseen anatomy, this time inside the body. Acupuncturists are trained to sense through touch the life energy (called chi) pulsing in the body's energy pathways; they take the pulses in the patient's wrist, through which all the pathways (called meridians) pass. By reading these pulses, acupuncturists assess the patient's health and determine where to put their needles. The meridians and the non-material systems they connect were extensively mapped by the ancient Chinese doctors (the Chinese call the non-material systems "organs," not to be confused with physical organs). These maps, which rival physiological maps of nerves, blood vessels, and physical organs in their intricacy, are the same ones relied upon today by modern acupuncturists. While Western medical ideas can't account for acupuncture, only the stodgiest of doctors deny that it can be effective. An extensive body of literature documents its successful use and many Western physicians have observed dramatic procedures—for example, anesthesia for major surgery—accomplished by acupuncture.

So the unseen anatomy is hardly unknown. Despite the inroads made by acupuncture, however, Western physicians haven't spent much time investigating its implications. Thus, they may be overlooking health's "missing link," because, in my view, such energy systems help account for the way that thought and emotion influence our bodies.

## Ancient Theories of the Unseen Anatomy

Exploration of the body's energy fields may be in its infancy in the West, but its history goes back thousands of years in such countries as India, Tibet, and China. In all of these ancient cultures, the unseen anatomy was widely described in both medical and spiritual texts. For example, the Vedas, the ancient spiritual writings of Hinduism, discussed the energy body, including its source in spiritual energy, 3000 years ago.

Obviously, these descriptions predated our modern scientific method, but that does not make them less reliable. Energy medicine, for instance, was carefully studied and documented in the laboratory of personal experience and borne out in applications with patients. One of the most confirming aspects of the energy anatomy is its continued relevance today, even to highly trained medical professionals. For example, in China, ancient energy practices such as acupuncture are used in modern hospitals alongside, and often in conjunction with, such high-tech procedures as surgery.

The energy system accessed by acupuncture is not the only body energy system with implications for health. Ancient Hindu and Buddhist texts from India, China, and Tibet all speak of a system of subtle body energy centers called chakras. According to these texts, there are seven chakras, or energy centers, located in the human body. Each center corresponds to a certain level of consciousness, or certain pattern of energy. Each energy center is a receiver and transmitter of electromagnetic patterns of energy, many of which are quite subtle and yet to be clearly documented by Western science. In other words, each center can receive energy from the world around us, and, transmit energy outward from within us. When all chakras are functioning fully with no blockages to energy flow, the person has fully mastered the human condition and is said to be in a state of enlightenment, which is the goal of human life. A handful of avatars and great spiritual Masters have reached this level of experience.

Most of us, on the other hand, have various degrees of blockages in the chakras, leading to disturbed function, usually at multiple levels. Blockages arise from the physical and emotional traumas of childhood, as well as a variety of less severe, but certainly invalidating experiences to the young child. Children are also taught dysfunctional beliefs about themselves and the world around which are maintained into adult life, leading to disturbed chakric energy flow.

For a more comprehensive study of the chakras and how they function, I recommend a book by Anodea Judith, titled *Eastern*

*Body, Western Mind, Psychology and the Chakra System as a Path to the Self.*

At the base of the spine is the first chakra, or Survival Center, which is concerned with the basic ingredients of survival, or the right to exist, breathing, digesting food, as well as feeling safe. We usually don't think too much about these fundamental aspects of our lives, but when we concentrate on thoughts of fear, insecurity, and lack of trust, we interfere and obstruct the natural flow of energy in the Survival Center. This can in turn lead to bowel and other health problems.

The second energy center is located below the navel and is the Sexual/Creative Center. Healthy sexuality, procreation, and creative expression are governed by this center. But all too common patterns of guilt, fear, and repression block the flow of energy in and out of this center, thus setting the stage for problems of sexual dysfunction in both sexes, as well as gynecologic problems such as fibroids, and urologic problems in men, such as prostate enlargement.

The third center lies in the solar plexus and is the Power Center through which you create your life experience through your will and personal power. The desire to achieve and accomplish moves through this center. However, once again, thoughts of fear, shame, inadequacy, powerlessness, and confusion block this manifesting power. If these blockages are sustained, then diseases, such as ulcers, can develop in this area.

The fourth center sits in the center of the chest and is called the Heart Center. It is the center that love and compassion move through. Love is considered by the ancients to be the glue of the universe, an energy that "pulls together." Thoughts of sadness, isolation, grief, fear and self-hate block the function of the Heart Center, setting the stage for heart disease.

The fifth center is located in the throat and is called the Communications Center. It allows creative expression. Thoughts of self-criticism, unworthiness and fear disrupt its function, interfering with communication and eventually causing disease, such as thyroid problems.

The sixth center is located at the middle of the forehead and is called the Psychic Center because it permits seeing of a higher order, such as intuition, imagination and psychic ability. It serves as a connection between the spiritual world and the physical world. Fear of the unknown, feelings of isolation and inadequacy interfere with this powerful center, leading eventually to headaches and other medical problems.

Finally, the seventh center is located at the top of the head and is called the Crown Center. It is the entry point for knowledge beyond the known, or knowledge from a Higher Power directly. It allows wisdom, mastery and the experience of God. Thoughts of inadequacy, fear and cynicism block the flow of energy in this center, leading to thought disorders and possibly headaches.

According to the ancient texts, true health, physically, mentally and spiritually, depends on the balanced flow of energy in all the centers. And in order for this to occur we must heal our storehouse of fears, inadequacies, self-hate, resentments, guilt, shame, and other emotional wounds that we carry in the unconscious and conscious minds. Emotional wound healing, as we have discussed, is a natural process in the bodymind, as we create life experiences unconsciously in order to feel and release the stored pains from childhood.

### The Unseen Anatomy and Modern Science

Most Western biologists and medical researchers think of the human body in strictly material terms and don't even exhibit much curiosity about subtle body energies. But a few maverick scientists have forged careers reminiscent of the ancient doctors and researchers of the Orient. In 1930, Professor Harold Burr, a neuroanatomist at Yale University, described "fields of life"—L-fields for short—within and around the human body. To measure these fields he used highly sensitive vacuum-tube voltmeters such as those found in physics laboratories, along with special silver-silver chloride electrodes. Burr believed that L-fields are likely created at the time of conception. According to his theory, they then direct both physical and psychological functions for the organism during the rest of its life.

Burr believed that changes in L-field voltages could give advance warning of future symptoms in the body, and applied his ideas to several realms of human health. For example, with an eye toward helping couples planning pregnancy or having problems conceiving, he used his approach to determine the exact time of ovulation for a woman in her menstrual cycle. He found that "ovulation is preceded by a steady and substantial rise in voltage, which falls rapidly to normal after the egg has been released." He also noted that ovarian cancer could be detected by measuring L-field changes; in fact, the changes showed up before any clinical sign of the cancer could be observed. He wrote about his research on L-fields and the promise they held for future medical practice in his book, *Blueprint for Immortality.*

Unfortunately, Burr's colleagues did not share his enthusiasm for the value of energy medicine. Thus, little research was done in this area until 20 years later when Dr. Robert Becker began looking into the bioelectric nature of life. An Orthopedic surgeon, Dr. Becker was initially concerned about the healing and regenerative systems in the body and how electrical currents could influence them. After decades of research, he concluded "... that a more primitive, analog data-transmission and control system still exists in the body, located in the perineural (around nerve) cells and transmitting information by means of a semiconducting DC electrical current." Becker maintained that this same electrical current controls cell activity. He also believed that bioelectric energy regulates our levels of consciousness and is involved in our decision-making processes. His ideas and research are described in his book, *Cross Currents—The Perils of Electropollution, The Promise of Electromedicine.*

## What Physics Has to Say about Health and Consciousness

When we talk about energy and healing, we inevitably find ourselves thinking about physics, because physics is the science that explores energy. On the surface, physicists, healers, and spiritual sages sound like they are carrying on different parts of the same conversation. As described in many spiritual and healing philosophies, the universe is like a sea of energy, with living things like waves that rise and fall on that sea. This story bears striking similarity to the story of the universe told by modern physics.

Where health fits in this discussion is pretty straightforward, at least from the spiritual point of view. If spiritual energy—essentially, consciousness in its purest state—is the ultimate building block of everything in the universe, then all phenomena can be explained in terms of the movements of that energy. This means that health, too, can be understood in terms of both the movement of energy and consciousness.

Most physicists might not go so far as to call the fundamental energy of the universe conscious, or to see its application to healing. But many of physic's greatest names have been struck by the similarities between the universe their experiments describe and the universe described around the world by Hindu, Buddhist, Taoist, and other mystical sages. Some go farther and assert that physicists, energy healers such as traditional Chinese doctors, and spiritual masters are all talking about the same universal essence.

The noted English physicist, David Bohm, was one such scientist. So is University of Vienna-educated physicist Fritjof Capra, whose immensely popular book *The Tao of Physics* spread the notion to the general public when it was published in 1975. The writings of American physicist, Fred Alan Wolf, also helped popularize the physics/consciousness connection. Seven years later, physician/author Larry Dossey explored the parallels between physics discoveries and healing in his 1982 book *Space, Time, & Medicine.* All of these ideas must be regarded as speculative. Not all physicists believe that physics and consciousness can be as easily knit together as Bohm, Capra, and Wolf do.

Nevertheless, the physics/consciousness connection is such a provocative—and intuitively sensible—notion that it can't be ignored. Plus, as we've already seen and will see further throughout this book, medicine is replete with phenomena that are hard to account for with ordinary biological models. For instance, many types of cancer have a clear, material reality with tumors, severe disruptions of function, and so on. Yet in the case of spontaneous remissions, those tumors and their associated symptoms sometimes quickly disappear. How can this be? Sometimes a patient will experience a life change— a new relationship, involvement in an exciting new activity, a personal revelation—and the life-threatening condition she was suffering from, such as heart disease or lupus, will subside into nothingness. Such startling turnarounds defy our ordinary understanding of the nature of physical reality. But they seem much more plausible when we view physical reality as modern physicists do. So let's reconstruct, in lay terms, the journey that Bohm, Capra, Wolf, and other physicist/mystics have taken and see why the physics/health connection is so compelling.

The framework for modern science was established in part by the seventeenth-century philosopher René Descartes, who proposed that matter and mind were separate. This philosophy of *dualism* was crucial to science because it meant that scientists could study the material world as something distinct from their own consciousness. According to dualism, the world they observed was real in and of itself and unaffected by what they thought about it. Freed by this philosophy, scientists began seeing the universe as composed of objects that were part of a vast machine. The machine operated according to natural laws and scientists saw their job as figuring out what those natural laws were. One of the followers of this so-called mechanistic world view was Sir Isaac Newton, whose ideas, known as Newtonian mechanics, formed the basis for classical physics.

For over 200 years, Newtonian mechanics was thought to be the final word on natural phenomena. But the discovery of electrical and magnetic forces, unaccounted for by Newton, showed that Newton's ideas were limited. Essentially, they only applied to the motion of objects composed of large numbers of atoms, and only when those objects moved at speeds well below the speed of light. In other words, Newtonian mechanics was an approximation that was only accurate under certain conditions. New theories were needed that considered smaller objects and higher velocities.

Thus was the way paved for Einstein's relativity theory and quantum theory, the twin pillars of twentieth century physics and the reason that physicists and mystics seemed to suddenly be speaking the same language. Relativity theory proposed that space and time weren't constants and separate, as the mechanistic world view supposed. Rather, they were intimately related to each other in a continuum Einstein called space/time. From this idea, Einstein derived his famous formula, $E=MC^2$, which showed that matter and energy were equivalent and that one could be converted to the other.

Einstein also contributed greatly to quantum theory, along with an international group of physicists including Max Planck, Niels Bohr, Erwin Schrodinger, Werner Heisenberg, Paul Dirac, Louis De

Broglie, and Wolfgang Pauli. Quantum theory deals with the subatomic world of matter, i.e. the electrons, protons, and neutrons that
make atoms. When physicists began investigating matter at this level,
they found that it neither appeared nor behaved like the solid objects
of Newtonian physics or ordinary, consensual reality. Instead, paradox was rampant and reality hard to pin down. Depending on how
physicists viewed them, subatomic entities would appear sometimes
as particles, sometimes as waves. Light demonstrated a similar dual
character, showing up sometimes as electromagnetic waves and
sometimes as particles.

Heisenberg and Bohr in particular helped resolve these paradoxes
but only by showing that at the subatomic level, the concepts of the
mechanistic world view no longer applied. Entities weren't particles
or waves exclusively at any one time. They had the properties of both
and the way they appeared at any moment was a function of the
experimental situation or apparatus used to study them. Nor could
they be tied down to definite points of time and space like objects in
the Newtonian world. They could only be described in terms of
mathematical probabilities. That is, physicists were forced to talk
about subatomic matter in terms of "tendencies to exist" and subatomic events in terms of "tendencies to occur."

Although the modern physics he helped create was moving in the
opposite direction, Einstein still held on to many aspects of the
mechanistic worldview. However, work by physicists John Bell and
Neils Bohr helped sever physics' remaining ties to this Cartesian (that
is, Descartes-based) view of things. A famous experiment by Bell
showed that two particles were instantly "in communication" with
each other and simultaneously reflected what happened to each, no
matter how much space—even a whole solar system—separated
them. This implied, as Bohr had been asserting for some time, that
the universe was an inseparable whole, not a collection of distinct
objects. It also implied to many physicist/mystics that their science
was discovering a universe that the ancient sages had known all along.

David Bohm's ideas brought the worlds of physics and spirituality closer still. Starting from Bohr's premise that the universe was an
unbroken whole, Bohm proposed that at its deepest level, or what he
called the "implicate order," the whole of the universe was enfolded

in each part of its parts. He then brought consciousness directly into the equation by stating that mind and matter were interdependent. One didn't cause the other; rather, both were enfolded in each other and derived from a higher reality beyond both mind and matter.

"Tendencies to exist," "tendencies to occur," "implicate order"— the weird language of modern physics is almost impossible to fathom with ordinary thinking. It adds up, however, to some basic notions that may have profound implications for understanding our existence, including our health. One of those notions is that at the subatomic level, solid objects are exposed as an illusion. They are not solid at all but mostly space. They are also not isolated entities but rather part of a complex web of interconnections in a unified whole. In such a universe, it seems more plausible that changes in consciousness will be reflected in changes in the physical universe, including one's own body.

Despite the startling advances in physics, biology and medicine have stayed put philosophically, as if Descartes and Newton were still the final word. In the biomedical model, our bodies are viewed as constellations of separate parts—organs, cells, biochemicals, and so on. Medical science focuses on these parts to help us cure our illnesses. Doctors use drugs to alter the chemistry of the body and surgeons remove, alter, and occasionally replace organs. But physics demonstrates unequivocally that if you look deep enough, the universe is unified and holistic. Medicine's tendencies to ignore the health effects of a patient's psychology seem even more shortsighted in this context. So does its tendency to treat only symptoms and diseased organs and such, rather than treat the body as a whole, integrated system. The side-effects problem in conventional medicine is just one obvious and unfortunate byproduct of medicine's resistance to a holistic worldview.

Before we leave this topic, it is important to give credit where credit is due and point out that the mechanistic world has been far from a total failure in medicine. Viewing the body in a Newtonian way as a mechanism of various parts has enabled medicine to develop brilliant surgical techniques, drugs, and other technological accomplishments that have saved countless lives. This underlines a point that Capra himself makes. The Newtonian is not "wrong," any more than relativity and quantum theory are "right." All three theories are approximations of different aspects of reality. Thus, each has its limitations but each works very well in the situations to which it is appropriate. For instance, Newtonian physics is still the physics of choice for large objects moving at sub-speed-of-light speeds (as in, for instance, space travel). It no longer applies at the subatomic level, where quantum mechanics comes into play; and when velocities exceed the speed of light, then relativity theory has to be figured in.

In the same way, mechanistic medicine also works well in certain applications but it, too, has its limitations. One of those limitations is in improving overall health. Mechanistic medicine does an excellent job at addressing certain acute medical emergencies and other conditions but it often fails at preventing illness or creating a thriving state of health. One big reason may be that doctors haven't yet accounted for the effect of thoughts and emotions in health, a holistic approach more in tune with subatomic physics.

This bears some relation to where physics is at today. Physicists are forced by the results of their own experiments to consider that the universe they are trying to explore and the consciousness they are exploring it with are not separate. In other words, true objectivity may not exist, even though it is considered the foundation of science. The next breakthroughs in physics may well come from resolving that dilemma.

### Thoughts and Healing—The Reality and the Potential

We saw earlier how thoughts and emotions can compromise or enhance the functioning of our immune system. Thoughts and emotions are both potentially powerful tools in our internal healing arsenal. They are not the same, however, even though the boundaries between them aren't always clear to us. And they are used quite differently in Edgework, or any healing process that takes them into consideration.

Perhaps nothing more clearly distinguishes humans than sophisticated thinking. The ability to think at high, analytical levels separates us from most, and perhaps all, other animals. Consider the role of thought in creating the human experience. Humans discovered the nature of electricity, gravity, physics, and chemistry—and how to utilize them for human benefit—through the process of penetrating, analytical thought. We create our daily experience, too—from the trivial to the crucial—largely by directing and focusing the personal force called thought. How we perform our work, which clothes to wear, where to go today, whom to call, which car to buy—such decisions define our day-to-day lives and all are birthed by thought.

But only rarely do we start from scratch when we think. The direction our daily thoughts will travel in is largely determined by "packages" of prior thinking called attitudes, opinions, and beliefs. These packages become controlling forces in our lives, setting limits within which we live (unless we believe we have no limits, which can open things up considerably!). Those with similar attitudes and beliefs become our friends and colleagues, reinforcing our way of thinking and helping to convince us that we are "right." We also share many attitudes and beliefs in common with our community, adherents to our religions, and society-at-large, which again can delude us into believing that we must be correct since so many other "reasonable" people agree. Of course, in many societies including ours, not everyone does agree—in fact, our culture today is marked by striking disagreements about basic ideologies and morals, which are themselves complex thought packages made up of attitudes, opinions, and beliefs strung together in a (supposedly) coherent whole. Thus, when as social animals, we gather with others in our area to think through social guidelines and controls that will allow us to live together, we often have trouble reaching a compromise that is satisfactory to all. As William Shakespeare said, "there is nothing good or bad, but thinking makes it so," but we become so attached to our thoughts that things can seem extremely good or bad to their core.

If you ask them, most people in my profession will say they have difficulty accepting that these same thoughts that form so much of the underpinning of our daily life and ongoing social relations can also produce illness or help restore health. Most subscribe to the prevailing medical model, which implies that patients are barely responsible for their illness. People accidentally "catch" a cold from something completely outside them, a virus or "bug." And people are almost always treated with pills, surgery, and other such techniques rather than dealing with the complexity of their stress, beliefs, and attitudes.

Nevertheless, most doctors are well aware of circumstances where psychological factors do have undeniably potent effects on the body. Below we examine one of the most clear-cut examples—placebo research—of thought altering the course of bodily events. Why doctors don't integrate the implications of this evidence into their overall medical philosophy is itself a fascinating study in the power of thought—in this case, entrenched thought!

## Placebos—Hard Proof of the Healing Power of Thought

Some of the most direct evidence for the ability of thought to produce bodily change comes from study of the so-called placebo effect. A placebo is a treatment that produces a positive result simply because the patient believes the treatment will work. The placebo itself has no intrinsic medicinal properties to produce that benefit. The most common example occurs when the doctor gives a patient a pill that he says should help alleviate the patient's condition when in fact the pill is composed only of sugar. Another common use of placebos occurs when a patient requests antibiotics for a disease that does not respond to them. The doctor goes ahead and prescribes the drugs in the hope that the patient's belief in them will do the healing. As we'll see below, even surgery can be used as a placebo. Placeboes have been shown in endless medical studies to produce a 35-45 percent improvement in whatever medical condition is being treated. Even doctors who are otherwise skeptical about the psychological aspects of illness accept, and often utilize, the power of placebos.

A dramatic example of the placebo effect occurred with the cancer drug Krebozian back when it was being touted in some media stories as a potential new miracle treatment. A patient with metastatic lymph node cancer had been told by his doctor that he had only two weeks to live; when he heard of Krebozian, he insisted on being included in clinical trials for the drug. After ten days on the medication, the man's tumors shrank and he was discharged from the program. Two months later, he heard a news report that the Krebozian trials were producing discouraging results; shortly thereafter, his tumors reappeared. His physician, well aware that his patient's beliefs were at the bottom of this yo-yo effect, told him that the batch of Krebozian used in the trials was later discovered to have been defective. He then injected the man with water, telling him that he was getting fresh, intact Krebozian. Once again the patient went into remission. He remained in good health until two months later, when he heard that Krebozian was "worthless" in the treatment of cancer. Two weeks later, he died of his original disease.

When the tranquilizer Valium was at its peak of medical use, 30 million Americans annually were taking it to reduce their stress and anxiety. Since then, however, 30 double-blind studies have shown Valium to be no more effective than a placebo. Similarly, the drug Aureomycin was hailed as an effective treatment for atypical or viral pneumonia. It was given to thousands of patients over a four-year period until a controlled study showed that it too had no advantage over placebos.

The placebo effect has been demonstrated even more dramatically with surgery. Consider the following experiment conducted in 1958. At that time, obstructive coronary artery disease was treated by sewing the internal mammary artery, an artery in the chest wall, into the heart to improve blood flow to it and thereby reduce angina pain. Half the patients in the experiment received the full surgical procedure while the other half received only a skin incision with no arterial graft. Of course, the patients weren't let in on the ruse—*both groups believed they had received the same, complete surgery.* Following the operation, the two patient groups showed equal improvement in their angina symptoms, required less of the medication nitroglycerin (a common treatment for angina), and performed better on treadmill stress tests. In fact, clinical outcomes across the board were exactly the same for both groups.

In 1981, a similar project was carried out with patients in Denmark suffering from Meniere's disease. The symptoms of Meniere's disease can be very debilitating with constant dizziness, buzzing in the ears, and eventual deafness. Thirty patients underwent surgery to receive an inner ear shunt to treat the symptoms, but unbeknownst to them, only fifteen actually received a shunt. At the three-year follow-up point, 70 percent of the patients in *both* groups were experiencing significant symptom relief.

Numerous other studies have confirmed the power of placebos, which is really the power of belief. For example, one third of people get as much pain relief from placebos as they do from morphine. In other research, placebos:

- reduced gastric acidity in ulcer disease;
- proved more effective than aspirin and cortisone in the treatment of rheumatoid arthritis;
- lowered blood pressure; and
- suppressed coughs as effectively as codeine.

Although we think of modern medicine as a highly scientific discipline focused on physical treatments, doctors often practice much like shamans, who use deception and other manipulations of the patient's belief system as primary tools. In a 1974 *Scientific American* article entitled the "Ethics of Giving Placebos," the authors stated that "35-45 percent of all prescriptions are for substances that are incapable of having an effect on the condition for which they are prescribed." Dr. Halstead Holman of Stanford University has noted that "three of four of the most commonly prescribed drugs treat no specific illness."

Despite their willingness to take advantage of placebo power, however, most physicians still act as if it is some sort of special case or parlor trick. Mainstream medicine has yet to integrate the implications of placebo research or systematically explore other ways in which patients' belief systems can be accessed to improve their health or recovery. But clearly the placebo effect is not some medical anomaly. It graphically demonstrates exactly what we noted at the start of this chapter, that there is no clear boundary between body and mind so that therapy based on thoughts or emotions can be a potent method for treating medical illness. Our power to heal ourselves with thoughts and emotions can be tapped unwittingly as with the placebo effect, but those who are aware of this ability can also consciously summon it.

There's yet another implication of placebo research that modern medicine has yet to fully acknowledge: that our conventional medical methods such as drugs and surgery, even though they have undeniable physical effects, work in part because we believe they will. While most doctors are not ready to take this philosophical leap, physicians who work in shamanistic cultures in other countries or on Native American reservations here know that shamans are often able to achieve results with their people that conventional physicians can't. It's not unusual to find shamans on the staff of a conventional medical clinic in those circumstances because the doctors realize the importance of engaging their patients' beliefs.

## The Anatomy of Healing Thoughts

Medical science is still wrestling with its own belief system about placebos and other evidence of the power of thought in the body. Nevertheless, it appears to be well on the way to uncovering the pathways by which thought works its bodily magic. Thoughts, especially those energized by feelings, influence the body's chemistry and physiology by forming chemicals called neurotransmitters. First discovered in the 1970s, neurotransmitters are essentially the brain's messenger service because they enable the brain to talk to the rest of the body. They are chemicals that transmit nerve impulses across the synapses that separate nerve cells throughout the body. Also called neuropeptides, they include chemicals with specialized functions that go by such names as lymphokines, cytokines, and growth factors; many of the body's hormones are neurotransmitters, as well.

The sum total of all this neurotransmitter activity creates what has been termed a neuropeptide network, allowing thoughts to influence the bodymind's physical processes. Your immune system, digestive tract, muscles, heart, and all other organs "listen" to your thoughts via the messenger service of the neuropeptide network and react just as directly as if you were sending a mental message to your hand to lift a finger.

Researchers are now beginning to penetrate the universe of the bodymind beyond the level of the neurotransmitters. Using a sophisticated new tool called positron emission tomography, or PET, scientists can now explore tiny events inside the brain. PET studies have shown how thought physically activates the brain with changes in regional blood flow as well as changes in the flow of regulatory hormones and the powerful neurotransmitters. This new field of scientific research, the "psychobiology" of thought, bridges the previously wide gap between psychology and medicine and reveals even more convincingly than the discovery of neurotransmitters themselves that the movement of consciousness is a physical—that is, electrochemical—event in the bodymind. Every thought that flows in your endless stream of consciousness and self-talk can potentially make a significant impact on your bodymind's physical systems (although the effect is greatly muted by the self-opposing nature of thought, as we'll see below).

Indeed, if we were more aware of the impact of thought on the bodymind, we would take greater care to think "healthfully." Even those of us who have heard about the new advances in bodymind research tend to ignore the effects of our thoughts because thoughts are such a familiar and constant part of our daily experience. No matter what we are doing, we must endure the endless mental chatter inside our heads. Most of it seems rambling and inconsequential, and even ridiculously contradictory. We want this and then we want that instead, and then we think we don't deserve any of it. One moment, our thoughts bring us down with worry, resentment, and self-criticism; the next moment, they make us giddy with inspiration, creativity, and excitement. It appears to us as if our thoughts just add up to inner background noise that cancels itself out and amounts to nothing in the end.

But if we "do the math" on our own thoughts or just listen to ourselves and others around us, we discover that each person has definite patterns to their way of thinking. Some are pessimistic about any opportunity that presents itself, some optimistic. Some fret about every bump that appears in their path, some take even big bumps in their carefree stride. Clearly, if thoughts make a difference to our health, we would want them to be as positive as possible. Yet at various times, even the cheeriest among us are weighed down by self-imposed limitations, discontents, concerns, and pain.

It simply is not possible to control all of our thoughts and make them positive—there are way too many of them. But we can be aware of the tone and content of our thoughts as they stream by and redirect them to be more uplifting. We can "re-frame" thoughts and turn half-empty glasses into half-full ones. And we can even concentrate and focus our thoughts on specific goals, including healing ourselves. (The Exercises at the end of the book will help you look carefully at your patterns of thinking.) I believe that science will eventually discover that no drug has as much power over our body systems as focused thought.

## Emotions and the Bodymind

Emotions are the other major component, with thoughts, of your consciousness. On a day-to-day basis, I believe they are even more important to understanding health and disease than are thoughts. As we just discussed, thought can have almost laser-like power when we focus it, but few of us do. Most of us, in fact, dissipate the bulk of our thought power because of the careless manner in which we use it. And I'm not being critical here, just literal, when I say "care-less." We have so many thoughts that it would take far more discipline than most of us can manage to exert control over our entire thought stream. Nevertheless, because our thoughts tend to conflict with one another instead of all flowing in the same direction, the net effect is greatly reduced and sometimes all but nil. Attitudes and beliefs, on the other hand, are consistently held patterns of thought, and do have a steady effect on our lives as well as our health.

In contrast, the emotions that arise in us do make a tangible difference that we can feel. Neurotransmitter research and PET studies show that thoughts are indeed biological and biochemical events, but not on the same level as emotions. We have all felt emotions suddenly emerge in consciousness from deep inside us; they can grip our entire being with dramatic physical conse-quences—tears, quickened heartbeat, perspiration, laughter. Often these emotions show up without even being provoked by outside events, and are precipitated by thought and memory. Thoughts "pop" into our minds, too, but not usually with that same force and body arousal.

In fact, emotions have such a direct connection to the well being of our bodymind that we can rely on them to guide us to the healthiest, most satisfying path through life. We have all had "gut feelings" about things as if the feeling were speaking only through the body without thought. And by and large, that is exactly what is happening. If you are established in a job or career now, for instance, think back to the time when you were deciding which employment track to pursue. No doubt you entertained thoughts telling you to go with the track that promised the most income, the most security, the most prestige, and so on. But perhaps there were other tracks that interested you more, even if they weren't the most practical option, in which case your gut probably tugged at you to make a more "heartfelt" (notice the body connotation) choice. This is sometimes spoken of as the difference between listening to your head and listening to your body, and career choices are a perfect example, although some of us are fortunate to find work we love that also supports us in the manner we prefer. I firmly believe that those who listen to their bodies have much healthier bodies as a result. It is as if through the language of emotions, our bodies are telling us what is good for them.

Emotions are the fire of consciousness, and it is a fire that can either purify or damage us. The positive emotions of happiness, joy, inspiration, and love can optimize our body functioning more efficiently than any dietary or exercise regimen. The emotions of fear, anger, sadness and pain will eat away at the body if we do not deal with them appropriately. But in either case, feelings are there to be felt. If we don't allow ourselves to fully experience emotions, we deny ourselves the healing potential of the positive ones and harm ourselves by not releasing the negative ones.

One of the problems of some New Age therapies is the obsession with positive thinking, which seems to presume that negative emotions can be disarmed by changing the negative thoughts associated with them. It is true that changing your thoughts to more positive ones can sometimes make you feel better about things. But positive thinking is often just a form of denial, like covering up rotting flooring in a house with brand-new linoleum. The floor is still going to collapse one day because the underlying problem was never dealt with, just hidden behind a shiny new face.

Every system in the body feels the same emotions you feel with your consciousness. When patterns of negative emotions are sustained, they contribute to illness. From headaches to high blood pressure, from indigestion to ulcers, from fatigue to cancer, the body will express emotions that are not allowed free flow through it. I often tell my patients: "either you express your emotions, or your body will."

In fact, I believe that emotions are more important to understanding health and disease than thoughts. For most of us, the power of thought is usually dissipated because of the manner in which we use it. The conflicting nature of our thoughts reduces the net effect. Sustained beliefs and attitudes, however, have a more consistent effect on the body.

Also, we generate our most potent thoughts when we focus our mind on something and begin to think about it. To a large extent, we choose what we think about, so most of us are unwilling to sustain a train of thought that doesn't feel very good. We entertain negative ideas, but only the bleakest among us find satisfaction in staying with them for long.

Emotions on the other hand often arise uncontrollably from deep within us. Sometimes powerful emotions grip us without even being provoked by outside events—leftover sadness from the long-ago loss of a loved one, for example. Thoughts "pop" into our minds, too, but not with the force and body arousal that feelings can.

The powerful influence of emotion over our lives and our bodies has to do with the fact that emotions that are not fully experienced are stored in the unconscious mind for future replay. They will arise to consciousness again and thus give us another opportunity to experience and release them because it is the intention of the bodymind's wisdom that we fully experience these emotions, no matter how many tries it takes. But that's not an ideal scenario. Because emotions are bodymind events, they are affecting our bodies during the time they are stored there, and the long-term effect of long-stored negative emotions is damaging. Far better that we experience these emotions the first time they show up or at least in one of the early replay rounds rather than after they have eaten away at us for a while.

The way this damage occurs can be seen in the physiology of emotions. As we saw in Chapter 2, scientists believe that emotions are produced within the hypothalamus and limbic system of the brain, the same system that controls appetite, hormone levels, water balance, sexual rhythms, and the autonomic nervous system. No wonder our emotions affect our appetite and sexual drive, among other things!

The emotions, like thoughts, cascade into the body through the neurotransmitter network, eventually touching every cell in the body. Emotions energize us so I like to think of them as "e-motion" or energy in motion—that is, energy that has to go somewhere. The biological plan for emotion is for it to flow outward and be felt just like electricity traveling down a wire. When we suppress emotion, we prevent it from flowing so it is stored as a type of potential energy, or energy waiting for release. If we keep it in storage and never allow it to express itself, then it starts negatively affecting bodily tissue and function and becomes the mechanism for psychosomatic disease. To use another analogy, emotions are like a stream flowing out of the mountains; if you damn it up, it will wreck the terrain.

## Multiple Personalities—
## The Power of Consciousness, Case by Case

Perhaps the most astonishing evidence of the impact of thoughts and emotions on the bodymind comes from research on what is called multiple personality disorder. Most people who suffer from this condition were subjected to severe sexual, physical, or psychological abuse in childhood. Apparently to defend themselves against the pain, they compartmentalize their minds into two or more distinct personalities, each with individual characteristics. It is as if several people are living inside the same skin.

Intriguingly, each personality has a unique grip on the body and can produce different symptoms and illnesses that are only present when that particular personality is dominant. By the same token, an acute medical condition tied to one personality suddenly vanishes when another personality takes over. For instance, Dr. Bennett Braun of the International Society for the Study of Multiple Personality has documented a case in which all of a patient's personalities except for one were allergic to orange juice. If the man drank orange juice when one of his allergic personalities was in control, he would break out in a severe rash. But when the non-allergic personality took over, the rash would instantly fade and he could drink orange juice without problems.

Dr. Francine Howland, a Yale psychiatrist who specializes in treating multiple personalities, writes of a patient who was stung by a wasp, causing his eye to swell shut and producing great pain. While arranging for an ophthalmologist to see him, Dr. Howland was able to draw out another of the patient's personalities, which then took control of his body. This personality hadn't experienced the wasp sting, so the pain and swelling disappeared.

In another case, a patient was admitted to the hospital with out-of-control diabetes, or diabetic ketoacidosis. This condition can have widespread and devastating effects on the body (I have worked in emergency departments and seen it wreak havoc first-hand). However, much to her doctors' amazement, the patient's symptoms disappeared completely when a non-diabetic personality took control.

Among other dramatic accounts about multiple personality patients:

- Epileptic seizures have disappeared when a non-epileptic personality took over the mind;
- A scar, burn mark, or cyst that appears on the body when one personality dominates goes away when another personality takes its place;
- One personality may be right-handed while another is left-handed;
- One personality may be colorblind while another is not;
- Even eye color can change from personality to personality.

To me, the clinical data of multiple personality disorders provides undeniable evidence that illness is largely a drama of the psyche played out in the biology of the body. Each of the medical conditions described above is a complex process. Some involve the immune and endocrine systems. Some involve digestive, respiratory or other complicated functions. And, yet all change almost immediately when the governing forces of consciousness also change.

### Spontaneous Remissions—What They Tell Us

Every so often, patients with advanced cancers recover completely. The medical annals are peppered with hundreds of such case histories. Although few physicians have any way of accounting for them, no one doubts that these recoveries occur. In most instances, the patients have been x-rayed or undergone exploratory surgery so the tumors have been observed and documented. Often, the patients are thought to be beyond the possibility of cure and are advised grimly to put their affairs in order. Years later, they are not only still around but in shockingly good health and cancer-free, a fact that in many cases has also been medically confirmed.

While the medical establishment has treated these so-called spontaneous remissions as freak incidents and given almost no further thought to them, some independent-minded researchers have studied the cases for clues that might apply to cancer in general. What if these remarkable patients have something in common that would benefit everyone trying to combat this fearsome illness?, they ask. And while the answers they've come up with are not conclusive at this point, they have found indications that give everyone motivated to recover their health some hope. The best news is that not only do psychological states appear to make a critical difference, but there isn't any particular personality type that is favored over others. That is, surviving cancer doesn't necessarily depend on gifts only available to a special few. All of us have the internal strengths required to win the battle against one of the body's most persistent foes, if we so choose. We'll examine the particulars about the psychology of cancer survival in later chapters.

But it's a constant frustration for those attuned to consciousness issues in health that the medical community hasn't made a more concerted effort to understand these fascinating events. Researchers G. B. Challis and H. J. Stam studied spontaneous remission cases reported in medical journals from 1900 to 1987. They noticed that article contributors would routinely offer physiological and other medically acceptable rationales for the recoveries, but they almost never suggested psychological, lifestyle, or sociological explanations—perhaps, Challis and Stam write, because the physician/authors were unwilling to risk their reputations. Beyond the general bias in medicine against non-medical and less-concrete disciplines like psychology and spirituality, there is a marked lack of curiosity about spontaneous remissions. There are no medical journals devoted to them or even an evolved method of studying them. Medical schools all but ignore teaching about them. As a result, a source of potential revelations about cancer survival remains almost entirely untapped.

Spontaneous remissions, along with multiple personality research and the placebo effect, shouldn't be swept under the rug in modern medicine. They all point to healing resources within us that we might be able to access with something as commonplace as thought, the healthy expression of emotion and considerations of the healing power of happiness and passion. We haven't yet found a way to cure every major illness with psychological techniques. But a lot of progress has been made, as we'll see in later chapters. And the realm of psychology may contain the key to the floodgates, for it just may be that when our belief systems in this society can truly accept medical miracles, they will begin occurring with much more frequency.

# 5

# CANCER—
# THE PSYCHOLOGICAL
# ASPECTS

*Cancer is a symbol, as most illness is, of something gone wrong
in the patient's life, a warning to him to take another road.*
Elida Evans (Jungian analyst), *Psychological Study of Cancer*

*There are no incurable diseases, only incurable people.*
Bernie S. Siegel, MD, *Love, Medicine and Miracles*

We have reached a crossroads in our society's understanding of
cancer's origins. For reasons that are political and economic as much
as medical, our society has looked first at physical causes such as genes
and hormones and other such differences to explain why some people
get cancer and others don't. We've paid less attention than we should
to environmental factors such as chemical carcinogens in large part
because chemical companies have used their political and financial
clout to divert attention from those factors, both in the cancer
research establishment and the public at large. The pharmaceutical
industry also has a major stake in the status quo. For one thing, it
makes its income off of cancer treatment, not prevention, and is
obviously more interested in research that might lead to lucrative new
products than research that won't. For another, many of the leading

producers of anti-cancer drugs are owned by those very same chemical companies that make the suspected carcinogens.

In a similar way, another vital clue in the cancer mystery that has nothing to do with external factors is also being overlooked by mainstream medicine. I'm talking now about the role that consciousness plays in the onset of cancer. I think it is crucial that environmental carcinogens be thoroughly studied and restricted as appropriate. But while we're walking down that path, we also have to pay equal attention to psychological issues, which are even more neglected than those nasty chemicals. The fact is that of all the people who are exposed to a particular chemical in the environment, only a small proportion will get the disease. Clearly, something else is at play.

As we noted in Chapter 1, many experts feel that serious diseases such as cancer result from a complex interaction of factors such as genes, lifestyle choices, environmental conditions, and such. That helps explain why some people get sick and others don't when they are exposed to the same chemical. But emotional and attitudinal issues tend to be discounted in this equation or ignored altogether despite the intriguing information pointing to their importance. Recall the study we looked at in Chapter 1 that showed that emotional issues were even more important than smoking history in determining who got lung cancer. We're going to examine much more research on the psychological aspects of cancer in this chapter, research that backs up my own observations from my medical practice. Although there is much more study that can been done of this matter, I feel confident in saying, based on what I've already seen, that consciousness issues are the deciding factor in cancer. What's more, I think we already know enough to identify emotional *patterns* that describe a typical cancer personality. And this means that we also know enough to suggest to patients a way of living their lives that will help prevent this dread disease.

### The Cancer Personality Profile

In 1971, President Richard Nixon launched his famous "war on cancer" with the passage of the National Cancer Act. Now nearly thirty years and $25 billion dollars later, cancer death rates continue to rise. In 1970, 907 people died every day from cancer. In 1997, the number of daily cancer deaths was 1,547. Some scientists believe that by 2005 cancer will afflict one out of two people in this country.

It just may be, however, that death rates are staying at high levels because the cancer establishment is barking up the wrong tree. Despite all the effort and money spent on developing them, chemotherapy, radiation, and surgical therapies have not greatly improved survival rates for most forms of cancer and they create intense side effects that themselves sometimes produce fatalities. If the body is the messenger for emotional issues, then cancer therapy may be one of the most egregious examples of killing the messenger. To me, our failure to make dramatic breakthroughs in cancer treatment after all this time and expense indicates that we should investigate other avenues. The most promising path in my opinion is to help patients heal emotionally and attitudinally while giving them treatments that enhance their immune system. (Conventional treatments, of course, tear down the immune system, a very risky approach that often backfires.)

In my experience, cancer demonstrates the unity of mind and body more consistently than any other disease. Drawing both on my own background in medical practice and extensive research literature, I believe the majority of adults with cancer will exhibit the following patterns:

• Significant childhood stress, either from major traumatic events or diffused throughout early life;

• Repression of emotion that begins in childhood and continues in adulthood, thus thwarting the efforts of the unconscious mind to discharge its stored contents (shadow projection);

• The inability to handle repeated shadow projections and other stresses of adult life, resulting in a sense of being trapped and the eventual feeling that "this is too much, I can't take it any more";

• The inability to find a sustained creative purpose that generates a passion for life;

• The sustained stress and the attitude of giving up suppress the immune system to the point that death, via cancer, offers the only way out of the pain.

Certainly, cancer is a complex disease and people are infinitely complex as well, so I have observed many variations on these patterns.

Children with cancer sometimes fit the above pattern but often do not. Nonetheless, the model is a useful one that I have seen reflected time and time again in most of my patients with the illness. This model also echoes loudly in psychological studies of cancer patients. So let's go through it, step by step.

## Childhood Stress

Several studies have found that the childhoods of cancer patients are frequently marred by major emotional trauma. For instance, Scottish researcher David Kissen, who examined the personality traits of lung cancer patients, discovered that a large number of them had lost an important loved one such as a parent, brother, or sister during their childhood. He published his research in the British Journal of Medical Psychology in 1967. Other researchers have noticed that cancer patients commonly suffered a break in their family's unity during their childhood due to divorce, death, or prolonged separation from one or both parents.

My interviews with cancer patients have often uncovered similar emotional blows. Patients will mention loss of, or separation from, a parent, as well as other parent-based traumas such as emotional, physical, or sexual abuse. All such incidents unleash tremendous anger, pain, guilt, or other powerful emotions in the young child's consciousness. The pain is too great and the child too young for the storm of strong emotions to be felt and released, so the child represses them, simply to survive. (Repression is an unconscious process while suppression is a conscious choice not to express emotion.) Even infants can experience these intense feelings. For example, the newborn separated from her mother and given to adopted parents seeds the pain of the loss of the most important person in her life into the shadow of her unconscious mind.

The childhood stress that contributes to adult cancer need not be so focused on particular events. In fact, chronic stresses such as lack of parental affection are sometimes even more devastating to the child's developing psyche. All of us need love to thrive, but children need it most of all. Ideally, parents will offer their children the unconditional support, nurturing, and loving attention that builds self-confidence and esteem. Indeed, healthy personality development depends on this. When a child can take his emotional problems to a loving parent, the emotions are expressed and he comes to understand his problem and grow from the experience. Over time, children in such families learn that feelings are natural and that it is okay to be angry or cry and be vulnerable. Thus, instead of being suppressed into the shadow of the mind for future replay, the inevitable traumas of childhood are released naturally—the best possible outcome for both health and happiness. Just as importantly, these children learn *how* to express painful emotions and they better understand the difficult lessons in life.

Unfortunately, most cancer patients have lived a different past, one that is often wanting in parental love and support. For various reasons, their parents weren't capable of loving to the extent that a child requires and deserves. Often the parents were overly strict, emotionally distant, and unable to express love. Finding no outlet for emotional pain, the child learns to stuff feelings, steadily adding to the brimming stores of the unconscious mind. If this pattern is not reversed, it lays the foundation for serious illness or other bodymind damage later in life.

The residue of this syndrome show up in research. Psychologist Lawrence LeShan interviewed 250 hospitalized cancer patients and then compared his findings with interview results from 250 patients hospitalized for other diseases. When he analyzed the data, he found a striking consistency among the cancer sufferers. They recalled a grim childhood during which they felt lonely and isolated. Their described their relationship with either or both parents as tense or hostile. The lack of parental closeness made them feel that deep relationships weren't possible with people outside the family, either.

It's actually more common to find lack of parental love and nurturing in the backgrounds of cancer patients than focused emotional trauma such as divorce or a parent's death. For example, psychologist Claus Bahnson at the Jefferson Medical College in Philadelphia interviewed cancer patients and found that their childhoods were generally marked by "cold, strict, aloof relationships with their parents." Another study examined psychological and personality traits of 1500 physicians and looked for associations with the development of illness over a period of 25 years. The strongest relationship revealed by far was the tie between a variety of cancers and lack of closeness to parents.

## Suppression of Emotion throughout Life

Research on the psychology of cancer patients consistently reveals a pattern of suppressing emotions, a harmful impulse I'm convinced starts in childhood after recurrent emotional pain. In fact, *the nonexpression of emotions is considered a hallmark of the cancer personality.*

In the late 1970s, psychologist Lydia Temoshok studied 150 patients with malignant melanoma at the University of California, San Francisco School of Medicine. She noticed a distinct similarity between them—they were "so nice" and never seemed to air negative emotions of any kind. Even in the face of terminal illness, they failed to voice fear, sadness, or anger.

Two decades earlier, Dr. Eugene Blumberg had studied cancer patients in a Veteran's Hospital in Long Beach, California and drawn similar conclusions. He wrote: "We were impressed by the polite, apologetic, almost painful acquiescence of the patients with rapidly progressing disease as contrasted with the more expressive and sometimes bizarre personalities of those who responded brilliantly to therapy with remissions and long survival."

Dr. Lawrence LeShan also noted cancer patients' lack of truthful emotional expression. They are almost "too good to be true," he observed in a 1961 issue of *Psychiatric Quarterly.* In his book, *Mind as Healer, Mind as Slayer,* Dr. Kenneth Pelletier wrote: "... cancer victims are frequently described by their friends as exceptionally fine, thoughtful, gentle, uncomplaining people." There is certainly nothing wrong with being thoughtful, gentle and uncomplaining, but when these traits serve as a cover for suppressed anger and pain, they may invite illness.

The emotional denial I have seen in my own cancer patients sometimes reaches ludicrous proportions, particularly with female breast cancer sufferers. As I often say to my patients, you could be standing on the toe of someone with breast cancer, ask her how she's doing, and she would reply "Fine." Everything is fine with some people with cancer, it seems, but they use their sweetness to divert others from what is sometimes a lifetime of anger and pain hidden within. It may be more socially acceptable to cover true feelings with a façade of niceness, but the medical consequences can be serious. The nature of the bodymind offers us a stark choice: express your feelings, or your body will.

## When the Stress of Adult Life Becomes "Too Much"

As I discussed in Chapter 2, I believe that emotional wounds stored in the unconscious mind seek release and healing by replaying themselves in our lives. I call this process emotional wound healing, which is similar to physical wound healing which occurs, for example, when you cut a finger. In other words, our unconscious emotional pain will influence our conscious choices in life, leading us to unknowingly set up circumstances that will allow us to experience the original traumatic feelings. For instance, if a child is abused or abandoned, there is a lot of pain, tears, and hurt that may be too much for the small child to fully release, so the pain is repressed into the unconscious mind. Later in life the pain will resurface when the person unknowingly creates a similar experience of abuse or abandonment. Now the person can feel and release the pain, or deny it again. If the person denies these feelings and explains them away with all kinds of reasons, the hurt is suppressed back into the unconscious mind and the process of emotional wound healing has failed.

Replayed circumstances often differ somewhat from the original source of the emotional wound, obscuring the fact that the emotional dynamics of both circumstances are the same. For example, after a failed relationship, we may start a new relationship with someone whose personality appears to be entirely different. But eventually we find ourselves confronting the same issues we failed to resolve in the previous go-round. Or we will find ourselves facing self-esteem issues at work that have their origin in problems with our parents. Even though the circumstances are different, the emotions are the same. It is our consciousness' intention that we will finally allow ourselves to take responsibility for our part in creating the events that trouble us, and fully experience the emotions those events engender. If we do this, our emotional wounds can heal and the formerly bound-up energy dissipates and stops eating away at our bodies. Our psyche's persistence in offering us the opportunity to re-own our traumas, which we call "shadow projection" in Edgework, is perhaps the most powerful tool for self-healing available to us.

This tool is no less available or effective for the cancer patient than anyone else. Unfortunately, though, it is the nature of the cancer psyche for patients to feel that fully experiencing any deep emotion would open a floodgate that would overwhelm them. In the majority of cancer patients, the shadow is bulging with pain, anger, and other uncomfortable emotions associated with a difficult childhood. Human consciousness is wise enough not to give us more than we can handle, so shadow projection can be trusted to parcel out emotion in bite-size chunks, but it is understandable that cancer sufferers would fear otherwise.

With the cancer patients I've interviewed over the years, I document the stresses in childhood and how they were recreated in adult life. Usually the stressful events crescendo in the ten years or so prior to the cancer diagnosis. I then ask my patients if they express feelings easily or if they tend to hold them in. Invariably, the answer is something like, "Yes, it is difficult for me to express my emotions." I next ask if they have ever felt like the stresses in their lives were too much to take. The vast majority respond with a faint trembling in their voice that yes, they have felt like the difficulties in their lives reached such intensity at times that they felt they were too great to bear (although, they often add in the next breath that, despite their stresses, they hadn't considered suicide).

I have seen the "too-much, I can't take it" syndrome so often that I consider it a risk factor for the development of cancer. The syndrome results from a collision between the healing tendencies of the psyche and the dysfunctional, emotion-denying tendencies of the pre-cancer patient. Basically, the shadow is relentless in trying to discharge stored emotion, and most pre-cancer patients equally relentless in denying emotions whenever they emerge. As a result, these people begin to feel trapped by the replay-denial cycle. If just once they would allow themselves to experience some of the replayed emotions, the pressure would subside, and they would see that feeling their emotions works. But rarely do eventual cancer patients take this risk. Instead, these people feel hopeless, helpless, and victimized, unaware that they are caught in a snare of their own creation.

Dr. LeShan noticed several features of this pattern in cancer patients he studied, leading to what he called the "despair syndrome." In a paper published in The Psychiatric Quarterly, titled "A basic psychological orientation apparently associated with malignant disease," he writes the following:

> . . . a barren and hopeless state, in which the afflicted individual experiences an extreme sense of unrelatedness to everything around him. Despair engulfs him to such an extent that love cannot bridge the gap, nor can he express such emotions as anger, resentment, jealousy and hostility in order to ease the loneliness. He sees no possibility of ever attaining any satisfaction or meaning in life, and in spite of any effort he may make, there is no hope for the future.

Dr. Goldfarb and his colleagues at the St. Vincent's Hospital and Medical Center of New York found similar psychological symptoms in their testing of cancer patients. They characterized it as " … preneoplastic [pre-tumor] feelings of hopelessness, helplessness and despair, as well as inability to express hostility and inability to accept loss of a significant object."

Many other researchers share these same conclusions. My sense of how pre-cancer psyche leads to cancerous tumor growth is as follows: Since the cells of the immune system are in constant communication with emotions through the bodymind's neurotransmitter network, they "feel" the pre-cancer patient's despair and hopelessness. If the message is sustained long enough, the natural killer cells (designed to kill aberrant cells such as cancer) and other immune cells acquiesce to the demands of consciousness and loosen their vigilance against cancer, permitting the illness to develop in the body. It is as if the immune system responds with primordial sympathy, "Okay, just as you wish, you won't have to take it anymore. Cancer will solve the problems in your life."

## The Inability to Find a Sustained Creative Purpose

As we've seen, it is not stress alone that causes the pre-cancerous suppression of the immune system. It is also the inability to express, and thereby discharge, the intense emotions associated with the stressful experiences. But the effects of stress can be offset by a life lived with creative purpose. People who "follow their bliss" find that their chosen vocation or avocation generates enthusiasm, creativity, and passion for life, like a battery that never seems to run out. They are so pumped up most of the time that they can endure considerable stress without being beaten down by it.

This almost inexhaustible zest is not necessarily the same thing as happiness. We all know of the despair and torment that can characterize the life experience of the artist, poet, writer, or philosopher. Van Gogh's agony was part of the psychic fire that birthed his wondrous art. The existential anxiety of Nietzsche and Kierkegaard compelled them to write treatises on human nature that still inspire us to this day. Indeed, descending into the stored pain of the unconscious mind can even spark the creative process when the person is inspired to illuminate his pain in a way that helps others understand their own. The painful experiences in life are meant to be lessons for us all. Creative people not only learn from their own pain but pass on the lessons to a wide public in many cases. This sense of mission, of assisting others, stokes the fire and makes the creative person's passion burn that much brighter.

Living life with passion nurtures the body almost across the board, improving immunity, digestion, and cardiac function, and relaxing the body's musculature among other benefits. (We'll examine the health effects of satisfying work and other positive states at length in the latter half of the book.) Every cell in your body has a powerful sense of purpose. The cells in your lungs absorb oxygen and release carbon dioxide. Your brain cells manage bodily functions, store and recall information, and create ideas, plans, and other thoughts. Skin cells defend you against invasion from the environment. The list goes on and on. But although we don't know how, we can see both from research and through our own eyes that the bodies of people who aren't dedicated to a purpose begin to deteriorate. If you, the sum of those 100 trillion cells, have no inspired purpose for living, it somehow affects the cells to lose their own passion to do a good job.

So it is with many pre-cancer patients. Their purpose in life has been lost or never discovered in the first place. Perhaps the death of a loved one cost them their enthusiasm for life. Perhaps after an accumulation of childhood traumas, they shut themselves down emotionally and never even considered the possibility of creative satisfaction. Perhaps feelings of unworthiness from a childhood lacking in affection and support led them to feel that they didn't deserve a more inspiring life. Cancer patients don't necessarily lead lives that look different on the surface; they have jobs, families, and typical outside activities. But their living is often colored with a sense of obligation, drudgery, and depression, lacking the animation, direction, and drive of a meaningful existence. Certainly, there are many exceptions to this pattern—people of great ambition and vitality whose lives are cut short by cancer for reasons no one can understand. But I have seen the profile just described so often that I would be remiss not to mention it.

We cannot leave the subject of passion without mention of the deepest passion of all—spirituality. Clearly no experience can ignite the fires of passion more than a personal experience of God. History is replete with examples of great power and accomplishment coming on the heels of a divine inner revelation. National polls show that 90% of Americans believe in God and the importance of religion in their lives. And, medical research is repeatedly showing the healing power of faith, prayer and contemplation of a higher power. Perhaps the fire of religious conviction can be rekindled, or ignited for the first time. More on this topic will come in Chapter 12.

**The Only Escape from Pain: Death**

At John Hopkins University School of Medicine, psychologists Pirkko L. Graves and John W. Shaffer and their colleagues carefully followed the health of 1000 medical students between 1948 and 1964. Over the course of the study, the subjects completed detailed questionnaires about their mental attitudes; their answers were compared to their illness patterns over the sixteen-year research period.

The results showed that people who considered themselves "loners" and went through life with little expression of emotion had the highest cancer rates; those that "acted out their emotions" had the lowest rates (although they weren't necessarily psychologically healthy—they tended to be anxious and easily upset, for instance). The authors of the study concluded that the *"personality profiles of the cancer patients were very similar to those that committed suicide."*

Decades earlier, another study, also of Johns Hopkins medical students, had reached similar conclusions. Beginning in 1946, Caroline Bedell Thomas correlated five conditions—coronary heart disease, hypertension, mental disorders, malignant tumors, and suicide—to the life habits of the subjects as they reported them on questionnaires. The profiles of those who developed cancer and those who later killed themselves were strikingly similar. They tended to be "low-gear" types who rarely expressed emotions and who had colder, more remote relationships with their parents than subjects who developed the other conditions studied. Perhaps cancer is a socially acceptable way of committing suicide for those who find the pain of life too much to bear.

The noted psychologist Lawrence LeShan discovered similar findings in his research on cancer patients. In *You Can Fight for Your Life, Emotional Factors in the Treatment of Cancer,* Le Shan writes: "To make the point even more strongly, many of the patients specifically expressed the idea that for years they had felt there was no way out of the emotional box they found themselves in, short of death itself."

## Cancer and the Mind—A Tentative Conclusion

The model I have presented above is meant to be a tool. In my experience it is a useful tool for the majority of adult cancer patients that I have seen in my medical practice. It also fits with a substantial part of the research literature. But you cannot use one tool for every job. The child with cancer may present a different picture and may not fit this model. And, certainly, the newborn or infant with cancer is a special case. I believe that to fully understand the infant with cancer requires a spiritual perspective that is not available to most of us yet.

It would be nice if we could say that, since we're honing in on the psychological attributes of the cancer personality, we could heal cancer with psychotherapy. But we're not there yet. We still have lots to learn about the exact psychology of cancer and the precise bodymind mechanisms by which psychological processes become disease. Nonetheless, the research literature and my personal experience with patients clearly shows that psychological healing, whether in individual psychotherapy or in group therapy, can favorably influence the course of illness for cancer patients. It has been shown to prolong life and to improve the quality of remaining years, and in some cases to lead to a cure. Perhaps as time goes on we will be able to focus precisely on the key emotional and attitudinal issues for the cancer patient and get better results. The Edgework Exercises are designed to hone in on key issues in the formation of disease.

I believe psychological intervention should be a part of every cancer treatment plan. Reducing fear, expressing emotions, releasing dysfunctional beliefs, reviving enthusiasm for life, improving self-esteem, and forgiveness can offer powerful and transforming experiences to anyone, and they may be what the bodymind is calling for with the experience of cancer.

And what we're learning about the cancer personality certainly does indicate steps that all of us are wise to take if we want to prevent disease. That starts with taking responsibility for the things that trouble us and expressing emotions as they occur. I can't promise that everyone who does this will be disease-free all their lives, but certainly expressive living is far more healthful, emotionally and otherwise, than the alternative.

We should also seek to create work that fulfills us, that enables us to use our creativity, that has meaning for us, and that is aligned with our larger, perhaps spiritual, purpose in life. If for any reason we can't do that right away, we should certainly try to fill our lives outside work with those same qualities, through an avocation, volunteer work, or whatever. Optimal health depends on an optimal life. Again, I can't guarantee that a satisfying life will inevitably be a long, healthy life, but I have certainly seen over and over that, when people want to be here, their bodies tend to do everything in their power to help them achieve their wish.

# 6

# The Mind and Heart Disease

*Through love, all pain will turn to medicine.*

Rumi

It doesn't take much of a stretch, even in a society obsessed with physical causes, to imagine that *the mind* would have something to do with heart disease. When we see people we care about, driving themselves hard at their work or straining under constant emotional stress, we worry that they will damage their hearts. It is also common knowledge that people who have suffered heart attacks in the past should try to keep themselves emotionally calm.

Nevertheless, the media and medical experts still focus their warnings primarily on the physical risk factors for heart problems—smoking, high-fat diets, lack of exercise, obesity, and so forth. So it's natural to assume that those who take poor care of themselves physically are the ones at greatest risk.

Not necessarily so. Of all the people who get heart attacks, only 30 to 40 percent have the traditional risk factors just mentioned. Clearly there must be other risk factors involved that don't appear on the usual lists. This is not to say that the physical risk factors don't matter. Indeed they do—they are called risk factors because those who have them are more likely to experience heart problems. But there is also such a thing as "protective factors"—aspects of a person's psychological or emotional make-up or social situation that help

insulate them from trouble even when they are seemingly undermin-
ing their health in every other way. Heart disease is a complex
condition like cancer in which a number of things including lifestyle,
psychosocial factors, and genes interact to produce a health problem.
But as with cancer, it may be that emotional issues are the thing that
tips the balance.

In this chapter, we examine the evidence to see if we can discern
a "heart patient personality," just as we saw the outlines of a cancer
personality in Chapter 5. As you'll see, this is important not only in
preventing heart disease but in reversing the illness if you already
suffer from it.

### Driving the Highway to Heart Disease

For over three decades, researchers have pursued the idea that so-
called Type A personalities—hard-driving, ambitious types who feel
constantly pressured by time, who overreact to even minor stresses,
and who may also be hostile, aggressive, and compulsive—are heart-
attack prone, especially when compared to more laid-back "Type
Bs." The notion garnered so much attention from the popular press
that "Type A" has become part of common language, with all kinds
of mistaken notions attached to it, including the notion that Type A
behavior is an automatic red flag for cardiac trouble. The fact is that
the research on Type As has yielded conflicting results. While some
studies clearly point to an association of Type A behavior with heart
problems, others show no correlation whatsoever, and one study in
the 1990s even found that among heart attack sufferers, Type As had
a higher survival rate.

When researchers began looking more closely at the data, however, they found within the Type A personality a factor—hostility—
that does point more clearly to heart disease risk. Hostility, in the way
the researchers are considering it, embodies many qualities—anger, a
chronically cynical or mistrustful outlook, aggression, an impulse to
oppose other people, and a desire to hurt others. Hostility may be
expressed outwardly, with verbal insults or even throwing punches,
or it may be held within as angry, cynical, or suspicious thoughts and
feelings.

Studies do show a clear correlation between people who are outwardly hostile and heart disease risk; although the correlation is a little weaker, hostile feelings and thoughts also appear to increase the chances of heart problems. For instance, people with cynical or hostile attitudes or suppressed anger are both more likely to have atherosclerosis and blockage of coronary arteries and more likely to have heart attacks. In one study, 255 physicians were given a battery of psychological tests when they were students at the University of North Carolina Medical School and then followed for the next 25 years. Those who had scored higher on the hostility scale had four times the incidence of heart disease. Yes, it's true that hostile types are more likely to smoke and drink, which also increases heart disease risk. But even when researchers "control" for these factors—that is, use statistical techniques to make sure the factors weren't tilting the data—hostility still shows up as a warning sign of future heart trouble.

Just as hostility is a part of the constellation of Type A behaviors, there are probably some aspects of hostility that are the real "toxic" factors as far as heart disease is concerned. Researchers hope to hone in on those factors in coming studies. But in the meantime, current research suggests that if you can find a way to release your anger and hostility without hauling off and popping someone in the mouth or having it turn you sour on the inside, your heart will be much healthier for it. I believe the best approach is to recognize the hurt feelings that usually exist just below the anger, and if people acknowledge the anger and then look to express the hurt, then the damaging effects of anger are avoided. We will look at this issue later in the chapter.

## The Long-term Effects of Long-term Heartache

We often describe lonely people as having aching hearts. That turns out to be a pretty astute perception, medically speaking. Consider social isolation, which appears to be one of the most stark emotional risk factors for heart trouble. Fortunately, the opposite of isolation—companionship, connection to a community, emotional support from family members and friends, and so on—seems to offer substantial protection against heart problems even in the presence of life stresses and all the usual physical risks. Researchers group these factors under the term "social support," which means there is someone around to talk to about your problems. Such support is more likely to lead to emotional expression and self-understanding. It is widely recognized as contributing to health and well being.

One of the most dramatic demonstrations of the value of social support occurred in the town of Roseto, Pennsylvania, which had a substantial Italian-American community. Despite the fact that most Italian-Americans there were overweight and ate a diet loaded with saturated fats, the rate of myocardial infarctions (a heart attack in which heart muscle dies because of blockage of the blood supply) was stunningly low. When members of this ethnic community did suffer heart attacks, death rates were just half what neighboring towns and the nation at-large experienced. Intrigued, medical professor Stewart Wolf went to Roseto to study what might be different about it. He found the community to be unusually cohesive. Members maintained strong ties both to relatives and to the community as a whole and relationships were notable for their mutual support. But inevitably, this tight little social structure began to unravel as younger generations moved away or adopted more contemporary lifestyles, and among those who did loosen their bonds with the community, heart attacks occurred at the same rates experienced in the rest of the country.

An English study of civil servants turned up similar results. The subjects who had the weakest social connections with neighbors, relatives, and friends had the highest death rates from coronary heart disease (CHD). Social isolation appears to have comprehensive ill effects on the body, not just the heart. Dr. Dean Ornish points out that people who feel isolated have three to five times the death rates from all causes, not just heart disease, compared to those who feel socially supported. And this is generally true regardless of their blood pressure, blood cholesterol levels, or smoking history. Again, the overwhelming majority of those who have the standard physical risk factors for heart disease don't ever contract it. As in Roseto, Pennsylvania, researchers have observed that feelings of being supported socially seem to help protect those who would otherwise seem to be strong candidates for illness.

Social support or lack of it isn't the only dimension in which heartache seems to relate to heart disease. More intimately, some studies suggest that a child's relationship with his parents—the primary "heart connection" of his life—can affect his cardiac health decades later. For instance, in 1997 Drs. Harry Russek and Gary Schwartz published research that demonstrated a tie between the quality of parent-child relationships and the child's health later as an aging adult. The study began with Harvard students in 1952 and 1954, when 126 healthy men were randomly selected from those years' graduating classes. In questionnaires, the subjects were asked to grade their relationship with their mother and father, from "very close" on one end of the scale to "strained and cold" at the other end. Thirty-five years later, the authors examined these same men's medical records and medical and psychological histories. The results were striking: 91 percent of the men who said they didn't have a warm relationship with their mother had suffered serious diseases in mid-life, including heart disease, high blood pressure, and alcoholism. This compared to only 45 percent of the men who said they had a warm relationship with their mother. Similarly, 82 percent of the men who felt distant from their fathers had serious disease in mid-life compared to only 50 percent for those who felt close to their father.

The profound emotional impact of losing a parent during childhood can also reverberate in adult cardiac health. Dr. Claus Bahnson examined data from the Middlesex County Heart Study and the Midtown Manhattan Mental Health Study and found that a significant number of cardiac patients had lost their fathers prematurely, usually when the son was between 5 and 17 years of age. In similar research, Drs. George Engel, William Greene, and Arthur Schmale interviewed patients hospitalized at the Rochester Medical School with various diseases. They found that early in their lives, a significant number of the patients had experienced the loss of one or both parents. When new losses occurred in their lives as adults, many of the patients grew deeply depressed and came down with physical illnesses. Common among those illnesses was heart disease.

These and other research show that the heart patient often has tremendous emotional pain in childhood. There are myriad ways children are ignored, humiliated, abandoned, criticized, neglected and abused by parents who usually do the best they can, but are too wounded themselves to be the ideal loving parent. And the child is completely dependent on the parents for physical, mental, and emotional care. The child believes what they say and do to him, and naturally, forms his or her sense of self-worth based on the stream of parental interactions in those early years. (I will use a masculine model as most heart attack patients are men.)

It is easy to understand how devastating it would be for a child to lose a parent early in life. Losing mother is the most injurious as she has been his source of life, both physically and emotionally. His grief would be unimaginable as the most important person in his life is now gone. Regardless of what Dad does and what other caregivers offer, the world has become uncertain, dangerous, and untrustworthy. As time goes by, he knows that he must be strong and take care of himself. But most important in terms of future experience, he has seeded tremendous grief into the shadow of his unconscious mind. His ego will structure itself to avoid feeling emotions in general because of this extreme pain lodged in his own shadow. His defenses against feeling his feelings will harden in these early years, much like his arteries will harden later in life. He has begun the emotional blockage that could set the stage for coronary blockage decades later.

As he grows into manhood, he will interact with the world primarily in a logical manner, for logic and reasoning are safe and don't hurt as much as emotion. He is driven by achievement, as he believes that he will be loved for what he accomplishes. As he strives to succeed at any cost, he ignores his own levels of satisfaction or fulfillment, as his only goal is to accomplish more for himself and his family. But the anger and the pain of his early loss still reside within, under pressure and wanting to heal. He will find himself in relationships where the girlfriend or wife will leave him for whatever reason, as his unconscious mind projects scenarios to heal the grief of parental loss. But instead of screaming in anger or crying the loss, he will deny his feelings consciously (suppression) or unconsciously (repression), as he stays well-defended by explaining away the current loss with a host of "good" reasons. The loss of a relationship in adult life will further harden his distrustful beliefs about people and how "you can't rely on anyone," and he will move further toward a life of emotional blockage and isolation. He will further doubt his own ability to be loved and taken care of by anyone, as his self-esteem deteriorates, heading him in the direction of depression.

Of course there are many variations possible in the example I have given, and it is based on one of the most damaging things that could happen to a child—loss of mother. But a similar scenario can be created for a much more common childhood problem: the cold or distant mother who doesn't know how to love, and the mother who neglects the child. In these situations, the abandonment is emotional, instead of physical, but the damage can be just as debilitating. The distant mother probably had similar experiences in her childhood and never learned how to love and nurture. The neglectful mother often has an emotional problem of her own, sometimes manifesting in alcoholism or workaholism. She may be physically ill, or dealing with major problems in her marriage such as an alcoholic or abusive husband. A child raised in such an environment often doesn't get his physical or emotional needs met. He feels insecure and may be exposed to anger or rage. He wonders what is wrong with him that his mother doesn't want to take care of him, and his self-esteem starts out at very low levels. He isn't taught the importance of feelings in an emotionally supportive environment, but instead is exposed to feelings that are out of control and scare him. For the child whose mother dies, the pain is seeded into the unconscious mind in a focal manner. For the neglected child, the sadness, fear and anger of not having his needs met on a daily basis, of not being loved day in and day out, will be pushed into the unconscious mind, creating a complex of wounds just as debilitating as our first example. And in both cases, these wounds are set for replay in the future, hopefully for emotional healing, but all too often for repeated denial and eventual physical disease.

As the child matures into manhood, he carries with him a low sense of self-worth and believes that only he can take care of himself, and he works hard to do so. He has become distant from his own feelings and likes to rationalize away problems instead of feeling the emotions underlying them. He tends to isolate himself whether married or not, and will not confide his problems with others. He is familiar with anger but that is as far as his emotional range allows, and his thinking about his problems can easily escalate his anger into resentment and hostility. The core grief and sadness of missing parental love and nurturing never comes to the surface, creating an emotional stagnation and blockage that is held in his energy body, and eventually creates the blockage in his coronary arteries, leading to a heart attack.

## Depression, Hopelessness, "Vital Exhaustion" and Heart Problems

We saw in the previous chapter how depression can be an emotional risk factor for cancer. But it's not particularly healthy for hearts, either. Medical research has identified an association between depression and heart disease, and in particular acute myocardial infarction (MI), for over 30 years. In one study, researchers out of Duke University Medical Center followed 730 Danish men and women over a period of 27 years. The subjects completed psychological tests at the start of the research and then again at the 18-year point. Those who described themselves in terms that indicated despair, low self-esteem, difficulties in concentrating, and low motivation were 70 percent more likely to have heart attacks and had a 60 percent higher risk of dying than the rest of the subjects. As we saw with the hostility studies, subjects with these qualities were more likely to smoke, drink, overeat, and take up other habits not friendly to their hearts, but that didn't account for all the heart disease. For example, the rates of heart disease and death were higher than smoking would explain.

Hopelessness—the opposite of hope or optimism and a distinguishing feature of depression—also strongly correlates to heart illness. In one study of 2800 then-healthy men and women, hopelessness was measured by a question from a psychological test measuring signs of depression. Subjects with high hopelessness indexes were much more likely to suffer either nonfatal or fatal ischemic heart disease (IHD). Another study, this time of over 2400 men, found that those with high hopelessness scores and no previous history of heart trouble had a significantly increased risk for a first MI. High scorers also had four times the risk of dying from cardiovascular disease. By the way, hopelessness also significantly increased the risk of getting cancer and of dying from it, not to mention death from external causes such as violence or injury.

In recent years, medical researchers have begun to pay attention to a mental state called "vital exhaustion," which encompasses feelings of hopelessness and demoralization, excessive fatigue, and irritability. This condition too correlates with coronary disease in both men and women.

## Surprise! Living Your Life Without Heart Is Bad for Your Heart

The same Stewart Wolf who did the Roseto, Pennsylvania research also studied some 10,000 American workers while on the faculty at Oklahoma University Medical Center. He found that those who went through life, joylessly striving without any real sense of satisfaction, had a significantly higher risk of MI.

In a somewhat related project, medical researchers in Sweden studied male twins and their subsequent development of heart disease. Twin studies are used to eliminate the influence of biology or genes; if twins develop different illnesses across a significant number of pairs, then something other than biology or genes is probably at play. The researchers found that in each pair, the one who was more dissatisfied with his childhood experiences, educational level, and achievements in life had significantly more severe coronary artery disease. The authors concluded that life dissatisfaction better predicted heart disease severity than did such traditional risk factors as high blood pressure, cholesterol and obesity.

## Looking Deeper into the Heart Disease Personality

As we have seen, hostility, social isolation, low self-esteem, and depression are associated with heart disease, as is the lack of fulfilling and satisfying work experience. In my opinion, two common elements underlie all of these issues: first, the inability to express emotion in a healthy, natural manner and, second, adherence to dysfunctional belief systems about one's self, usually developed in childhood. Hostility may seem to be an exception to the rule about inability to express emotion, but that is deceptive. Someone who is truly open to their emotions passes easily from one emotion to the next and does not suppress any emotional state. In contrast, the hostile person tends to stay stuck in one emotion: anger. He is unlikely to cry when his feelings are hurt or when he is grieving a loss, and he may not even admit that he is hurt. He has trouble expressing love to those around him. He prefers to deny his fears rather than acknowledge them and bring them into the open.

Anger is a natural, powerful emotion that can be expressed healthily. It doesn't have to be abusive or sustained; it can simply be felt and released. However, with many people and heart patients in particular, anger seems to fuel itself. For instance, some people feed their anger with more and more thoughts that justify their indignation. The anger escalates to the point that it seems hard to release. Eventually, it sours into hostility or resentment, which can last for days, months, or even a lifetime.

Note, too, that for many people, anger is simply a reaction to another, deeper emotion, so unless the original emotion is also expressed, venting anger won't achieve a full emotional release. We most often get angry when our feelings are hurt in some way. Take, for instance, the executive who rages at a manager who didn't complete a much-needed report on time. Perhaps underneath that anger, the executive feels hurt that his deadline for the report wasn't taken seriously enough. I consider anger to be a superficial emotion in most cases. With my patients, I compare it to the lid on a garbage can. I advise them to look inside the garbage can and see what pain or hurt precipitated the anger. Expressing hurt feelings in a vulnerable manner can produce a healing release, a far better result than allowing anger to just birth more anger.

The suppression of emotion in cardiac patients was documented in research done by Dr. J. Denollet in 1996 and published in the Lancet. He administered personality questionnaires to 618 coronary patients who were participating in an outpatient cardiac rehabilitation program. The questionnaire identified "Type D" behavior as "negative affectivity, social inhibition and alienation, chronic suppression of negative emotions and frequent depression." Then Dr. Denollet followed these patients for six to ten years and found that 24% of the Type D group had died while only 7% had died with other personality profiles.

Depression is the other major psychological risk factor for heart disease, along with many other diseases. As reported in the professional journal *American Psychologist* in 1987, R. S. Friedman and K.S. Booth used a statistical method called meta-analysis to correlate the findings of a large number of research studies on the relationship between personality and disease. The authors concluded that heart disease, asthma, ulcers, arthritis, and headaches are related to depression, anger/hostility, and anxiety. These findings don't surprise me because all of the psychological states mentioned are marked by an inability to express emotion (in the case of anger, again, that means the full content of present emotion). This is most obviously so with depression. Instead of experiencing and voicing their feelings, depressed people withdraw and become apathetic. They lose interest in life, and eventually become weighed down with fatigue, guilt, and hopelessness. As with all of us, depressed people have life stresses that naturally spark emotions, but they won't let the feelings flow, so the emotions simply build up like water behind a dam. It appears to many clinicians that depressed patients, despite their apparent lack of energy, in fact invest tremendous amounts of energy to keep the dammed-up emotions from bursting through to the outside.

I often tell my patients, who are holding in feelings, to imagine a closet that is so full that the door is bulging out and ready to break, and they are pushing against the door to keep it from breaking under the pressure. I also point out to them that the same energy used to hold in all that feeling could be used for more fully living.

I have seen thousands of heart patients over the years and the majority of them are tough, capable men who work hard to support their families, doing whatever is necessary to bring home a paycheck. This, too, does not surprise me. Who is more likely to hold in feelings than the man who has bought society's stereotype that a "real" man is strong and positive, doesn't cry, plows ahead with his work no matter what he feels, and otherwise avoids any display of vulnerability? Telling these men in their 50s and 60s to begin expressing their feelings can be a challenging task indeed, especially when their cardiologist says that surgery and drugs will fix them right up, and no one else in the health establishment has connected the dots between their blocked emotions and blocked blood vessels.

### The Good News in the Bad News

The above information may alarm those of us who haven't been able to rein in our hostility, who are more socially isolated than we'd prefer, who are depressed or overcome by feelings of hopelessness, who usually suppress their feelings, or who trudge through life without satisfaction, inspiration, or joy. But none of these conditions is a death sentence. Far from it, in fact. I don't want to underestimate the effort and difficulty of Edgework or other forms of psychological and spiritual transformation. Emotional and spiritual work isn't called "work" for nothing. But the good news here is that in almost every case the means to prevent illness is within our control. We may need the outside assistance of a therapist to help us reverse behavior or emotional tendencies that have become so ingrained that we can't see our own way out of them. But that too is within our control. The Edgework exercises are designed to lead a person through the key issues of emotional expression, healing emotional wounds from childhood, identifying dysfunctional beliefs and exploring deeper considerations about work and relationships. As we discussed in the previous chapter, the real key to therapy is motivation. If we want to change, we will find a way. In fact, once we are motivated to improve our lives, we have already turned the corner.

In focusing on the psychological side of heart disease, I'm certainly not suggesting that we ignore the physical risk factors. Smoking, drinking, high cholesterol, high blood pressure, weight problems, and sedentary living do predispose people to illness. Even if psychological issues are the deciding factor, a significant number of those done in by them still come from the population of people who have put themselves physically at risk as well. Yes, some people do all the wrong things—smoke like chimneys, drink like fish, and all the rest—and outlive every "health nut" in their town. But we're talking about an extremely small number of folks here. It may well be that these people lead model lives from a psychological standpoint. Many of them do appear to me to be remarkably serene, sensible, good-humored, wise individuals with excellent social support. But they may also possess genetic or other internal protections that the rest of can't count on. So we shouldn't. Note that Dr. Ornish, holistic heart doctor, has achieved his success in reversing CHD with a program that combines stress management and psychosocial support on the one hand with a very low-fat, low-cholesterol diet, exercise, and smoking cessation on the other.

By the same token, Dr. Ornish is the first to point out that some of his patients get better even when their physical numbers haven't improved that much. Thus, he feels strongly that the psychological tools in his program may be even more potent than the physical ones. That's my feeling about the matter, too. We give ourselves the best chance for health when we take care of ourselves physically as well as mentally, emotionally, and spiritually. But if health is a deck of cards, the mental-emotional-spiritual cards trump the physical ones nearly every time.

# 7

# TURNING
# THE CORNER ON
# SERIOUS ILLNESS

*The diamond cannot be polished without friction, nor the
man perfected without trials.*

Chinese proverb

*The discipline of suffering—of great suffering, know ye not
that it is only this discipline that has produced all the elevation
of humanity?*

Friedrich Nietzsche

To this point in the book, we've looked mostly at how repressed
emotions, dysfunctional beliefs, and other psychological factors can
make us ill. All of this information is vital to preventing serious
conditions like cancer and heart disease. Staying healthy, as we've
learned, takes more than improving our diet and exercise habits
alone. It means healing our emotional wounds, assessing our beliefs
about ourselves and others, maintaining strong social ties, and meeting our creative and spiritual needs as well.

But what if we're already sick with cancer, heart disease, or
another serious illness? What if our doctor only has a dire prognosis
and some unattractive, and possibly futile, treatment options to
offer? Can Edgework or other similar methods restore our health?

The short answer is yes. The long answer is more complicated. In the remainder of this book, you will read many case histories drawn from my own medical practice that demonstrate that people have reversed the course of serious illness after attending to their mental/emotional/spiritual selves. As I stated earlier in the book, however, neither Edgework nor any other therapeutic system can *predictably* turn around so-called terminal disease. The problem has less to do with the effectiveness of these systems than the nature of the challenge. As I've already emphasized, healing is a question of personal responsibility. That means that the primary generator of healing lies within the person, not the system the person chooses for therapy. If someone wants to get better with every fiber of her being and will do whatever it takes to make that happen, there are very few diseases in creation that can stand up to that determined an assault. People have conquered cancer through Edgework, through chemotherapy, through Christian Science, through exercise, through meditation, and even through abandoning all forms of therapy and just living a more fulfilling life. The only common ground between all these methods is the intention, belief, and dedication of the patient.

Also, I must make one point clear: the psychological healing offered by Edgework is not meant to stand alone in the treatment of disease, but rather to complement and improve the effects of other treatments. Once the body is ill, then treatments for the body are needed, along with explorations into the issues of consciousness that helped to create the illness.

I don't believe in the concept of terminal illness—when someone survives, the illness wasn't terminal, and there are very few diseases that some people haven't beaten. It is true that some diseases will usually terminate in the patient's death, but that is a mathematical, statistical statement that has little relevance to an individual's chances. Remarkable people do remarkable things; they represent the flip side of the statistic, the exception that proves the rule *but is just as true as that rule.* Medical history, not just my practice, is replete with stories of exceptional patients who have defied the odds. So the doctor who tells a patient her illness is terminal is misusing statistics. A truer statement would be, "Most people who get this illness have not survived. Some have, although we're not sure why." What also concerns me is the chance that telling a patient that she has three to six months to live can become a self-fulfilling prophecy, turning her thoughts in a fearful direction that further tears down her body and robbing her of the hope that would inspire her to do the things that just might save her. I believe, as do colleagues of mine, that more people die from the fear of cancer than from the cancer itself.

Thus, I find myself in the delicate position of not robbing people of hope but also not giving them false hope. So, yes, Edgework has helped many people make dramatic recoveries, but with any individual case it is impossible for me to predict what the outcome will be. What I tell patients is, "It's up to you. Healing yourself emotionally and spiritually is not simply a matter of writing positive affirmations. It may require you to make substantial and comprehensive changes in your life—changes in the way you express yourself to others, changes in the quality of your relationships and maybe a turnover in your relationships themselves, changes in the way you approach your work and maybe a change of work entirely." Not everyone is willing to commit to that level of transformation despite their insistence that they'll "do anything" to recover.

In addition, a psychologically and medically complex disease like cancer may require you to dig out layer after layer of emotional trauma buried deep in your unconscious mind, much of which goes all the way back to your early childhood. It may require you to eliminate faulty beliefs that have been part of your consciousness for a lifetime. On the mental level, it takes a lot to develop an illness like cancer; in turn, it takes a lot of effort to heal these psychological wounds. Will you have the energy and commitment to stick with all that psychic work? Does your body have enough time left on its clock for you to get that work done?

I can't answer those questions for people. But I feel that Edgework is valuable for my seriously ill patients to undertake whether their physical bodies recover or not. Personal growth is an essential part of the soul's journey, whether the body in which that soul is encased is glowing with health or sliding into oblivion. And that goes to the heart of our next discussion.

## The Difference Between Healing and Curing

In one of the most oft-cited studies of psychological cancer treatment, Dr. David Spiegel and his colleagues investigated the effect of one year's worth of "psychosocial intervention" on 86 patients with metastatic breast cancer. Spiegel, a specialist in hypnosis and dissociative disorders at Stanford University, divided the women into two groups—a control group that received no special attention and an intervention group that met for weekly mutual support sessions and was also taught self-hypnosis techniques for pain control. The women cried, laughed, and shared their fears together and buoyed each other's spirits. Spiegel set out with modest goals: he wanted to see if the intervention affected the women's quality of life in their remaining time. Sure enough, the intervention group reported lower levels of pain (even though the frequency of pain was the same) and better coping ability.

Pleased that their assumptions proved correct, Spiegel and his associates published their study. But Spiegel himself gave the research no second thought until he became annoyed by sensationalistic media stories about people who seemed to "wish" their cancer away. Determined to disprove that notion, he did a follow-up study of the breast cancer patients ten years later, certain that he could show that intervention did nothing to actually prolong the women's survival. Sure enough, he learned that 83 of the women had died. When he began to break down the numbers, however, some astounding facts emerged. For one thing, all three of the women still alive at that point had belonged to the intervention group. For another, while every member of the control group had died within four years, one-third of the intervention group was still alive after that period. Overall, the intervention group members had survived an average 36.6 months, virtually twice as long as the 18.9 months of the control group.

Clearly, the intervention had in fact prolonged many lives. In fact, Spiegel's analysis had also turned up what researchers call a dose response—that is, the more therapy sessions the women attended, the longer they lived. The therapy group featured many qualities we've already identified in these pages as having a healing effect:

- The women often expressed intense emotions—from their anger at having cancer to their love of their families to their caring for each other and themselves.
- They faced their fears about death and dying.
- The sessions helped overcome whatever social isolation the women were feeling in their outside lives.
- The women encouraged each other to be true to their feelings in the way they lived. With the group cheering her on, one woman left her husband and focused her attention on her children; another woman fulfilled a long-held desire to become a poet, even publishing some of her work in her remaining life. Reinforced by each other's support, the women took more assertive hold of their lives in other ways, too. The four longest survivors, in fact, proved their independence by defying their doctors' recommendations about their care. Two refused to undergo mastectomies; two turned down chemotherapy, and another stopped it mid-course.

Of course, the most salient aspect of Spiegel's work to many readers will be that all the women eventually died, no matter what path they took. The group sessions had a profound effect on the participants' bodies, but not so profound that the progress of the disease could be completely halted. The question that must be raised is how effective and precise are the healing tools offered to the seriously ill patient. Group therapy sessions are often loosely guided as members present what they feel is important, and, consequently there may not be sufficient focus on the complex and layered issues for each participant.

Dr. Dean Ornish and others have achieved great success in reversing a coronary heart disease (CHD) with a lifestyle change program consisting of very low-fat, low-cholesterol diet; stress management techniques; moderate exercise; smoking cessation; and psychosocial support. (See Chapter 6 for more on this.) But a somewhat similar program operated for cancer patients by Michael Lerner, perhaps the nation's leading expert on alternative cancer therapies, and physician Naomi Remen, yields less dramatic results. The Lerner/Remen program combines spiritual, psychological, nutritional, and physical (e.g. exercise) self-care. People who take part improve their quality of life and tend to live significantly longer, but the program hasn't produced cures. Lerner explains this in part by making a distinction between healing and curing. That is, what is healing to the mind isn't always sufficient to cure the body. In a nutshell, says Lerner, patients who have a better quality of life and take better care of themselves do better, but "better" doesn't always add up to a complete recovery.

I don't disagree with Lerner on any of this. But I think there is more to this phenomenon than the notion that cancer does greater damage than heart disease so it's harder to overcome. Heart disease has a rather simple pathology—atherosclerotic blockage in the coronary arteries which reduces blood supply to the heart. What initiates the blockages is not as well understood, but the disease mechanism is clear. What also seems clear to me is that heart disease occurs in people who are emotionally blocked, who find it difficult to be vulnerable and accept emotional support from others. In short, they have a hard time expressing and receiving love. Yes, they have physical risk factors such as overeating or smoking, but the emotional blockage is what turns risk into disease. If these people establish supportive social connections and also make lifestyle changes, the disease will usually begin to reverse. That is what Ornish's dramatic results show.

Cancer, on the other hand, is much more complicated physically and psychologically. It is also more complicated in our society's beliefs about it—that is, most of us find it much harder to believe that the physical damage of cancer can be reversed than believing that arteries can become unblocked. And this makes a critical difference because belief plays such a vital role in healing.

As we discussed in Chapter 5, the pre-cancer patient often has tremendous childhood trauma, such as abandonment, abuse, neglect, rejection or similar intense experiences. Since a child cannot feel and release such intense feeling, it is automatically repressed into the unconscious mind for future replay at a later date when the person is older, more mature and, therefore, more capable of handling the pain. This is the process of emotional wound healing that we have discussed. While one person will cry and yell in pain during the reproduction of the pain denied in childhood, the pre-cancer patient consistently refuses to permit the feeling to release, thereby prevent-ing the mind's attempt to heal itself. Eventually the pain and stress of denied emotional wound healing becomes so intense that the pre-cancer patient decides, "I can't take it any more." In some primal way, his immune system hears his decision and offers him a way out of the pain by creating cancer, in effect saying to the patient, "If life is so painful that you can't take it anymore, now you won't have to." In other words, for most adult patients, cancer is a way out of a life of intense pain and stress, but it comes with an escape clause.

Should the patient choose to exercise that escape clause and work on his psychological issues, he has his work cut out for him—and generally only a small window of time, perhaps months, in which to pull it off. The psychological burden of the cancer patient is so deep-rooted and tangled that the generic group therapy approach can only have limited effect. Group therapy will certainly be helpful, as Spiegel and Lerner/Remen have demonstrated. But will it cure? Usually not, because more specific, individualized therapy is needed. Dr. Johannes Schilder of Rotterdam's Helen Dowling Institute has long pondered what form of psychotherapy might produce a cancer cure. As he told authors Caryle Hirshberg and Marc Ian Barasch, he has concluded that it would probably take a new form of therapy for the field, one that is highly individualized for the patient and geared toward recreating life experiences. I agree. I also believe that the detailed and multi-pronged approach recommended in the Edge-work exercises, as well as in individual psychotherapy, will focus the healing work directly on the emotional blockages and faulty belief systems for each person.

The other crucial part of surviving cancer is believing that it can happen. As we'll see below, cancer survivors don't buy their doctor's prognosis of "six months to live." They believe that they can be the exception to the rule. As more and more people "beat" cancer in this society, it will become easier for everyone to believe that it is possible. Until England's Roger Bannister did it in 1954, track and field experts thought it was probably impossible to run a mile in less than four minutes. Then Bannister edged past the mental barrier with a time of three minutes, 59.4 seconds. A societal belief threshold was crossed and soon every elite miler was racking up sub-four minute times. As I write this, the record is now about 3 minutes, 43 seconds and few doubt that the 3 minute, 40 second barrier will eventually fall. That is how belief works. Change society's agreement about what is possible, and most people start thinking differently, too, with dramatic effects in the material world.

But we're not there yet on cancer, so I certainly join Michael Lerner in feeling that emotional work is valuable to do no matter what the eventual outcome of the disease. If one's life is going to end anyway, who wouldn't want to fill their remaining days with personal fulfillment and the thrill and joy of personal discovery and growth rather than resisting life right down to the last breath? And that is what is meant by the difference between healing and curing.

There is also a spiritual way to regard this issue. Many people the world over, myself included, believe that our soul and consciousness exist separately from our bodies and continue to evolve after death, often in other human incarnations. From this point of view, cancer may just be a way-station for some people in their soul's spiritual path. That is, the disease spurs them to work on themselves and reach a state of inner healing and peace. They then shed their body, and move on to the next incarnation, carrying with them the knowledge gained in the previous ones. Because the soul survives death, it is not necessarily important to it whether its current body or identity (ego) survive, since those are transitory anyway.

### What Spontaneous Remissions Tell Us

Some of the most intriguing information we have about how to cure cancer comes from the stories of people who have apparently made complete bodily recoveries from advanced cases of the disease. Examining the details of their lives during the time they were fighting and winning their battles against their illness provides valuable clues as to what can work for the rest of us.

As recounted in their book, *Remarkable Recovery,* writers Caryle Hirshberg and Marc Ian Barasch examined fifty cases of spontaneous remission to see if the cancer survivors possessed common attributes. Was there a personality type that better equipped some people to win this battle against long, long odds? Using a "mind-style" test devised by former Columbia University professor Herbert Spiegel that separates people into three clusters of personality traits, they found cancer survivors in each of Spiegel's three camps. Some of the patients were people of the heart who navigated their lives more by their feelings than their minds. Some were the reverse, analytical and concrete. Some found a balance between the two extremes. Apparently, Hirshberg and Barasch concluded, survival is more a matter of each person finding their "right path" than having the "right stuff."

But the authors did find some commonalties among the survivors, even if they expressed themselves in different ways. As with the breast cancer patients who survived longer in David Spiegel's study, these survivors demonstrated "congruence"—that is, they lived true to their thoughts and feelings. Most of them actively engaged with their disease, too, instead of just passively submitting to treatment. The majority fought to live or otherwise embraced the cancer as a challenge. They took responsibility for healing themselves rather than bemoaning their fate as tragic victims. They refused to accept that cancer was a death sentence. They believed their struggle would result in a positive outcome. Most were spiritually oriented as well and attributed their recovery to faith, meditation, or prayer.

Hirshberg and Barasch's findings echo in other studies of spontaneous remission cases. Dr. Yujiro Ikemi and associates searched for common psychosocial traits in five cancer survivors; they found that all had accepted responsibility for resolving their crisis themselves and four of the five exhibited a passionate religious faith. Dr. Paul Roud interviewed nine patients who were in remission after they had been diagnosed with terminal cancer. In each case, the patient's physician confirmed that survival had been highly unlikely. Patients gave similar answers to Roud's questions, listing the following explanations for their recovery: taking responsibility for both their illness' onset and outcome; taking responsibility for their quality of life; changing the way they interacted with others; realizing the value of close relationships and support; letting go of fear and worry; and having a strong desire to live.

My own patients who have made dramatic recoveries exhibit the same psychological attributes we see in spontaneous remission cases. The remainder of the book will examine such crucial strategies as taking responsibility for your own life, self-love, satisfying work, satisfying relationships, and spirituality. But I have to say that if there is one bottom line strategy from which all others flow, it is the importance of fully experiencing your emotions as they arise and reversing unhealthy attitudes. I'm not alone in concluding this. As we've seen, a great deal of research points in this direction, And it is also just common sense. It doesn't feel good to bottle up emotions, hold back emotional communications, or live in a way that runs counter to our emotional preferences. It also doesn't feel good to hold onto beliefs that limit our possibilities or the way we express ourselves in our lives. It doesn't take a genius to guess that these things might not be good for our bodies, either. As the noted medical educator Dr. Andrew Weil puts it, wherever nerves are, the activities of the mind can travel. Fortunately, the other side of this double-edged sword cuts on behalf of health, because the activities of the mind can also heal, as the following case histories demonstrate.

### Virginia's Story: Curing Lupus

Virginia, a social services director for a local hospital, came to my office in 1994 suffering from systemic lupus erythematosis, or lupus. Lupus, Latin for wolf, is so named because the pain can be severe like the bite of a wolf. A chronic degenerative disease that is difficult to treat, it requires medications that usually only takes the edge off the pain, and can be life-threatening.

Virginia had been in lupus' grip for the previous decade with pain in her fingers, hands, wrists, and ribs that had intensified over the years. She had taken the drug Prednisone for the past eight years, periodically increasing the dose when her pain worsened. (Prednisone is a potent chemical used to suppress inflammation, but it has the unfortunate side effect of suppressing the immune system as well.) The previous year, she had developed lymphoma (a tumor of the lymph nodes) in her right eye, requiring a seven-month course of chemotherapy.

In addition to her lupus, Virginia also suffered from leg edema (swelling from accumulation of fluid), allergic rhinitis (chronic stuffy nose), hypertension, hypothyroidism, chronic fatigue, leg cramps, intermittent rashes, and chronic low back pain. Needless to say, she had seen numerous medical specialists and was consuming a veritable buffet of medications.

After listening to Virginia recount her long and complicated medical history, I turned to the issue of stress in her life. Prior to the onset of lupus, she had experienced several years of marital troubles, and her relationship with her husband remained a problem area. The couple seemed to have little in common. They had different interests and difficulty communicating. Virginia said she was unable to express her feelings to her mate because he wouldn't listen to her. Her life in general seemed in no better shape than her marriage. She felt that everything was in turmoil and that she "couldn't do anything right." She described herself as having no self-esteem and said she felt constantly pressured.

As with all my patients, I then asked Virginia about her early childhood because I've found that adult problems are usually seeded in those fertile years. Virginia said that she had been sexually molested between the ages of three and four by both a brother and an uncle. She described this obviously traumatic time in a matter-of-fact tone, without emotion.

At the end of Virginia's first visit, I listed her numerous medical problems but, as with all my patients, stated her final diagnosis— suppressed emotion and chronic stress—in psychological terms. The treatment approach I offered began with physical strategies to strengthen her immune system, improve her digestion and assimilation of nutrients, and balance other biochemical problems in her body. I then listed for her the following emotional and attitudinal issues, which I felt, had contributed strongly to her many medical problems:

- Intense anger and pain arising from the childhood sexual abuse. Because she was so young when the abuse occurred, Virginia had stuffed the intense emotions threatening to burst her apart into the closet of her unconscious mind.
- The development of a personality that habitually suppressed feelings, especially anger. In fact, I believed Virginia's lifetime of suppressed anger had contributed to the painful inflammation in her joints, as if her very tissues were burning with emotion.

- Low self-esteem, which prevented her from standing up for herself and expressing her needs to others.

Virginia listened intently and I could tell by her body language that I had struck a chord in her heart—she seemed to soften and her breathing changed a bit. She recalled that a therapist had suggested similar conclusions to her in counseling sessions she had attended several years before. She wondered why it was so hard for her to express her anger. Why was anger so bad?

I worked with Virginia many times over the next several months. Motivated to rid herself of her bodily pain, Virginia modified her diet, took the nutritional supplements I recommended, and, most importantly, began to observe her own personality in action. For instance, she noticed that whenever her feelings were hurt, she buried her wrath. In the solitude of her bedroom, she practiced yelling at those who infuriated her. She remembered that her previous counselor had encouraged her to hit a pillow to unblock her rage, and began doing that as well. She noticed how much better she felt after "practicing" her feelings and realized for the first time that it was better to get the anger out than keep it in her body.

I spoke with Virginia not long before writing this passage. She no longer saw herself as a victim of her disease. She told me that her lupus had been a learning process for her, but now it was completely dormant and she was off all medications. She was leading a normal life, she said, and felt "better than I have in 15 years." She said that she no longer fears that her anger "will wreak havoc" and was now able to tell others how she felt. She acknowledged that she was still having a few problems with her husband, but said she was able to express her feelings "naturally" and urged her husband not to "take her anger personally."

Virginia made a healing journey of the highest order, confronting what previously seemed to her to be insurmountable barriers. Lupus became her own personal mountain and she relentlessly pursued the peak. The climb was intimidating and uncomfortable but she had quickly determined that, unlike a mountain of rock and earth, this one would probably be more painful not to climb. She realized she could go on as she had, enduring the discomfort and taking all her symptomatic medications. Or, she could take the emotional risk of living differently. She chose the latter, and lupus ceased to be the wolf and became her teacher.

## David's Story: Lessons from the Heart

David was a 56-year-old banker who came to my office seeking additional treatment for his coronary artery disease. Some six months prior, he had a small heart attack while playing tennis. During his hospitalization, a coronary angiogram showed significant blockage in three arteries and he underwent a triple coronary artery bypass procedure. His heart was strong, according to his cardiologist, and he did well post-operatively, taking medications and participating in a supervised exercise program. However, approximately three months later he noticed a pressure in his chest while exercising. His cardiologist adjusted his medicines, which included nitroglycerin, and did not feel further intervention was necessary.

He came to me based on his interest in a good nutritional program and supplements to complement his current medical therapy. As I listened to David, I was struck by the angry tone of his voice as he reviewed his medical history. He was an assertive and strong-willed man, who was angry at himself for having had a heart attack and bypass surgery. He didn't have many of the traditional risk factors for heart disease and he prided himself in staying thin and exercising regularly. His father had had a heart attack late in life, but David did not smoke cigarettes, his blood pressure was slightly elevated on occasion, but required no medications prior to the heart attack, and his cholesterol and triglycerides were fairly normal. He admitted to high levels of stress in his work, but said he "thrived under the pressure."

I explained that the majority of cardiac patients do not have the classical risk factors for heart disease, so we need to look a bit deeper into his history for answers. David was divorced some thirteen years earlier after a marriage of sixteen years, which produced two children. I asked about the divorce and he said that his wife left him because he was "shut down and she wanted to live with a husband, not a banker." They had tried marital counseling, but David "couldn't get into it." I asked David what he felt about her decision and he said that it angered him initially, because he had provided for her and the family so well, but later he could understand her choice better. I asked about other relationships in his life and he said that he had girlfriends on and off, but his business travel made relationships difficult. I suggested that intimacy in his marriage might have been just as important as a good income, and David looked a bit puzzled and said nothing.

I then asked what his childhood was like. David was raised on a farm and he was the first born with two younger brothers. He said his mother "ran the family like a drill sergeant," and he found it hard to please her. She was not very emotional and David had problems communicating with her. His father was very strict and always busy with the endless chores of making a living in the farming business. David felt like he really didn't know his father. He couldn't recall one time when his father told him that he loved him. David felt like he had been working since the age of twelve, non-stop.

I then asked David if it was easy for him to express his emotions. (I already knew the answer to this question, but I wanted to see what he would say.) He said that he felt a lot of anger and got frustrated easily, but that was about it. I asked if he had ever cried, and he said he "broke down and cried like a baby" when his wife and family walked out the door, but he had never cried otherwise since childhood.

And then, as I always do with patients, I asked if he enjoyed his work. David said that he loved the excitement and challenge of the banking world in the early years, but the constant pressure and travel had become a grind and he wondered how long he could take the "constant battle." He had felt depressed on and off over the past several years, but he "could pull himself out of it." He had spent many a lonely evening in hotels while traveling and felt there was more to life, but he wasn't sure what he could do.

At the end of our first hour, I summarized his medical problems: coronary artery disease, problems with digestion and absorption, especially of minerals like magnesium, food sensitivities, and weakened adrenal glands from all the stress. I then listed the following emotional and attitudinal issues, which, I believed, contributed to the medical problems just mentioned:

- His childhood was practically devoid of the most important nutrient of all—love, producing in the child intense pain, which was buried in the unconscious mind, as well as the feeling of "what is wrong with me that my parents don't love me."
- He then developed a personality that avoided emotions, except for anger, and he felt much safer dealing with the world through his intellect.
- He had low self-esteem and felt deeply inadequate at not being loved by his parents and compensated for this by achieving more and more in his professional life. Perhaps he could be loved if he worked really hard and accomplished a lot.

I told him that his body had certainly gotten his attention with the heart attack and his heart was "aching" in more ways than reduced blood flow alone. There are more aspects to the heart than its blood pumping function. I then explained that I believed that the biggest risk factor for heart disease was emotional blockage, which always precedes coronary blockage.

I hoped I hadn't overloaded this "no nonsense guy" with my expanded version of cardiac function, and I watched carefully as he sat quietly, head down, for a few moments. I reminded him of how well he can meet a challenge if he sets his mind to it. And this challenge of opening his heart and learning to feel will take far greater courage than any macho external task I could think of. Perhaps this was what his heart pain was calling for.

I also briefly explained emotional wound healing to David and suggested that the loss of his wife's love for him and her departure was an unconsciously created opportunity to own the pain of his loveless childhood.

David was fairly quiet during the rest of our session as I set up a diet and supplement program. I suggested that he think about counseling and recommended a friend of mine who I knew would do a good job.

At our next visit, a month later, David said that he had contemplated my words a lot and had decided to give counseling a try.

Over the next year, I saw David occasionally. He said that he had learned a lot about himself with the counselor and he was making big changes in his approach to life. He felt "more alive" as he learned to express a wider range of emotion than anger. He had cut back on his work, especially the travel, and was spending a lot more time with golf and other sports that he enjoyed. He had met a beautiful woman and his relationship with her was "richer and deeper" than he had ever had before. And, he hadn't had an angina pain for over six months.

## Patty's Story: Putting Leukemia into Remission

Patty, then 55, first came to my office in late 1998, six years after being diagnosed with chronic lymphocytic leukemia (CLL). Her tonsils had been enlarged her entire life, she told me. When she finally underwent a tonsillectomy in 1992, a biopsy of the tonsils revealed CLL. Lymphocytes, a type of white blood cell, play a critical role in the healthy immune system because they make antibodies against invaders. As we saw in Chapter 3, the immune system is like a huge combination police/military force. Antibodies are the missiles in the system, fired at viral, bacterial, or other foreign attackers if the police (macrophages) are unable to defeat the enemy through close-in street combat. Once an antibody attaches to an enemy cell, it weakens or otherwise disables it, making it vulnerable to the macrophages. With CLL, however, the lymphocytes over-reproduce and are immunologically incompetent, unable to produce antibodies. The large number of circulating lymphocytes gradually collect in the liver, spleen, and lymph nodes, causing them to enlarge. They also collect in the bone marrow, replacing the cells that make red blood cells. As a result, the patient eventually becomes anemic and susceptible to infections, which eventually cause death.

When I first saw Patty, she was already past the median survival time—6 years—for CLL patients and I was impressed by her vigor and the assertive way she was pursuing her treatment. She was an active, inquiring patient with her oncologist; had consulted with the esteemed leukemia experts at Stanford University; had traveled to the alternative Hoxsey Clinic in Mexico; and had studied macrobiotics, intensive herbal therapies, and more. All along, she would observe what lowered and what raised her white blood cell count (WBC), the key parameter in CLL. By the time she reached my office, she was anemic with a hemoglobin of 10 grams/deciliter of blood (normal is 12 to 16) and WBC of 66,000 cells/microliter of blood (normal is 5,000-10,000), and she complained of fatigue.

After taking Patty's medical history, I turned to her psychological background. The cause of CLL is considered unknown by medical researchers. In my opinion, that's because they're looking in the wrong places for answers. The research focus is always on some physical process or mechanism that has gone wrong—a chemical, a faulty gene, or so on. For me, the answer often lies in the unconscious mind and a complex web of repressed emotions and self-defeating beliefs that originated in a troubled childhood.

And my expectations were certainly fulfilled with Patty's stress history. Over the next 20 minutes, she mentioned physical abuse by her father and emotional abuse by her mother and four older siblings (the closest to her in age was eight years her senior). Patty's mother had "lost control" with the older children and felt they were "mean-spirited," so she "clamped down on me." Mom tried to isolate Patty, too, keeping her at home and not allowing her to have friends, as if grooming her to take care of her in her old age. She made Patty the "center of her world," but in the process Patty lost her childhood. She also told Patty frequently from the age of four on that "I'm old and I will die," leaving her frightened daughter to wonder, "if Mommy dies, where will I go?"

Meanwhile, the other siblings resented all the attention focused on Patty and were emotionally brutal toward her. Dad had no time for his children and would solve behavioral problems with belts and spankings. Patty recalled her mother telling her to "wait 'til Daddy gets home," an ominous warning, when she was upset with her daughter. She remembered feeling that she had no power over her life as a child and no sense of security. To make matters worse, this was a family that habitually hid feelings.

Patty said she concluded that her life was too much to take as early as 14 years old when she would "ask God not to wake me up in the morning." She eventually married but described her 30-year relationship with her husband as distant. She tolerated it by focusing on her children and her work. In 1989, however, her husband's personality changed, she said, and became "mean and vicious." She dealt with that too by burying herself in her work and, as always, "stuffed her feelings inside." But then her employer tried to get rid of her, even though she knew that she was doing a good job, an experience Patty described as "devastating." Her "I can't take it any more" thoughts surfaced with a vengeance as she tried to squelch her anger. Patty's recounting of the doctor's call telling her she had leukemia makes clear her emotional deadness at the time. The doctor told her that she had cancer but that he couldn't fit her into his appointment schedule for two weeks. Patty told me she hung up the phone and went right back to work.

As with most cancer patients, Patty had passed up many opportunities in her adult life to express the tears and anger she had accumulated over the years. I commended her for the way she had involved herself in her treatment but suggested that something was missing: emotional and attitudinal healing to heal the wounded little girl living in her unconscious mind. Patty sat quietly as she contemplated our discussion. She considered herself a spiritual person and she recognized that her healing journey was about to take a different turn, a turn within. She knew she had to change in order to continue living.

Over the next year, Patty began seeing a psychotherapist to help her understand her psychic pain and, more importantly, to help her experience emotions that needed to be felt. It was always a pleasure to have this vital person walk into my office excited about some new discovery about her inner life. Bit by bit, she was making sense of what once seemed to be such a senseless childhood. With her therapist, she was pushing hard to release limiting belief systems and was now allowing herself to express feelings "with certain people." She felt that, through her therapy, she was regaining the personal power she had lost as a little girl. She was unfolding spiritually as well, working with a meditation master and having visions of her life in the past.

By the time of our final visit, a year and a half after she first came in, she was no longer anemic and feeling much stronger. Her WBC tested consistently lower than it had for some time, indicating that her CLL was in a quiescent state. She knew her healing journey wasn't over, but she was eager to learn more about herself and see what effect that had on her health. The dark cloud of cancer had inspired a journey into the light of self-realization.

## Bob's Story: Healing the Wounds of War

Bob was 71 when he first made an appointment with me for the intermittent atrial tachycardia that had troubled him for 10 years. Atrial tachycardia means rapid heart rate that can come on suddenly and unannounced. The state can last for minutes, hours, or even indefinitely, requiring medical treatment to terminate it. Those who suffer this condition feel weak and dizzy because the heart is beating so fast that it doesn't have time to fill and pump an adequate supply of blood. The most disturbing feature of this fairly common problem is the anxiety and panic that it produces in patients. They fear that something has gone terribly wrong with their heart, and the resulting adrenaline rush just makes the heart beat that much faster.

Bob had seen a cardiologist for his condition and, after proper testing, was told that his heart was basically okay and the problem was not life-threatening. The doctor had given him medications designed to prevent the problem, but the condition was still occurring with upsetting frequency.

Bob's life was severely hampered by his tachycardia because it tended to strike at particularly inconvenient times such as when he was about to do something new and exciting. For example, just before coming to see me, he and his wife had traveled to Alaska, where they had booked a cruise in the state's spectacular coastal waters. In their hotel room the night before the ship departed, Bob's heart once again started racing at about twice the normal rate and he was overcome with the usual gloomy thoughts: "Is this time different?" "Am I having a heart attack?" He certainly couldn't start the cruise like this.

After waiting futilely a couple of hours for his heart to slow down, Bob and his wife went to the local hospital's emergency room. An EKG was taken and he was hooked up to the cardiac monitor. This time, however, the problem had changed. He was now in atrial fibrillation, where the heart not only beats too fast but also irregularly. Atrial fibrillation concerns doctors because blood clots can form on the heart's quivering walls, dislodge, and travel to the brain, causing a stroke. To prevent this, Bob was started on a blood-thinning medication.

The doctors at the hospital also gave Bob other drugs to slow his heart. They eventually took effect. After several discussions with Bob, his doctors decided he could embark on the cruise as planned if he stayed on his medicines. Bob enjoyed the voyage overall, but the peace he felt from the tranquil Alaskan scenery kept being interrupted by a new set of fears about his health.

When Bob came to my office, I took the usual medical history and then turned to the critically important issue of life stresses. Bob's tales added up to a picture of extraordinary tensions. When he was 12 years old, his mother died and his life "fell apart," he said. Later, he served as a medic during World War II, piling up severe emotional and physical wounds. Day after day, he would pull gravely injured soldiers from the battlefront, carrying them back to the hospital tent where doctors would frantically, and often unsuccessfully, try to save them. For 50 years, he had been unable to rid himself of feelings of guilt and inadequacy about his war experience; a sensitive man, he believed that if he had somehow known or done more, he could have prevented at least some of the deaths. When he related his war memories, I could see his eyes begin to moisten, but he always held the tears back.

The war scarred Bob physically, too. One day, while carrying a wounded soldier on a stretcher, he was shot in his left buttock. The bullet fractured his left hip, sending him to a hospital for the next two years and ending his front-line action. He left the military with no mobility in his left hip or knee and a left leg two inches shorter than his right one. He needed a cane to walk, a daily reminder of his wounds decades before. Later, as a civilian, Bob developed stomach ulcers on several occasions as he dealt with the stresses of raising a family and working as a traveling salesman.

I explained to Bob that stress affects the body in many ways and undoubtedly contributed to his atrial tachycardia. I also told him that buried or suppressed emotions don't go away until they're released by fully experiencing them. Even though his emotional war wounds were decades old, he could still heal them by simply allowing them to flow outward, as emotions are designed to do.

Bob acknowledged that he always kept his emotions inside and tried to avoid thinking about his war years. But he couldn't really forget. "For no reason," he said, war memories would suddenly pop into his mind, often triggering his heart to pound hard in his chest and occasionally producing his tachycardia. He also had dreams that recreated the agony of the war and he would awaken in terror. As he related this, his sadness and pain was palpable.

At the end of our session, I outlined Bob's medical problems for him and then described what I felt were his deepest emotional injuries. His mother's death when he was at the vulnerable age of 12 planted the unconscious fear that "things won't be okay." Responding to the overwhelming pain, his ego developed the automatic protection of avoiding emotions, a protection that still persisted. But emotional wounds, like physical ones, try to heal, which is why his sense of foreboding and the tremendous accumulation of emotional baggage from the war kept pushing their way to the surface in his later years. Fears of any kind will trigger the stress system, producing adrenaline and other hormones. These can contribute to ulcers as well as tachycardia.

As I explained these hidden factors to Bob, his voice began to waver, and I could see tears forming in his eyes. Despite his long habit of avoiding emotions, he agreed to seek counseling and let his feelings flow whenever possible. I told him that this healing was long overdue and that it required courage not unlike that of his military years. Bob's life had pushed him to the emotional edge many times, but not realizing he could handle the pain, he had always gotten cold feet and retreated. He seemed relieved and encouraged now to walk a different path.

As Bob walked into my office months later, he quickly reported on his successes in psychotherapy with an apparent sense of pride and accomplishment. He had cried repeatedly over his war experiences, initially with the help of his counselor, and recently on his own. He now understood that his years of repeated denial about his wartime pain did not make it go away. He also knew what I had meant when I said months earlier, "either you express your feelings, or your body will." He realized that his fear, when his heart raced, was like the fear he felt in the war—a fear that he would die. He said that he now understood that the only real way to forget about the war was to acknowledge his pain and heal his emotional wounds by simply feeling them, thereby releasing them from his unconscious mind forever. I reminded Bob that the greatest medicine is to love and accept all that you are, including the pain. And, happily, he reported that his tachycardia had become much less frequent recently and he believed he could eventually stop it entirely. And, the chronic muscle and joint pains in his low back, hip, and left leg had also lessened significantly.

## Different Strokes

Virginia, David, Patty, and Bob each present quite different psychological pictures and I don't want to minimize those differences. Hopefully, some day we will have devoted the same amount of study to psychological causes of illness that we have to physical causes. At that point, it may well be possible to tie specific patient psychological profiles to each medical condition. We are making progress, but we are not quite there yet for a lot of medical diagnoses. Nonetheless, introspective people can often identify the emotional issues associated with their condition by asking themselves what was going on in their lives or what emotions dominated their consciousness prior to the time they became ill. But as we've seen even in the research described in these pages, the same psychological state—depression for example—may precede cancer in one person and heart disease in another. I've concluded from my experience with patients that the healing journey is highly individualized—what is true for Ruth may not be so for Tom.

So the most important conclusion to draw from Virginia, David, Patty and Bob's stories is a comprehensive one: that when they moved forward and began to work on themselves, their bodily conditions moved too—toward better health. In his book, *Natural Health, Natural Medicine,* Dr. Andrew Weil describes two of his female patients who, like Virginia, were diagnosed with advanced cases of lupus. Both were suffering from kidney damage, high blood pressure, and drug toxicity because of their prolonged treatment with dangerous medications. Neither appeared to have much of a future, but both eventually went into complete remission. Immediately preceding their recoveries, one woman had converted to fundamentalist Christianity and the other fell in love and married. So what did the healing? Each apparently filled an important gap in her life but it wasn't the same gap. Same disease, same recovery, with more or less (their cases were somewhat different, obviously) different paths. Yes, one could argue that love is a form of spirituality or vice versa, but while there is certainly truth there, the more important point, I think, is that each person did what was best for *her*, and it produced a similar, magnificent result. As we examine the various aspects of emotion-based healing in the next few chapters, keep this in mind. It is not important that you be a perfectly enlightened being leading a perfect life to be healthy, or that you do everything that has worked for someone else. It *is* important that you not turn your back on the personal issues that are shouting to you in body and mind.

# 8

# TAKING RESPONSIBILITY AND RECLAIMING PERSONAL POWER

*As ye sow, so shall ye reap.*

Jesus

*When we have done our part within, the exterior will unfold itself automatically.*

Johann Wolfgang von Goethe

Holistic health advocates have long pointed out that conventional medicine focuses more on understanding the physical mechanism of disease and relieving symptoms than on understanding what causes the problem in the first place. And they're absolutely right, which became abundantly clear to me early in my medical training. From pathology classes to ward rounds in my clinical rotations, my professors discussed how disease functions in the body. In my classroom studies, I learned about the biochemical and cellular disturbances that underlie illnesses; I saw them firsthand in laboratory tests, X-rays, EKGs, CT scans, and the like. When I interviewed patients, my questions focused on the physical experience of the disease. When did it start? How long had it lasted? Where was the pain located and how intense was it?

123

In those early years, I rarely asked patients about stressful life events or other psychological issues that might have helped bring on their illness. After all, I was taught that my purpose was to treat the patient's diseased body with the tools of modern medicine: drugs and surgery. My focus was supposed to be the disease, not the patient. Few of my professors seemed interested in the life experiences of the person who had the disease.

Then, while still in medical school, I came across a quote by Sir William Osler, a prominent physician who had authored a classic textbook on internal medicine. Dr. Osler wrote, "It is more important to know what sort of patient has a disease than what sort of disease has a patient." It took me 15 years of medical practice to get the importance of what he meant.

My subsequent experiences, especially my curious predilection to listen to patient's stories, have led me to conclude that one of the biggest of modern medicine's many failings is its view of disease as some quirk of fate. Patients are led to believe that they are helpless victims of disease and that the disease itself is an unfortunate but otherwise meaningless event in the context of their lives. Sure, doctors now make some effort to show heart attack patients that they ate too much fat over the years and that cigarette smoking was damaging. Those afflicted with cancer are told they may have a genetic predisposition, and perhaps their diet played a part in the onset of the tumor, but beyond these superficial and disjointed insights, little light is shed on the question of "Why me?"

Another revealing failing of modern medicine is its focus on drug therapy. The body's natural wisdom and enormous self-healing capacities depend on a mysterious and complex interplay of vitamins, minerals, amino acids, and fats, plus a staggering array of other factors. Conventional doctors spend little effort assessing imbalances in this system and restoring them to healthy levels. Instead, more and more drugs are prescribed as they endlessly flow from the highly profitable and influential pharmaceutical industry. The drugs address symptoms almost exclusively, not the process generating the disease, and actually increase internal imbalance, leading to more symptoms and often more drugs.

More to the point of this book, drugs also cover up life issues at the base of disease, much like an alcoholic drowns his sorrows. From my perspective, the body uses symptoms and diseases as messages to get your attention. The physical disturbance is intended to slow you down a bit so that, hopefully, you'll consider the state of your life and move toward greater balance. Thus, to mask a symptom with a drug is to deny your body's efforts to heal itself.

## Health and Responsibility: The Deeper Meaning

"The body is never ill or healthy, for it does no more than express messages from our consciousness," write German psychologist Thorwald Dethlefsen and physician Rudiger Dalke in their brilliant book, *The Healing Power of Illness.* These simple words capture what I believe is the most important principle for responding to the challenge of illness: we have created it and, therefore, we are responsible for healing it.

Oliver Sacks, a prominent neurologist, says much the same thing in his book, *Awakenings:*

> . . . our health is ours; our diseases are ours; our reactions are ours—no less than our minds or our faces . . . expressions of our nature, our living, our being here.

For those caught up in conventional medicine, the issue of self-responsibility in disease remains controversial, should generally be avoided, and can only lead to the damaging emotion of guilt. In holistic health, on the other hand, responsibility is a core principle, so many people today accept it without question. But even in holistic health, the notion of personal responsibility is often presented in a modest form that I find inadequate. Yes, it's important that patients take responsibility for their health by eating well, exercising, getting enough rest, and avoiding toxic habits like smoking, but that's just the common-sense level. There is a much deeper notion that I feel is just as crucial: we are responsible for all the experiences in our lives, even the ones that seem outside our conscious control.

Many would say that I have gone too far now. How is the driver who is blindsided at a stop sign by a drunk responsible? How is the employee responsible who was unwittingly exposed to toxic chemicals by his employer's negligence? How is the person who is poisoned because of a foul-up in the city's water system responsible?

I agree that it's not always easy for us to see how we might have played a role in our own illness or injury, particularly when we've been conditioned to see things otherwise. We live in a society that promotes the notion of victimization, the opposite of responsibility. Webster's dictionary defines victim as "a person who suffers severe injury from another; one who is cheated or duped." But one can be injured by another, cheated or duped, and still be responsible. At first glance, everyone in the above examples appears to be a victim, but it's not hard to postulate how each might be responsible for his fate. In the first example, all of us accept the risk of being injured by reckless drivers when we step into an automobile. In the second example, perhaps the employee had reason to suspect that his employer would be less than vigilant about safety procedures and didn't take proper precautions or investigate the matter or, for that matter, leave the job. In the third example, perhaps the poisoned person never thought it important to vote for politicians who cared about the city's environmental quality and safety, or never supported the local environmental group that monitored the city's water system. These are conscious factors that could contribute to each challenging experience, but the deeper level of responsibility lies in the unconscious mind. We will get to that in a moment.

Acknowledging that we are responsible does not mean accepting blame. It simply means that we are not passive players in any scene of our lives, and we play a role in creating everything that happens to us.

Admittedly, this view violates our sense of logic and how the world works. How can a child be responsible for the divorce of her parents or an illness at the age of three? How were the citizens of Hiroshima responsible for the atomic bomb? These questions are not easily answered from our ordinary frame of reference. But when you base responsibility on unconscious motivations as well as conscious ones, then things become a little more understandable. When it comes to health or otherwise improving our lives, however, if we can at least accept the premise that we are responsible, we can move past blame or victimization and into taking responsibility for healing ourselves. And if you are sick, isn't it more important to you to heal than to figure out who's culpable for your problem? The issue of personal responsibility in disease is the foundation upon which healing firmly rests. If I have the power to create illness, then it follows that I have the power to reverse the process—that is, heal the disease.

One final criticism of the personal responsibility philosophy must be answered. With health in particular, some commentators have argued that self-responsibility inevitably leads to feelings of guilt, as in "I created my cancer. I'm such a jerk." Yes, you may feel guilty if you own the creation of your disease, but that doesn't mean that it's an accurate assessment of the situation or that you're stuck with the feeling. The purpose of accepting responsibility for your illness is not so you can beat yourself up about it. Besides, not blaming others does not mean that the blame lies with you. Disease is not about blame. It's about an opportunity to reclaim the power to dramatically influence your health. It's also about opening yourself up to learning the life lessons your disease offers you. I'm not suggesting that you try to reason away the *feeling* of guilt. But you can allow yourself to experience it, be fully aware of it, and then forgive yourself and others and release it from your system.

## Responsibility, Personal Power and Unconscious Responsibility

Assuming responsibility for our experiences is effectively an exercise in reclaiming personal power that we have given away to those we blame, or to fate, or whatever. Although it may take a leap of faith for you to do this at first, assuming responsibility is the only way to discover your personal power and take it back. Your power is your birthright and as precious a possession as you can have. Here's how to make it yours again.

Start by considering why the issue of personal responsibility is so challenging. Our society leads us to believe that the reasons for our problems lie in what others do to us. The problems at work are due to the boss. Problems at home are caused by our spouse. If we slip and fall in the supermarket, we blame the store for putting too much wax on the floors. We are even encouraged by our legal system to try to prove that we are helpless victims, by hiring an attorney who will establish the point in a court of law.

Unfortunately, blaming necessarily creates two major problems. The first, again, is powerlessness. We become the powerless victim of another's actions and are left nervously awaiting future crises because of our belief that the sources of our troubles lies outside us. The second problem is that by refusing to look at our own role in creating our life experiences, we sacrifice the option of gaining understanding and meaning about those experiences.

Responsibility becomes easier to accept when we realize it can exist on two levels: conscious and unconscious. That is, sometimes responsibility is more apparent than others. For instance, many health problems occur because patients consciously choose unhealthy behaviors—drinking heavily, smoking, overeating, eating fatty foods, and so on—despite being aware of the risks. Yes, as we've seen in earlier chapters, emotions and thoughts may be the most critical factors, but with many illnesses such as diet- or smoking-related heart disease, the lifestyle choices establish the necessary preconditions. That is, they lay the groundwork for thoughts and emotions to finish the job. Each of us creates our lifestyle based on freely made, conscious choices, and thus we are responsible for the consequences.

The unconscious level of responsibility is where the issues become cloudy, where personal responsibility is not so obvious. Yet this is the area where most of our personal power lies, because the vast majority of our mental activity is unconscious, actually 80 to 90% according to psychologists. That means that you are using the 10% to create a day for yourself as you like it to be. But the 90% is the shadow and contains all the repressed pain, fears, anger, limitations and inadequacies since childhood, and it has an agenda too. The agenda of the unconscious mind is emotional healing; it wants to create circumstances that would allow you to feel and own some of the issues it is storing. The unconscious mind is subtly influencing your conscious choices to create decisions that set up the "accidents," unexpected circumstances, things going wrong and the like that we all experience from time to time. Perhaps the original design for human experience is to gradually reduce the unconscious 90% into a conscious 100%. If we are creating our experience largely based on unconscious forces, then by dedicating ourselves to developing greater self-understanding, we can reclaim the largest stores of power available to us.

## Upon Reflection

Again, the first principle in healing—or with any problem in life, as far as I'm concerned—is to accept that any situation that you find yourself in is exactly what you want at that moment. Another way of saying this is that your outer life reflects your inner life. William Thackeray stated this point with poetic clarity when he wrote: "Life is a mirror: if you frown at it, it frowns back; if you smile, it returns the greeting."

No, I'm not suggesting that if you grin at life, tensions in the Middle East, the Balkans, and Africa will instantly dissolve. We'll leave it to the metaphysicians, mystics, and philosophers to explain collective responsibility at that level. But I can testify that the view of personal responsibility I'm suggesting to you is transformative when you apply it to your immediate experience. Your illness, or issues with the people in your daily life, are extremely specific reflections of how you think, as well as the contents of your shadow projecting into your world for the opportunity of healing. These reflections are also precisely what you need to see if you are going to start reflecting something more to your liking.

Recall our earlier discussions about the unconscious mind being the shadow, containing all the pain, anger, rage, and sadness that you've never allowed into your conscious experience, and all the personality characteristics that you've disowned. Recall, too, that emotional wounds have a natural healing mechanism, just as physical wounds do. That mechanism is the projection of the shadow contents into conscious life experience. The shadow is under pressure to discharge its contents and it will do so relentlessly, forever challenging you to become whole by accepting all that you are—the so-called bad, as well as the so-called good.

Let's look again at an example of shadow release, this time in the light of personal responsibility. An uncle sexually abuses a seven-year-old girl. The pain and anger generated by the incident seem overwhelming to the child. Too hurt and scared to fully express the emotions at the time, she consciously suppresses some of them into the shadow of her mind. She also represses them as well. This occurs automatically, because repression is an unconscious process designed to protect us from intense pain.

The nature of the shadow, however, is to push the emotions outward so they can be released. Later in life, the girl, now a young woman, will make choices about boyfriends that are influenced by her unconscious mind and the pain of early abuse, and she will draw to herself a sexually abusive experience with a boyfriend. This is a critical opportunity for her to take responsibility for her present experience and heal the childhood wound at the same time. As an adult, she is better able to fully express the emotions of her abusive experience than when she was a child because she won't find the feelings so threatening or overwhelming. She is also more capable of understanding the experience intellectually once the feelings have subsided. If she cries out her pain and expresses her anger, she allows the shadow contents to release, and simultaneous healing of the childhood and adult abuse takes place. If on the other hand, she denies her feelings again and focuses all her energy into blame of the other person, then the healing opportunity is missed. What's more, the shadow remains full and under pressure to recreate a similar experience in the future. Perhaps the new experience won't be as intense as the childhood incident, but the theme of the woman's relationships with men will likely center around mistrust or abuse of one kind or another, until she takes the emotional leap that ends the cycle. In short, her relationships with men will be compromised for years to come, as she unconsciously creates, and then denies, opportunities for shadow release and inner healing. She will play victim to men and in the process give away her power to create fulfilling, loving relationships with them.

I know that what I have just outlined could bring strong objections from many women in our society, as I have suggested the abused woman "asked for it." Let us be very clear here—she certainly did not ask for it consciously. No one in their right mind would ask for pain and abuse—only masochists do things like that. But I would say that she "asked for it" on the unconscious level because we all have self-healing mechanisms built into us. Our cuts heal automatically, and thank God they do, as I would find it very difficult to try to figure out how to do that intellectually. And our emotional wounds heal automatically too. The shadow recreates the painful experience from childhood in order to heal the emotional wound that wasn't permitted healing at the time it occurred in childhood. Healing, like religion, means to become whole—to accept all parts of ourselves including the parts we don't like, the painful and rejected parts, or the parts we have forgotten, all of which are hidden in the recesses of our own mind. By plumbing the depths of her anger, pain and tears in a sense of reponse-ability, the lady in our example will find greater personal power and she will have released her distrust of men and be much more likely to have fulfilling relationships in the future.

Shadow projection has only one purpose: self-healing and the building of personal power, a fundamental part of both psychological and spiritual growth. Abraham Maslow was instrumental in bringing the idea of self-realization—or self-actualization as he called it—to the field of psychology. Prior to Maslow, most psychological models were obsessed with disease rather than health, just like the medical models that preceded them. Writing about the element that he saw missing, Maslow stated, "I think it is fair to say that no theory of psychology will ever be complete which does not centrally incorporate the concept that man has his future within him, dynamically active at this present moment."

In addition to owning the reality you experience as your own projection, it's also important to realize that you may have thoughts, beliefs, and attitudes that limit you and are reflected in your reality. For example, the thought that "I can never have what I want" can blind you to ways that you can make your relationships, work life, and leisure time more satisfying. To improve the quality of your life, including your health, you need to identify and alter thoughts, attitudes and beliefs that don't support your continued growth and sense of self-worth.

A great spiritual teacher of mine once said: "Don't say I didn't want it (whatever experience, painful or otherwise) to happen. Be pleased by every occurrence in your life and the wisdom it provides you. Consider it your manifestation and don't run from your creation. Don't explain it, but gain your understanding through feeling, not words. Master the emotion of every occurrence. By rejecting the limitation or pain in any occurrence, you hold onto it, only to replay it again in the future. What is needed to be felt expands self-love, as every emotion eventually unfolds into 'I want to be loved.' The Soul expands through emotion felt." These words have reverberated within me over the years, but I can say from experience that there is no way to come to this understanding intellectually. It can only be gained through testing its validity in your life. Once you do that, I believe that you will see that it produces insights you could not have gained any other way.

### Responsibility and Emotional Release

For reasons rooted deep in our cultural history, our society has always stressed thinking and intellect over emotions and other feelings such as intuition. Our society favors the masculine approach in life with its aggressive and controlling nature over the feminine, which is more accepting, nurturing and balanced with feeling and intuition. As a result, we try to run our world almost entirely with our minds. We make heady plans, and try to execute them with sheer mental will, bulldozing past whatever feelings arise in the process. When the outcome fails to meet our expectations, we become frustrated, disappointed, and frightened. But because our emotional skills lag far behind our thinking ones, we deal with those feelings by resorting to more busy plans and hard work to make everything turn out right.

Many of us are simply afraid of our feelings. We weren't taught the importance of expressing emotions in childhood. Instead, we were told "Don't cry" and "Be strong." (This is true of boys in particular but not exclusively.) Our parents weren't intentionally trying to inhibit us, but many parents also misunderstand the important guiding force of emotion. As a result, many of us have developed personalities with elaborate defenses against feeling life's pains, from daily bumps in the road to life-changing disasters. Challenges in life that could strengthen us, if we accepted them, are misconstrued as fears that threaten us. Eventually, the web of inner defenses begins to entangle us, putting us into a survival mode in which we try to escape our problems *en masse* rather than confronting them and learning from them. The universe has equipped us with the inner resources to master life but, through misinterpretation of emotion and opportunities, we tap only a fraction of them. When we feel stress and excitement, we read it as a danger sign and beat a retreat. When we happen upon an opportunity for change, we foresee only change for the worse, and let the opportunity pass.

I believe that the solution to this dilemma lies in understanding responsibility. When we accept both real problems and apprehensions about future problems as our own creation, we are inevitably led to the emotions brought up by the experience. We are now sitting with the pain of the divorce or business failure instead of sidestepping it. That will bring on sadness, and perhaps tears, but the vulnerability and emotional openness also permits the self-healing mechanisms of the unconscious mind to work. Stored emotional pain is gradually released, reducing our need to create future adversity and thereby increasing the likelihood of future successful experiences. Just as importantly, we learn the value of paying attention to our feelings. We are more apt now to navigate life with a balance of heart and intellect instead of by intellect alone, leading to greater levels of maturity and self-understanding. Instead of defending ourselves against feeling with unrelenting busy-ness, we slow to the pace of our inner world, a pace at which the communications of the heart can be heard.

I in no way mean to discount the contributions of intellect to our world. Without intellect, we would not have science and technology, and where would the world be without that? But intellect devoid of feeling creates as many problems as it solves. Nuclear weapons and environmental destruction by profit-obsessed corporations are both examples where the products of intellect have triumphed over heart-felt living and common sense. In my opinion, true genius represents the proper balance of intellect and emotion. As Pascal said, "The heart has reasons that reason knows not of."

Not only do emotions guide us toward greater health and well being, they can lead us to unlimited depths of personal wisdom. The late psychiatrist, David Viscott, wrote: "Being in touch with your feelings is the only way you can become your highest self." Being in touch with feelings is impossible without personal responsibility, for feelings must first be owned as ours, not blamed on others.

### How Personal Power Is Lost and How to Get It Back

Just as personal power is gained by taking responsibility, denying responsibility for our experience dissipates what power we've gathered. And most of us don't have a lot to spare. We disperse much of the power that is our birthright as we grow up under the influence of family and society. Influenced by their beliefs about outside causes and outside authority figures, we give our power first to parents and teachers and religion and eventually to spouses, government, political parties, scientific experts, and so on.

By the time we enter young adulthood, most of our power is now invested outside of ourselves, and our fears prevent us from reclaiming it. The little girl who was afraid of her father becomes afraid of her husband. The little boy who was belittled by his parents grows up feeling inadequate, afraid he won't be good enough or won't have enough money. Fear fuels our anger, frustration, resentment, worry, anxiety, and depression, and it's an insidious trap because we also fear that we won't be able to handle our fears. So we bypass them as much as possible by seeking safe, unexciting paths in life, or we seek our excitement in ways that don't confront some of our most basic fears (for example, a mountain climber who avoids committed relationships isn't lacking in excitement, but he's still sidestepping one of his biggest challenges). Our attempts are futile, of course, because of the mechanism of shadow release. Inevitably, we will unconsciously arrange a replayed incident to give ourselves the opportunity to experience the fear and release it from the shadow. But most of us will let the opportunity pass with the excuse that "I'll do it next time."

The only way out of fear, however, is through it. Here's a technique that will begin eroding the storehouses of fear and other repressed emotions burdening your unconscious mind and move you toward taking 100 percent responsibility for what happens in your life. Consider for a moment something that has bothered or challenged you, perhaps repeatedly—a troubled relationship, an unfulfilling job, an illness. Then consider the issue as something arising from the creative power of your own consciousness. Consider it as something you personally designed to teach you a life lesson. Now contemplate and feel all the emotions that arise within you about the problem. Stay with the feelings and let go of all your previous explanations for the problem, simply nurture the emotions as they come up. Remember that if you have ever blamed someone or something for a problem, then you have given them your power. Imagine living life without blame.

In this manner, you begin personal healing of the highest order. You have taken some important steps toward moving from the victim to the master of your experience. You will soon understand what the Yaqui healer, Don Juan, meant when he told his student, Carlos Castaneda: "To the ordinary man, everything that happens to him is either a curse of a blessing. To the warrior, each thing is a challenge."

In Jungian psychology, an archetype is an image or pattern of thought with ancient roots in human culture that is present in everyone's individual psyche. The courage required to explore self amidst the jungle of inner fears and defenses is exemplified by the Warrior archetype. The warrior spirit embodies the qualities of self-responsibility, courage, bravery, and discipline in dealing with the challenges of life. We usually think of warriors as indigenous people, martial artists, or soldiers going to battle to protect family, tribe, or nation from an aggressive foe. But this is just the most superficial perspective on this complex image. While we all have an impulse to defend the weak and vulnerable in the outer world, we also have inside us an "awakened warrior" to fight the battle of consciousness within. As Tibetan Buddhist teacher Chogyam Trungpa puts it, "The key to warriorship is not being afraid of who you are. Ultimately that is the definition of bravery: not being afraid of yourself."

## Responsibility Pitfalls—
## Positive Thinking, Failing to Forgive, and Craig's Story

Now that we've established the importance of taking responsibility for creating our adversities, it's time to fine-tune this notion. Taking responsibility is a watchword of the personal growth movement that has been around since the early 1970s. But just like the super-religious sometimes miss the entire point of spirituality, the most fervent growth junkies sometimes use the very tools of growth to stop growing.

Take, for instance, positive thinking. As I've said throughout this book, thoughts can be important factors in causing disease or prolonging disease, particularly when they have coalesced into negative or otherwise unhealthful attitudes and beliefs. For example, one of the first steps in fighting cancer has to be reversing the belief that your disease is inevitably fatal. Psychologically based beliefs, such as "I'm not good enough" or "I'm not the kind of person that other people can love," can be part of the complex of thoughts and emotions that lead to illness and that must be turned around for healing to take place. But for many, positive thinking becomes an obsession that displaces other important facets of personal growth, including the release of repressed emotions. In fact, positive thinkers are often among the most dedicated avoiders of uncomfortable emotions such as anger and fear. Confusing emotions with thoughts, they protest that unhappy emotions are too "negative" and try to reverse them with positive affirmations or simply cover them up with a smile, albeit a transparently shallow one.

Nobody will do much growing without exploring the shadow side of their consciousness. But the consequences of misplaced positive thinking are much greater for patients with serious illness. As Lydia Temoshok points out in *The Type C Connection,* about the psychology of cancer, preaching positive thinking to cancer patients plays right into the syndrome that may have fed the tumor formation in the first place. That is, it reinforces what they are inclined to do anyway: cover up painful emotions. As I said above, the only way through fear is through it. That goes for other repressed emotions as well.

And that leads to a second pitfall of personal growth. Just like positive thinkers get stuck in one aspect of growth, those who explore their emotional selves can also get stuck, particularly if they do not forgive the source of their pain. I can illustrate this problem best with a story about one of my former patients. I always enjoyed seeing this man, let's call him Craig, when he came to my office. The owner of a successful computer software company with a lovely family, he is a bright, motivated, sophisticated patient who takes his health and life seriously, although perhaps too seriously at times. I never had to cajole Craig to explore his emotions. He had been doing it on his own for years in addition to his more worldly intellectual pursuits. But as we'll see, he sometimes got mesmerized by the fascinating twists and turns of his psyche and lost sight of why he was exploring it in the first place.

In his early appointments with me, Craig had complained of fatigue and occasional depression. He understood that his depression meant that he was probably avoiding emotions, like anger, and he wasn't surprised when our sessions uncovered some forgotten aspects about his childhood relationship with his mother. Craig was an only child, and his mother emotionally exploited him with her smothering form of love. He had read Patricia Love's book, *The Emotional Incest Syndrome: What to Do When a Parent's Love Rules Your Life,* and it struck home as he realized how his mother had turned to him as an infant to get her emotional needs met, needs that should have been fulfilled by her husband.

Emotionally incestuous parents violate the boundaries of their child's personality, confusing their child's emotional issues with their own. They enmesh themselves in every aspect of the child's life, negating his thoughts and feelings and only rewarding him when he thinks like they do. Their parenting style is so controlling that the child fails to develop an independent sense of self. Children of emotionally incestuous parents inevitably have relationship problems because any close relationship begins to feel like an invasion. That is, the barriers they erected against the invasive parent become barriers to intimacy later in life.

After exploring these issues for over a year on his own, Craig came back to my office complaining of sexual problems, especially his frequent inability to maintain an erection during lovemaking with his wife. Frustrated and worried, he wanted his testosterone levels measured and everything else checked out physically. I assured him that the source of his problem wasn't in his body; it was in his resistance to intimacy going back to his childhood. Craig wasn't happy with my diagnosis. On my recommendation after our last appointment, he had seen a counselor about the psychological wounds inflicted by his mother and done the exercises the counselor suggested on a daily basis. He had worked on resolving those issues with such determination that he felt the job should be done by now. He all but stormed out of the office.

I ran into Craig a couple of months later at a local coffee shop. After some opening chat, he told me excitedly about the progress he'd made with his issues. He had written his mother a letter telling her he forgave her, and told me he genuinely felt that he understood her wounded nature and that she did the best she could. Although he didn't send the letter to her, his forgiveness of her released his anger towards her, and what's more, a week or so later, his sexual potency returned to normal. He also realized that he needed to forgive himself as well as his mother. He maintained that, if we create our experiences in life for our learning and growth, then we need to forgive ourselves as well as for drawing the experience to us in the first place. It was now two months later, and his performance had been mostly just fine.

Craig's story makes several vital, and related, points:

- **You are not your problems. You can *resolve them* and you will still be here.** In contrast to those who resist doing inner work, some take to it like an exciting new hobby. They see counselors, attend as many growth workshops as they can fit into their schedule, and devour one self-improvement book after another. They venture into their emotional selves without fear, willing to cry out their repressed tears in front of an entire seminar group. But they come to identify with their problems so deeply that after a while there is little left to reveal and their issues become their "shtick." They are stuck in the past, their past emotional wounds. When you get a physical wound, you cleanse it, allow it to close up and heal, and then forget about it and get on with your life. You don't keep opening up the wound to look at it. So it goes with emotional wounds. If you confuse them with who you are and keep reopening them for another look, they are no more likely to heal than physical ones.

- **Growth is not a profession or a form of recreation.** The stereotype of the growth group junkie is pretty accurate at times. It is exciting to explore your personal issues to the nth degree, and it can be socially rewarding when you do it with a group of people who have the same interest and dedication. You can support each other in surmounting personal barriers and cheer everyone's progress. But watch out when the activity of attending workshops or reading the latest self-improvement book becomes more thrilling than the actual changes you are making in your life. Change is the bottom line, and if you're attending more workshops and changing less, you may be using your superficial commitment as just another excuse for avoiding your real issues.

- **When a wound doesn't go away, it may be because of a failure to forgive yourself and others.** We've talked extensively about the importance of fully experiencing your emotional pains from the past. But when someone else inflicted that pain, as in a case of emotional or sexual abuse, it is crucial that you forgive that person. Also, based on our expanded notion of self-responsibility, you need to forgive yourself for calling the abuser to you. Otherwise, the blame just keeps the wound from healing and you become stuck in the pain just like Craig was for so long.

Forgiveness is obviously an important part of taking responsibility. If you are responsible, then who is to blame? Again, just how you were responsible for something may not always be apparent to you, but the *stance* of responsibility is what will get you moving in a healing direction.

### Responsibility and Reincarnation

There are some situations in which the victim's personal responsibility is hard to figure. For me, the biggest example of this is the child, or even newborn, with serious illness. Many cultures around the world explain such phenomena by referring to the spiritual idea of reincarnation. That is, some events that seem inexplicable in terms of a person's personal responsibility in this life are explained as originating in the circumstances of a previous existence.

Put simply, reincarnation postulates that an individual soul inhabits many different lives over time. That is, after a life ends in one body, the soul begins a new life in a new body. It repeats this cycle of birth and death so it can complete karma and accumulate self-knowledge. The goal is self-realization and the discovery that God is within, or oneness with God.

The type of knowledge that a soul seeks through reincarnation is not intellectual learning. It is wisdom, the type of learning gained from illuminating life experiences. The challenges of each lifetime are based on individual karma, or "as ye sow, so shall you reap" in the Christian tradition. In other words, if you hurt someone, the laws of karma demand that you pay the debt and learn the lesson. When a karmic lesson is not passed before that lifetime ends, it is carried over into the next lifetime to give the soul another chance to succeed (sort of like repeating a test or grade level in school). The cycle of reincarnation goes on until all the karmic lessons are learned and complete understanding is gained about the human experience on earth. In other words, each soul enters a lifetime with a "course list" encompassing the pivotal experiences of that lifetime. Seen from this point of view, a young child with cancer, so tragic in our Western framework, may be repeating a karmic lesson carried over from a previous life. Perhaps there is an important lesson for the family of the child to learn. If the child dies, reincarnationists see him as having completed his "course list" in his current incarnation. His life may have been short because his "educational agenda" for himself and others for that lifetime was also short.

Reincarnation is viewed by many in Western society as a superstition but it is not merely the belief of uneducated peoples. In countries such as India, highly credentialed professionals and scientists commonly believe in reincarnation, finding no conflict between it and their academic education. Many prominent Western thinkers including Plato, the German philosopher Arthur Schopenhauer, and Carl Jung have also believed in reincarnation; Jung wrote about what he claimed to be his 18th-century incarnation in his *Memories, Dreams and Reflections.* Some spiritually oriented psychotherapists claim to "regress" their patients back through previous lifetimes to resolve issues in the current one. Brian Weiss, a Yale- and Columbia-trained psychiatrist, writes compellingly about his past-life therapy practice in his book, *Many Lives, Many Masters.*

Some spiritually curious researchers also claim to have uncovered evidence of reincarnation. For instance, Dr. Ian Stevenson, Carlson Professor of Psychiatry and director of the Division of Personality Studies at the University of Virginia, has collected some 700 case histories of children worldwide who astonished their parents with precisely detailed descriptions of the people they claim to have been in past lives. According to Stevenson, several of these exceptional children speak the language of the previous lifetime even though they have not been exposed to that language in their current life. Under hypnosis, the majority of these children also recall a violent death in their previous life; what's more, Stevenson reports that 200 of them have birthmarks at the exact location of the injury that supposedly caused the sudden and violent death.

None of the above is intended to convince you that reincarnation is a fact. Ultimately, despite all the intriguing accounts by authors such as Weiss and Stevenson, you must decide as a matter of faith whether reincarnation is something you can accept. I mention it only because it has been useful to me as a way of accounting for events in my life and others' that are not easily accounted for by personal responsibility. For me, personal responsibility has been an invaluable tool for helping me better understand my experiences and the experiences of my patients. In my life, it works brilliantly. To see if it will also work for you, I invite you to try it on for size.

## The Final Word on Responsibility: Compassion

One of the biggest objections to the philosophy of personal responsibility is a moral one. Many of those in society who proclaim the importance of personal responsibility use it to justify a lack of compassion. If everyone is responsible for their own circumstances, they ask, why should we care about the poor, the sick, the hungry, minorities, and other so-called vulnerable people in our world? "They should pull themselves up by their own bootstraps," the political ideologues sniff. Or in the New Age version, "They are just projecting their own negative thoughts." This "I've got mine" self-righteousness is one reason that so many others find the idea of personal responsibility repugnant.

But this is a debate between limited views, especially from the standpoint of human consciousness. Once you become aware of vulnerable people or other social problems, they become part of your reality. If you take responsibility for your reality, how can you responsibly turn your back on them? Seen this way, consciousness and personal responsibility is the beginning of compassion, not the end of it.

# 9

# THE IMPORTANCE OF SELF-LOVE

*We do not become enlightened by imagining figures of light but by making the darkness conscious.*

Carl Jung

*How we feel about ourselves crucially affects virtually every aspect of our experience, from the way we function at work, in love, in sex, to the way we operate as parents, to how high in life we are likely to rise. . . Thus, self-esteem is the key to success or failure.*

Nathaniel Branden

If there is one quality that sets the healthy adult apart, it is self-love. From self-love springs confidence, courage, spontaneity, creativity, expressiveness, will, and, of course, the ability to love others. People who feel good about themselves don't feel threatened by those who think differently than they do. They are not jealous of others' happiness or success; in fact, they applaud it. They do and say what they feel because they aren't driven by others' approval of them. That is, they don't need others' permission to live their lives. In relationships, they support their partner's desires and individuality not only out of love but because they are whole and don't feel threatened by another's happiness. No matter how content or successful they are, they are never complacent or afraid to reach for more because they know they deserve it. When faced with the opportunity to grow, they seize it—risk doesn't scare them, it excites them.

People who have self-love also tend to have exceptional health, because quite simply self-love is made up of healthful thoughts and feelings. People with self-love usually make more healthful choices in life as well, because they don't have conflicts about their self-worth that drive them to be self-destructive. By the same token, thoughts and feelings of unworthiness—the opposite of self-love—lie at the core of many adult problems, including disease. (Another term for unworthiness is low self-esteem.)

But self-love does not just happen to us. There is no self-love button to push on the human body. People who feel good about themselves either come from backgrounds of feeling loved and supported from their earliest childhood, or they are people who have aggressively worked on themselves, learning to appreciate their intrinsic worth through transformative personal growth.

Most of us have at least some personal issues related to feelings of self-worth, because no matter how much our parents loved us, there have been traumatic moments from our earliest consciousness where it appeared to us that the state of love in which we entered the world had utterly collapsed. Some of these go back to the birth process itself. In this chapter, we examine how birthing and child-rearing practices that are standard in our society damage our sense of self-worth and what can be done to reverse the damage, not only to improve our health but for a fuller experience of life itself.

### Birthing and the Inner Child

Since ancient times, the purity, curiosity, and innocence of the child's mind has captured the human imagination. In culture after culture and religion after religion, it represents curiosity, wonder, discovery, spontaneity, awe, immortality, and even enlightenment. In Greek mythology, the child-god Hermes captures the favor of his father Zeus with his creative cleverness. In Hinduism, there is the image of the Divine child Krishna, in Christianity, the Christ child. The same motif surfaces in modern thinking, too, in the influential works of Sigmund Freud, Carl Jung, Milton Erikson, and many other giants of psychology. Jung referred to the child archetype as representing a "wholeness which embraces the very depths of Nature."

But the child of innocence becomes the child of experience earlier than you might think—while still in the womb of mother. Research has shown that during the last three months of pregnancy the baby in mother's womb is a fully equipped infant that just needs to grow some more. He is ready for a lot of life's experiences at this tender pre-term age, and is listening, moving, grimacing, smiling, feeling, learning, making decisions, and most importantly, bonding with his mother.

Dr. Thomas Verney, a psychiatrist, reviewed much of the remarkable research on the unborn child and published it in his 1981 book, *The Secret Life of the Unborn Child.* Dr. Verney collected studies from around the world on mothers and their unborn children, including studies on healthy, neurotic, and even psychotic mothers. The research showed that the unborn child has primitive intellectual and emotional needs and that he has to feel loved and wanted, perhaps even more than we do. Basically, the more an unborn child is wanted and loved by the mother, the easier the pregnancy and delivery will be and the healthier the baby at birth. A lot of research supports this notion, including that of Dr. Gerhard Rottmann of the University of Salzburg, Austria. Dr. Rottman studied 141 women and divided them into four groups based on their attitudes toward pregnancy. Based on psychological testing, ideal mothers wanted their babies consciously and unconsciously. This group had the easiest pregnancies, the most trouble-free births and the healthiest babies, both physically and emotionally. In contrast, the mothers with the most negative attitudes toward their pregnancies, the Catastrophic group, had the worst medical problems during pregnancy, and bore the highest rate of premature, low birth-weight and emotionally disturbed infants.

So even while still in mother's womb, the child is beginning to learn about the world, and for many, its purity begins to fade and it begins accumulating the emotional issues that will become its life's project to work through. Many of these issues bear directly on its sense of self-love, which can be further damaged if the child experiences a difficult birth process.

While having gained early experience about life while still in his mother's womb, his lessons may gain in intensity during the birth process itself. Just prior to birth, he enters an extreme state of stress in preparation for his arduous journey into the outside world. Even at this early stage, he will use stress as a learning tool. His body is primed for birth by powerful hormones, especially the adrenal stimulating hormone, ACTH. This stress arousal creates new proteins and brain cell connections that will allow him to "understand" and receive the nurturing and support that he desperately needs to reduce the stress of birth.

In a normal healthy birth the infant moves through the birth canal in a steady, perhaps sensuous manner, usually entering the world without crying as he continues bonding with his mother in the hopefully dim light of day. For some though, the trials are more severe. Labor may be prolonged, the journey through the birth canal may be terrifying and even life-threatening. These painful experiences are felt by the infant and recorded in his unconscious mind, later to be expressed as timidity and fear about other transitional experiences in life.

Nature has done an excellent job of designing birth and complications only occur in about 10 to 15 percent of cases. Unfortunately, however, Western hospitals, following the dictates of modern medicine's disease model, have designed their birthing methods as a defense against those complications, which compromises the 85 to 90 percent of births that are normal. Pregnancy and delivery are regarded as dangerous, complicated, and painful, requiring high-risk medical interventions that themselves dramatically increase the risk of problems. (It is certainly true that hospitals are the best place to be if something goes wrong in birth, but it is ironic that hospital births themselves make complications far more likely.)

In medical birthing, the mother is put in awkward, unnatural positions for the convenience of the obstetrician; these positions slow down the birth process because they don't take advantage of gravity and thus make the use of contraction-inducing drugs more likely.

Many mothers in hospitals are given pain medication, either by choice or because the contraction-inducing drugs produce particularly painful labor; if the anesthetic is not localized, it will cross the placenta and enter the baby's system. The child, whose extremely sensitive eyes have never been exposed to direct light, is born under bright lamps, again for the doctor's convenience. Soon after birth, the baby is whisked away from its mother to the nursery where tubes are inserted in various orifices. Burning drops are put in its eyes and then, in many cases, the infant is observed in a nursery most of the day and night rather staying with his mother, as Nature intended.

Let's return to the ideal scenario, Nature's plan. The infant's most important need is love—if love is totally absent, it will die. And again, love and support by parents is the ground in which self-love grows. Nature intends that immediately after birth, the baby is held, caressed, fondled, and nursed, allowing him to feel loved and safe in his new universe. Bathed in maternal nurturing attention, his every need is attended to, and by the fourth day his levels of adrenal steroids fall back to normal. He is developing trust and self-worth, which, if sustained, will allow the emergence of a healthy personality.

But those of us born in hospitals are not so lucky. Although hospital births obviously don't diminish a mother's love for her child, they do dramatically diminish the opportunities she has to communicate it. Just focusing on what takes place right after the baby emerges, we can see that Nature's plan is thrown into disarray. If the baby has drugs in its system, it will take longer than its mother to shed them because of its immature body mechanisms. The drugged state will interfere with both bonding and breastfeeding, two ingenious, interrelated methods that Nature has designed for passing love between mother and child. Chances are that the mother will get little consistent help from the hospital staff to breastfeed anyway; only 60 percent of American mothers even try to breastfeed, and lack of encouragement and expertise in hospitals is a big reason why. Policies in many hospitals against babies "rooming in"—that is, staying with their mothers instead of in a nursery—also interrupt bonding, increasing the baby's feelings of fear, abandonment, and isolation.

Hospital staffs aren't intentionally cruel but they don't give the baby credit for being a conscious, sensitive being yet, nor do they give credit to Nature for knowing better than they do. As a result, they have developed procedures that are insensitive to the baby's emotional needs. The less-than-nurturing experiences that result become encoded into the child's mind, creating a matrix of insecurity and anxiety that will influence it for a lifetime. The groundwork for feelings of unworthiness has been laid.

Contrast our supposedly superior high-tech birthing methods with the no-tech, purely natural approach used by tribal peoples in Uganda. The pregnant woman in this culture follows her usual routines until about five minutes before the birth. She then retires to her home, squats, and delivers her child. Within the hour, she resumes her normal activities, her baby in a sling next to her bare breasts. Her infant is never separated from her, and she caresses, massages, and sings to him continuously. Mother is so attuned to child that every need is met before the child cries; she even anticipates when he needs to urinate or defecate and takes him to the bushes before he soils himself.

The result of all this close, loving contact is some remarkable children. In 1956, Marcelle Geber researched infant and child intelligence in Kenya and Uganda. In the latter country, she found some of the most advanced infants and children scientists had ever seen. At two days of age, the 300 home-delivered babies studied could sit upright with only their forearms held for support; focused and smiling, they gazed brightly into their mothers' eyes. At six to seven weeks, they crawled, sat up by themselves, and stared at their image in a mirror for an extended time. On these and other standard developmental tests, Ugandan infants were demonstrating functions that average American and European children aren't capable of for at least several months to a year later, a huge gap in developmental terms.

Tellingly, Geber also tested infants born to upper-class Ugandans in European-style hospitals. They showed none of the precocity of the naturally birthed Ugandan babies, ruling out the effects of heredity. Just as revealing is the fact that the home-birthed Ugandans' maintain their intellectual superiority to Western children for only the first four years of life. When their children reach four years of age, Ugandan mothers cut off attention to them without warning, ignoring them totally in deference to a custom designed to bond the children to their culture. At this point, the children's developmental advantage over Western children disappears. As Joseph Chilton Pearce, who writes extensively about the Uganda studies in his *Magical Child,* explains, the shock of abandonment is so great that the children's intellectual development is damaged for life.

The overriding lesson from these African studies, it seems to me, is the importance of love to the child in her most formative years. The Ugandan children learn from their first day in the world the foundation lessons of self-worth: "I am important," "I am worth it," "I am lovable." This rudimentary notion of self-empowerment helps optimize growth and learning by promoting release of the pituitary growth stimulant known as growth hormone.

Because the Ugandan parenting style of boundless love and support begins immediately after birth, bonding is optimized. With his mother always at his side, the infant can interact with the world from a base of security. The unfamiliar does not frighten or intimidate him nearly as much as it would an insecure infant, so he builds knowledge quickly and his intellect expands accordingly. From moment to moment, he may be surprised or alarmed by something he perceives as dangerous, but his mother is always there when he retreats and soon he is ready to venture out into the vast unknown again.

We have to remember that in his first years the child is a feeling being, not a thinking one. He can't distinguish between "good" and "bad" or "true" and "false." His mind is like a blank hard disk in a computer, and all experiences are programmed in indiscriminately. This is how his beginning self-awareness and self-understanding is formed and why constant love and meeting of his physical needs is so important. When his hunger is relieved and his other discomforts remedied, he registers the experience as "positive" and his self-worth is enhanced. If his needs are not met, even momentarily, he records the experience as "negative" and his sense of worthiness suffers.

Humans, including human babies, are remarkably resilient so it's not as if a few late feedings or diaper changes will scar the child for life. But Nature clearly intends that early child-rearing more closely resemble the Ugandan model than the contemporary Western one.

We can see this clearly from the vast benefits of breastfeeding and how much better kids do both health-wise and intellectually if they are breastfed for at least a year (ideal is probably several years). For a child to be breastfed on demand, he and his mother have to be in constant proximity. And, of course, the close skin-to-skin contact of breastfeeding communicates loving as well. It is as if Nature has designed a feeding system that not only includes physical nutrients, but emotional ones as well, thereby ensuring that the child will receive the constant loving attention that it needs to thrive.

As mentioned, loving attention stimulates the pituitary to release growth hormone, which stimulates both body and mind to develop. Children who receive only physical care—that is, who are only fed and changed, without the caressing, talking to, and other energies of love—will not grow. Without love, their growth hormone secretion slows and they "fail to thrive."

The problems with parenting in our society aren't so severe that failure to thrive is epidemic, but we also don't have the strong cultural agreements that Ugandans do, at least in the early years, about the importance of the parent-child bond. There is little cultural or institutional support for breastfeeding or for the importance of a parent spending as much time as possible with the child in the early years. Parents often return to work within weeks of their child's birth, either by choice or because of economic necessity. In many homes, plunking the little ones down in front of the TV has largely replaced another form of intimate relating to kids, reading to them. A significant minority of parents believe that attending to a young child's every emotional need, even feeding them on demand, spoils them. Many parents were themselves not closely nurtured when they were young and know only how to practice the same form of remote parenting practiced with them.

If a baby cries and her mother does not come to comfort her, she feels the pain of abandonment, just as she feels the happiness of her mother's presence when she is needed. If a child asks to be read to and her parent urges her to watch TV alone instead, that too sends a message that "I'm not worthy." If a child is disciplined too severely for misbehavior or judged unfairly, she might well conclude "I am a bad person." All of the above are well within the bounds of what we call "normal" parenting. And then, of course, there are the psychological consequences of severe traumas such as abuse or divorce or other abandonment, all of which a child will probably interpret and record in her subconscious mind as damning evidence of her unworthiness.

## When Children Are "Bad"—Discipline and Self-Worth

One of the most critical impacts on our sense of self-love comes from the way our parents handle it when we need disciplining—or at least when they think we do. Child discipline is a hot topic today because as one of the battles of the culture wars, we are locked into a debate about the virtues of permissive vs. autocratic—i.e. strict— parenting. It's a silly fight because psychologists and researchers are largely in agreement that neither parenting style by itself produces very good results. The preferred style, called authoritative parenting, combines the best aspects of both. From the permissive style, authoritative parenting employs loving acceptance, emotional attentiveness, respect for children's individuality, and encouraging children to express themselves. All of these qualities are crucial for children developing a strong sense of self-esteem, whereas their autocratic opposites—coldness, unresponsiveness, and quashing of individuality by requiring rigid obedience and adoption of parents' values, wishes, and ideals—tear self-esteem down.

Autocratic parenting does trump permissive parenting, according to most experts, in its approach to discipline, at least when its methods are practiced with moderation. Authoritative parenting draws its ideas of discipline from autocratic parenting. The basic concept is that children should be accountable, and this is instilled in them by clearly stating rules and consequences for not following those rules and consistently enforcing those consequences if rules are broken. When practiced as just stated, kids internalize their parents' disciplining of them and develop good impulse control and a mature understanding of what's okay to do and what isn't.

Again, discipline is something strict parents often get right and permissive parents, by definition, never do. But strict parents can also go overboard, in which case discipline becomes unduly harsh and unjust. Combined with the austere approach to the child's emotional needs and the disregard for her individuality, strict parenting can wreak havoc on the child's sense of worthiness. In her seminal book, *For Your Own Good,* the German psychotherapist and anti-abuse crusader Alice Miller describes the child-rearing methods popularized in Germany by a mid-nineteenth century author named Schreber. This best-selling writer recommended severe parenting approaches such as the following:

> The little ones' display of temper indicated by screaming or crying without cause should be regarded as the first test of your spiritual and pedagogical principles. . . Once you have established that nothing is really wrong, that the child is not ill, distressed, or in pain, then you can rest assured that the screaming is nothing more than an outburst of temper, a whim, the *first appearance of willfulness* (italics added). Now you should no longer simply wait for it to pass as you did in the beginning but should proceed in a somewhat more positive way: by quickly diverting its attention, by stern words, threatening gestures, rapping on the bed. . . or if none of this helps, by appropriately mild corporal admonitions repeated persistently at brief intervals until the child quiets down or falls asleep. . . . This procedure will be necessary only once or at most twice, and then you will be *master* of the child *forever* (italics added).

Miller postulates that this German version of "spare the rod and spoil the child" lies at the root of violent child-rearing in our culture too, and weakens the child's will and self-esteem for a lifetime. I would add that these same psychic wounds produce the seeds of later mental and physical disease.

In most families, of course, discipline and disapproval of children don't reach these extremes, but all of us can recall incidents from our childhood that affected our sense of self-worth. The toddler, who in his explorations of the world, knocks something off the table and is told he is "bad"; the little girl who is caught lying to her mother about using her make-up and told that "is a horrible thing to do"; the little boy who hits the family dog with his toy truck and is told he is "a monster"—everyone has such memories. And the reason we still have them is that the events they are based on are traumatic and indelible for children even though most parents dismiss their own behavior as trivial and neglect to reassure the child afterwards that he or she is still loved and perfectly okay. Children have a constant need for love and support as they pursue the intimidating task of exploring the world. When their faith in their own worthiness is shaken, it is written into their "software," showing up later in personality issues of inadequacy, lack of confidence, and poor self-esteem.

These everyday traumas don't ruin us for life, but they do leave "blemishes" in our consciousness that affect us until we do something about them. Even the most successful, confident-seeming people have such issues to work through. None of us gets through our impressionable years scot-free because no parent is perfect and children are acutely sensitive to all but the mildest criticism, especially when it comes from Mommy or Daddy God. This is why personal growth is so important for everyone who wants to live a fuller, healthier life and why the Divine Child archetype is so compelling. We all have an unconscious mind to unburden and the clean slate of the newborn's mind is a potent metaphor for our goal.

## When Inner Children Displace the Divine Child

Throughout this book, we've looked at how we store in our unconscious minds childhood traumas that were too painful to fully experience at the time. But now that we are looking at the nature of those pains in more detail, it's time to examine how they are recorded in the mind in more detail as well.

The various psychological wounds of childhood such as abandonment, betrayal, neglect, and excessive discipline and control each creates a unique mix of fear, anger, and pain. Each is recorded in the unconscious mind as unfelt emotion, but in an individualized way. Essentially, the mind constructs individualized barriers to protect against feeling the pain, and these effectively become sub-personalities of the adult personality. I call them inner children because they are formed in childhood from childhood emotional trauma.

You will recognize these inner children from your own behavioral life or the lives of others whom you know. The rejected child has problems with relationships, fears commitment, and may contribute to a person who becomes the "pleaser" or "overachiever" or "nice person," always trying to satisfy others to win their approval and heal his sense of emptiness and loneliness. New experiences and challenges in life frighten the fearful child. The wounded inner child feels unworthy of love and sees a lot of pain around him, and feels powerless to control the world. The abandoned child contributes to the person that becomes the "clinger," with an insatiable need to be close to others. Indeed, there are many variations in the problems represented by the wounded inner children.

Inner children live in the shadow of the unconscious mind, which psychologists agree constitutes the overwhelmingly largest share of our mental activity. These unowned parts of us become unconscious forces in our minds and, through the process of shadow projection, in our lives. Jung writes that it takes psychic energy to hold these inner children within the shadow and shield them from the light of the conscious mind. In fact, the amount of energy can be so great that it eventually leads to fatigue, depression, and disease in adulthood.

Where does this energy come from? Jung suggests that it is the energy of the Divine Child, but diverted to serve the purposes of inner children instead. When released through personal growth, the energy becomes the enthusiasm, spontaneity, creativity, and wonder that we often miss as adults. To re-own the power of the shadow is also to reclaim many of the glories of childhood.

### The Healing Power of Self-Love

The universe of psychotherapy provides us with countless philosophies and techniques to release the energies of the Divine Child. In the end, however, many of them come down to the same thing: the fire of awareness directed at self and the ownership of previously suppressed emotions. I believe the essence of this process is self-love, because we are in effect telling ourselves, "I will love and accept all that I am, including the pain."

Alice Miller describes self-love much the same way when she writes about the healthy personality in her book, *The Drama of the Gifted Child:*

I understand a healthy self-feeling to mean the unquestioned certainty that the feelings and wishes one experiences are a part of oneself. . . . This automatic, natural contact with his own emotions and wishes gives an individual strength and self-esteem. He may live out his feelings, be sad, despairing, or in need of help, without fear of making the introjected mother (aspects of mother in the child's unconscious mind) insecure. He can allow himself to be afraid when he is threatened, or angry when his wishes are not fulfilled. He knows not only what he does not want but also what he wants and is able to express this, irrespective of whether he will be loved or hated for it.

Self-love is the opposite of self-dislike or hatred, which engender self-judgment and denial stemming from an early childhood decision that "I am bad." And it bears no relation, either, to such superficial qualities as self-absorption, egotism, or boasting, which themselves can be defenses against inner pain. People with low self-worth judge themselves continually. They also compensate for their deep-seated pain by judging others as harshly as they judge themselves. Often they forget that they are in the same boat with those they criticize. This is why self-love is a necessary pre-condition for compassion. Only when we feel good about ourselves do we feel generous enough to feel good about others. Only when we own our pain do we have the capacity to feel another's hurting, too, and want it to heal.

Actually, once we are aware of the full dimensions of shadow projection, we can use our tendency to judge others to advance our personal growth and expand our compassion. Remember the basic premise of the bodymind's self-healing process: the shadow relentlessly tries to empty itself of the inner children's hidden emotions by pushing them into the light of our awareness. It does this by influencing our conscious choices in order to create life circumstances that reflect the wounded parts of our inner children. That is, we project our issues into the world, in order to see them once again, and, hopefully, to allow the stored emotions to be felt and released. *And one of the ways we do this is by noticing qualities in others that we don't like or would like to change in ourselves.* They are effectively a mirror of our own psyche. What we judge in others is what we judge about ourselves. If we understand this, we can let go of judging them—indeed, even silently thank them for reminding us to keep on the path of self-awareness and growth. They are essentially an indication of our need to correct our course, and when we make that correction, the reflection will change in kind.

Without the work of healing the inner children, Alice Miller wrote, "we continue to live our lives unaware of patterns we adopted when we were young, and thus we limit the scope of our living in the present." No one likes the child abuser, and yet we are all child abusers. We neglect and abuse our own inner children, by not allowing them to express their pain and keeping them in the dark closets of our unconscious minds.

But we can bring that abuse to an end through Edgework or other personal growth—that is, through exploring the edges of the unconscious and accelerating the process of shadow release. The Exercises at the end of the book will guide you in methods to listen to, heal, and re-educate your inner children. And then, by simply allowing the emotions that surface during the process to flow and fully experiencing them as we do, we can prevent future negative consequences in our bodies and lives.

"Owning" is another word for allowing emotions to flow and experiencing them. And owning is itself another word for self-love and forgiveness, for to own emotions is to accept them as our own and to forgive those we have blamed for our troubles. The painful scenarios in our lives continually change, but the basic, underlying emotions remain the same. Self-love breaks the cycle. It also keeps us moving forward in our growth process by allowing more deeply buried wounds to surface as other wounds are healed. It has been said, there can't be too much love in the world. Well, there can't be too much self-love in your life. In fact, there can't be much of a life without it.

# 10

# HEALING AT WORK

*I made a living, but I never really lived.*
The single most common regret of the terminally ill,
according to Elizabeth Kubler Ross

*Work is love made visible.*
Kahlil Gibran


The Tour de France, bicycling's premier competition, is widely described as the most grueling event in sports. It covers 2,290 miles and winds through two mountain ranges. The 1999 winner, American Lance Armstrong, had failed to finish the race in three previous tries, defeated in part by the brutal mountain stages. In 1999, however, it was his victory in the first stage in the Alps that paved the way for him to win the competition. But the real miracle was that Armstrong was able to compete at all. Just three years had passed since he went into remission for testicular cancer, a disease that nearly killed him.

After Armstrong was diagnosed in 1996, the cancer spread to his brain and lungs. His doctors privately held out little hope for his survival, although they told him to his face that his chances were "50-50." He received four rounds of chemotherapy and two operations, one to remove a testicle and another for brain lesions, but those close to his case say his recovery is miraculous. We can never know for sure how someone is able to beat the medical odds that Armstrong faced, but one aspect of his story seems clear to me: he was focused on something beyond his illness, a career that he loved and wanted passionately to resume. He is a dramatic and inspiring example of the health benefits of satisfying work.

Obviously, Lance Armstrong is not your typical wage earner. Only a very few of us who dream about being pro athletes or actors or musicians can make that particular dream come true. But that doesn't mean that we can't love what we do every day, and it certainly doesn't mean that we have to settle for dreary work that demeans or bores us. Too many of us think only about money or security when preparing for a career or seeking a job. Most of us simply don't believe it is possible to make a living doing something we love, so we don't even try. Like an arrow that lands where it is shot, these paths inevitably lead to work with few rewards beyond whatever they pay. What's more, they create a breeding ground for poor health.

In my medical practice over the years, I have learned that the background issues of consciousness can be vitally important in both perpetuating health or developing illness. Since the body is the messenger for illness that begins in the mind, it is important for me to know about the day-to-day tone of feelings, stresses, thoughts, and attitudes. This is why I always ask my patients if they enjoy their work. Most of us will spend more of our waking hours at our job than any other single activity, especially when we figure in the time we spend readying ourselves for the day and commuting to our workplace. In addition, work-related issues will tend to occupy our thoughts away from the job whether we enjoy our work or not. With so much of our lives committed to the job, the overall quality of our lives is inextricably tied to the quality of our work lives. Doesn't it make sense that if we just drag ourselves through the workday that our state of health might reflect that same mediocrity? Is it even logical to think that we could achieve a state of thriving health without work that we thrive on, too?

## Work and Health: What the Researchers Say

Satisfying work may be the most overlooked and underrated of all the factors affecting human health. Modern medicine says virtually nothing about it, although that's not terribly surprising since it all but ignores most emotional issues. Even most holistic practitioners don't give work-satisfaction near the attention it deserves. Researchers haven't exactly flocked to this topic, either, but what research does exist underlines work's ability to impact health, for better or worse. In fact, work-satisfaction has been found to be a consistent and widespread predictor of long-term health, perhaps second only to marital satisfaction.

We've already noted two relevant studies in Chapter 5, one conducted in Sweden and one overseen by Dr. Stewart Wolf in the U.S., in which low levels of life satisfaction, including satisfying work, strongly correlated to higher rates of heart disease. Studies of broader illness patterns show a similar relationship. In a study done at Cornell Medical College in New York, the illness patterns of 3,500 people were studied over a 20-year period of time. The authors concluded that those who were more dissatisfied and discontented with their work had more frequent illnesses. A study of employees and homemakers in Detroit revealed that those with the best health were those who were generally happy with their work and home life. The connection between bad health and dissatisfaction in this study was partially explained by the fact that both employees and homemakers who were dissatisfied with their lives tended to smoke, drink more, and report more stress.

Sometimes a number of employees will come down with similar symptoms in a workplace even though outside investigators can't find any physical cause to explain it. Often this occurs in newer, tightly sealed buildings with inadequate ventilation. Reports of nausea, dizziness, headaches, flu-like symptoms, and other problems are so common in sealed work-spaces that the complaints have been grouped together under the name "sick building syndrome." The condition doesn't strike all occupants equally, however. Those who are bored at work, having problems with the boss or other co-workers, have less control over their work lives, or have other job stresses are much more likely to feel ill, as reviews of illness outbreaks by investigating authorities such as city health departments and the National Institute for Occupational Safety and Health (NIOSH) demonstrate. In two cases in New York, one at the National Broadcasting Company and the other at New York University in Manhattan, reports of symptoms decreased after workers were given a greater voice in airing grievances and how to carry out their assignments. This doesn't mean that unhappy workers just imagine feeling poorly. Sick building syndrome is a real physiological phenomenon even if the physical factors leading to the symptoms aren't always measurable. The fact remains, however, that those who are happier at work don't suffer the syndrome nearly as often, and sometimes not at all.

Many women have trouble finding total satisfaction if they spend year after year as a homemaker with no employment or career to challenge them. Research shows that their feelings affect their health. A study of working women and homemakers in San Antonio, Texas found that the employees' cholesterol and triglyceride (fats that can increase heart disease risk) levels were healthier than the housewives', even though they had to juggle the roles of worker, wife, and mother. I'm not suggesting that all stay-at-home mothers rush off to work because, as we saw in the previous chapter, breastfeeding (often hard to manage when working) and staying with a child in the first few years are much better for the child's health, happiness, and development. But there's no question that many women pay an emotional price when they parent and keep house exclusively and it can affect their health and sense of vitality. I highly recommend that mothers in this situation pay extra attention to filling their spare moments with activities that stimulate them intellectually and give them pleasure. They should also acknowledge the intrinsic rewards that come from their dedicated form of parenting, especially the knowledge that they are doing what is best for their children. (Many women who have rushed back to work early in their new baby's life continually beat themselves up for not being more available to their child. In a society that does not support stay-at-home parenting, monetarily or otherwise, there is no easy answer to this dilemma.)

### Making Work That Is Satisfying Work for You

The late Buckminster Fuller wrote that at a time of desperate financial struggle in his life, he decided to trust that if he dedicated his life to supporting the Universe, the Universe would support him. This was the turning point that made his spectacular career as a paradigm-shifting inventor and philosopher possible. What Bucky didn't say, however, is that in his case, the Universe paid close to minimum wage. Fuller struggled to make ends meet most of his life.

The point is that if you work for love more than money, you may well have more love than money. Emotionally rewarding work is not always the most financially rewarding work. People who devote themselves to their passion often do so at great economic sacrifice—for example, the stereotype of the struggling artist is pretty accurate for most people who work at music, art, or writing. But they continue at it because they love what they do and can't imagine settling for less control and happiness in their lives. And that is a health-enhancing choice.

Contrast this with the "dream" that drives so many: choosing the job or career that pays them the most money possible, then dragging themselves to their uninspiring work day after day just so they can spend their money in their off hours. Is it any surprise that people who make these kinds of trade-offs in life often suffer a trade-off in their health as well?

By the same token, it is possible to have both money and satisfaction, particularly if you can accept all that good stuff in your life at once. We've discussed how thoughts and emotions can limit your health. They can also limit your income. I would counsel struggling artists to search their consciousness for beliefs that they necessarily have to struggle in their field. They should also ask themselves if they are attached to the romance of the struggle or to the company of other struggling artists. Also, make sure the feelings that arise within you in relation to low income are felt and released instead of explained away, thereby pushing them back into the shadow. Quite often these emotions can be traced back to childhood issues of unworthiness. All such mental frameworks can prevent more profitable opportunities from appearing. And this doesn't mean that one has to sell out to sell. While it is certainly true that many people compromise themselves to make money, there are many outstanding examples of artists and other people whose very success in the marketplace is based on their resolve to maintain their integrity at all possible cost. People who make a lot of money are generally those who intend just that. People who build a reputation for integrity are those who won't have it any other way. If you want both money and integrity, set your sights on both goals at once. You can't hit the target if you don't aim at it, and that's just as true in your vocation as on a shooting range.

## Making Your Work Edgework

Since we usually spend so much time at work, it is a fertile ground for the self-exploration offered by Edgework. Instead of playing victim and blaming the boss, or the schedule, or another employee for your problems, you take responsibility for the painful experience and backtrack into your shadow to find what feeling needs to be released and owned. This transforms an unfortunate experience into one leading to greater self-knowledge. As we discussed in Chapter 2, Edgework uses stress as a signal to look within to find answers. Perhaps the only beneficial aspect of unfulfilling or meaningless employment would be to use all the boredom, resentment, anger, and sadness as motivators to use the exercises of Edgework for inner healing. But eventually, as this process continues, such self-understanding would most likely lead to finding more fulfilling and passionate work.

In the long run there is greater advantage to making your passion your vocation: it is a much quicker path to personal growth. Anything in life can be Edgework, but your major occupation during the day is a much better "staging area" than most. When you spend as much time at something as you do at work, you will undoubtedly see many of your issues reflected in your circumstances there. There are unending opportunities to work on yourself as you work all those hours at your job. But this is even more true when you are working at your passion. When you are more emotionally engaged with your work, you challenge yourself more. Facing up to work challenges and overcoming them one after the other will build your personal power right through the roof. Why? Because advancing your career or business naturally puts you in position to face your barriers in relation to self-worth, success, happiness, and so on.

If you know many successful entrepreneurs, you have probably noticed that, whatever personal issues they may still have to resolve, they are extremely powerful people. They don't buy excuses—theirs or anyone else's—and as a result are able to produce change and progress where others see only obstacles. They can take an idea from its earliest stage and build it into a thriving enterprise. They are able to move employees to perform at a high level. They are able to persuade customers that their product or service is a fair exchange for the customer's money. I'm not saying that entrepreneurs are enlightened beings, but they are people who are accustomed to putting aside their fears and pushing through their self-imposed limitations (which is one reason they are impatient with everyone else's!).

Those of us who work at our passion are essentially entrepreneurs. Even if we work for a large company, we approach our work entrepreneurially. It is not the supervisor or the assignment that drives us, it is the intrinsic charge of doing the work itself. We don't just follow instructions, go home at five o'clock prompt, pop a beer and watch TV. We are engaged with our work creatively. We have ideas for improving products or processes or inventing new ones, and we act on our ideas. In short, we are alive at work—life is not something we put on hold until the work day is over.

So it should be even more clear to you now why working at your passion is so vital to your health. A bodymind that is fully engaged around the clock instead of being dragged around with the brakes on for eight or ten hours a day is far more likely to stay in peak operating condition. A mind that is excited about life will animate the body from the heart to the ends of the fingers and toes. A person who wants to be at work won't be sending her body unconscious messages to get ill so she can cash in a few of her sick days. A person who is utilizing her occupation as a growth process—and people who love their work do this as a matter of course, even if they don't conceptualize it as such—will use stress as an opportunity to unburden her shadow thereby giving the bodymind less reason to grab her attention with dramatic physical illness. Not only is it good for your health to like your work, it is impossible to maintain peak health without it.

# 11

# HEALING IN
# RELATIONSHIPS

*You fell in love because your old brain had your partner
confused with your parents!*
Harville Hendrix, Ph.D.,
*Getting the Love You Want: A Guide for Couples*


As I've been implying all along in this book, the principles of
Edgework, of taking responsibility for all our experiences in life,
owning the emotions that arise in shadow projection, and taking the
risk to grow beyond our self-imposed beliefs and limitations, can be
applied long before we experience the devastating effects of major
misfortune or serious illness. Yes, illness or other big problems
provide a picture window view of our shadow made manifest, but
they also offer dramatic evidence of a life lived unconsciously, of not
accepting the challenge to grow until damage reaches a critical point.
It is as if we are going through life denying the healing opportunities
we have unknowingly created for ourselves. Instead we defend ourselves and play victim, thereby giving away our power and yet another
opportunity for natural self-healing. Emotional wound healing via
shadow projection is a built-in method for bodymind growth and
healing that we can use on a daily basis.

Remember, Edgework can be about anything. It doesn't have to
be a spectacular drama. To live life consciously is to make whatever is
happening to us in the moment the focus of our growth process. That

being the case, the best opportunities for conscious living come from the things that occupy us every day. In the previous chapter, we noted how our work offers us the chance to explore and challenge ourselves. An even more accurate reflection of our inner selves is offered by our relationships, especially our close, romantic ones. Indeed, who we choose to be in a relationship with is often a direct reflection of our shadow issues. We discussed this earlier with the example of how the abused child will often select an abusive partner when she grows up. But it is widely recognized that, abused or not, all of us tend to select partners who have characteristics of our opposite-sex parent, so relationships are ripe for examining issues that have persisted since our childhood.

Does this mean that if you are not in a relationship, you don't have the same opportunities to grow? Hardly. If you don't have a relationship, the fact that you don't is probably a preoccupying concern in your life. If it is not, that may well be because you are avoiding issues that are uncomfortable for you. Either way, the topic of relationships is still primary subject matter for your personal process. Which means that the issues that you have not faced or resolved with regard to relationships are waiting for your exploration and understanding—this is the process of Edgework.

Relationships impact your health in another, and perhaps even more dramatic, way: the health-giving power of love. Love is the greatest healing force in the world. It is very difficult to maintain good health without it. For instance, the link between loneliness and heart disease is quite well established. We examined some of this evidence in Chapter 6, and we'll see more below. Babies die without love. And so do adults, only more slowly.

## The Healing Power of Love

Love is more than what we think. It is more than what psychologists call self-esteem or self-love. It is more than the warm feelings we feel for friends and family members. It is more than the magnetic attraction between lovers. Just exactly what it is, however, remains a mystery. Everyone who has experienced it knows in their heart that it exists, but no science can measure it and no language can even fully define it. The sages tell us that it extends beyond the mental and physical worlds and into the world of spirit. I have heard it described as the "glue of the universe." Indeed, scriptures world-wide declare that God is love.

So we're dealing with something of all-encompassing power, something far beyond Hallmark card sentimentality, when we talk of love. We're also dealing with something inextricably bound up with health. At the core of every emotional wound, every pain, and every tear lies the absence of love. As such, love also supplies the fundamental force behind true healing. The forgiveness and, obviously, the self-love that we have discussed earlier as being crucial to shadow release are both aspects of this force. So is the nurturing, support, and caring emanating from those who are close to us. Beyond any other emotional, mental, or spiritual need, love stands as the singlemost important requirement for human fulfillment. The father of modern medicine, Paracelsus, surely was thinking along these same lines when he wrote, "The true ground of medicine is love."

Traditional societies, in which shamans do the doctoring, also acknowledge the healing power of love. Disease in such cultures is often taken as a sign of poor social integration—in other words, the ill person is too cut off from other people, and thus love. Dr. Dean Ornish has taken much the same approach in his treatment of heart patients. His work has taught him that isolation from other people leads to chronic stress and ultimately to illnesses such as heart disease. He feels that humans have never been as socially isolated as Americans are today. Increased mobility has scattered extended families across the map. Churches, synagogues, and workplaces once played a far more important role in providing a sense of human connection and community than they do now, and nothing has arisen to replace them. Neighbors interact far less than they once did, for a variety of reasons. Even parenting can be an intensely lonely endeavor with two-parent households on the decline and no relatives around to help.

Ornish treats the pervasive loneliness he has observed in heart patients by making support groups part of his therapeutic program. He originally formed the groups so patients could encourage each other and also exchange recipes and shopping tips that helped them stay on the program's strict dietary regimen. But he soon noticed that the sense of community the group provided was making a difference in patients' health, so much so that in many cases it appeared to be even more important than the dietary and exercise aspects of his program. The groups don't attempt to provide formal psychotherapy in any sense. The "heart connections" that the patients make just by being together are therapeutic enough.

Dr. Ornish is not the only one in the medical and research universe to identify the health-eroding capacity of loneliness. Several studies have linked it to suppression of the immune system. Research at Ohio State College of Medicine found that students with the highest loneliness scores had reduced defenses against herpes viruses. Conversely, students with the lowest indexes of loneliness and stress had the highest levels of natural killer cells. Another study at Ohio State compared blood samples of divorced and married females to test their immune system responses. Women who had separated from their husbands had significantly weaker systems than those who were still married, and married women who described their marriages as poor had less immune capacity than those who rated their relationships highly. In a University of California, San Francisco study of patients with the AIDS-precursor ARC (AIDS-related conditions), those who scored high on loneliness and depression had significantly lower counts of helper T-cells and other immune system activity levels. Recall, too, that as we noted in Chapter 6, people who feel socially isolated have much higher death rates from all causes than those who don't.

What this implies is that loneliness is more than just a form of sadness; it is starvation for an essential nutrient of life. We can no more do without love than food, water, and oxygen. The tricky part of this is that for some people, close relationships constitute a risk they don't feel they can afford to take. They desperately want to be connected to others and to receive and give love, but for any number of reasons, fear they can't take the chance. Usually, the fears go back to childhood experiences—of being disapproved of, not good enough, rejected, abused, abandoned, and such.

If love is missing in your life, I suggest that you make it a point to address your lack. The Exercises suggested at the end of this book will help you identify and heal the emotional wounds that prevent establishing healthy relationships. You can also join activities with like-minded people or by getting together more often with your friends. If those ideas seem too chancy, try taking on the issue in individual or group therapy. Another strategy: get yourself a pet and dote on it. Think of these ideas as a form of health insurance—not the kind that pays for your health care, but the kind helps ensure you won't need it.

### Relationship, Relationship, on the Wall …

As mentioned above, the relationships you have with the people in your life offer you daily opportunities for emotional and attitudinal healing. And if you consistently heal the wounds within your consciousness, they will not precipitate into your body and cause disease. Such healing represents one of the highest forms of preventive medicine. In addition to emotional wound healing and personal growth, relationships offer the unparalleled experience of love, perhaps the greatest healing force of all. Let's look more closely at shadow projection in relationships to make sure we can make use of this powerful healing potential.

As an infant and child, your relationships with your mother, father, and other close family members generated most of the formative experiences out of which your psyche arose. But undoubtedly, things did not go perfectly no matter how loving and attentive your upbringing was. At various points, you suffered blows, however inadvertent, to your self-worth and sense of being loved. The traumatic experiences of childhood that you still have not resolved as an adult live on in your unconscious mind and their essential dynamics are replayed in your life circumstances. Your adult relationships, particularly your closest ones, constitute one of the primary "stages" on which those replays take place. And one of the main reasons for that is that you tend to form adult relationships based on the emotional wounds you suffered as a child and according to patterns that you learned as a child interacting with and observing your family members.

Harville Hendrix, Ph.D. is a well-known psychologist with over 20 years in marital therapy. He founded the Institute for Relationship Therapy, based in New York City and Dallas, Texas. The following quote is taken from his best selling book, *Getting the Love You Want, A Guide for Couples:*

> What we are doing, I have discovered from years of theoretical research and clinical observation, is looking for someone who has the predominant character traits of the people who raised us. Our old brain, trapped in the eternal now and having only a dim awareness of the outside world, is trying to re-create the environment of childhood. And the reason the old brain is trying to resurrect the past is not a matter of habit or blind compulsion but of a compelling need to heal old childhood wounds.

Let me give you an example of a healing opportunity that arose in the relationship of one of my patients. Lisa was an attractive 26-year-old woman who came to me complaining of fatigue, depression and weight gain. She was depressed about her weight and problems in her relationship. A previous boyfriend had left her and she was worried that her current boyfriend would as well. Later in our interview, she told me about her parent's divorce when she was only three years old. At the end of the hour, I summarized her medical issues as I saw them and then told her the following. The intense pain and anger of losing her father was seeded into her shadow, becoming an emotional wound. In the fantasy world of the child she may have felt responsible in some way and may have begun to doubt her own self-worth as the second-most important person in her life had abandoned her. She had the understandable belief that she couldn't trust men. Her fears that she would lose her mate caused her to cling tightly to him and in the end her clinging began to push him away. I suggested to her that when her previous boyfriend left her, she had created an opportunity to heal the intense pain of losing her father. Instead of blaming men for lack of commitment, she could look within herself to find the answers. I could see her eyes light up a bit and I referred her to a counselor who used inner-child writing as part of therapy.

Each time I saw her over the next several months, she was brighter and brighter. One day she told me that she felt she had healed the wound of losing her father by writing to the fearful and abandoned inner child and forgiving her father. And, she continued, she already saw a change in her boyfriend. Her weight loss was easy and she was no longer bothered by depression. She had learned to honor her feelings and take responsibility for any situation that arose in her relationship or otherwise. I thought to myself, how easy it is to treat people when they focus their healing at the causal level of consciousness.

Other dramatic episodes in your life will also present you with profound opportunities to confront and work through your psychological issues. But not even your work life offers you the day-to-day reflection that relationships do. With their ever-changing patterns of support, rejection, happiness, frustrations, expectations, intimacy, denial, and growth, relationships cover every emotion in the spectrum. Nothing else in life offers such rich material for self-study.

Of course, I don't mean to slight relationships as just a prolonged personal growth exercise. But the fact is that the same key to using your relationship for personal growth will also improve the quality of the relationship itself. *And that key is to accept that the situations you face in your relationships are an exact mirror of your inner state.* As I said in Chapter 8, I believe this is true of all experiences in life. But when you focus your attention on your partner, parents, or siblings, you are seeing a reflection of you and your issues that is literally closer to home and therefore more specific and tailored.

Again, the idea that you create your life circumstances is an admittedly mysterious concept that seems at times to defy logic. We looked at some of the standard objections to it in Chapter 8. In this chapter, I prefer to stick to the pragmatic. For now, just consider the mirroring concept as a tool for self-exploration and understanding. You have to try a tool to see if it works. Let's take this one for a spin by applying it to perhaps its most obvious target, marriage.

It is well known that 50 percent of all American marriages end in divorce. For many in the remaining 50 percent, the relationship persists out of sheer inertia, a repetitive, unfulfilling living arrangement completely devoid of excitement or joy. In fact, studies have shown that in forty to seventy percent of cases, one or both spouses goes outside of the relationship for the passion that once ignited the marriage. Statistics sometimes lie, but when it comes to marriage, it seems obvious that few of us are able to turn our original love into an enduring, happy partnership.

For the vast majority of couples, the love, excitement, and fascination with each other that characterizes the courtship and early stages of marriage loses its edge gradually. Eventually, problems, conflicts, and duties dominate the day-to-day experience of the relationship. For those who learned in childhood to suppress feelings, the anger and pain is denied and the marriage begins to stiffen and die. For others, anger about unmet needs continually builds, sometimes exploding in violence and abuse. Either way, the other person is blamed and the marriage deadlocks into patterns of denial.

Some spouses attempt to avoid the pain of dying relationships by escaping into their work. Some focus on their children and smother them with excessive attention. Some become obsessive about the tidiness of the house and yard. Many turn to numbing agents such as alcohol, cigarettes, tranquilizers, anti-depressants, and sleeping medications. Sometimes the bodies of one or both unhappy partners begin to break down under the stress of sustained emotional conflict and denial.

Of course, as the saying goes, the only way through the pain is through it. Those who "escape" their marriage via divorce usually find themselves facing the same problems in their next relationship. A mirror is brutally honest; it will reflect you just as you are—and after all, when you leave a relationship and start a new one, you bring yourself with you. The setting and characters may have changed, but the plot remains the same.

This widely recognized pattern need not repeat itself in your life, however. Nor does your current relationship have to be doomed to conflict, boredom, and mediocrity. If you create the problem, you have the power to alter it. Yes, it takes two to tango, so your partner also plays a part in creating marital troubles. But your point of access to correcting those troubles is to work on your own contribution to the problem. And fortunately, that is sufficient to resolve most difficulties, or at least get them moving in a healing direction. Besides, to berate your spouse for co-creating a problem would just be blaming and deflecting responsibility, wouldn't it?

The mirroring concept that I've suggested above as a way of viewing your relationship troubles is not just a philosophical idea. It can also be applied as a problem-solving and self-awareness technique, and when it is, it is the most effective tool I know for transforming relationships. Here's how it works:

When a problem occurs for you in your marriage, accept responsibility for it. Consider the issue as a call for inner healing co-created by you and your lover. Then focus on your emotions that arise from it and feel the emotions intensely and completely until they are gone. Do not analyze or think about the issue until the feelings are gone, and certainly do not judge or blame anyone for how you feel. By accepting the feelings associated with neglect, abuse, or whatever issue is at hand, you release the emotional charge stored within. By owning the emotion as your own, you release it from storage in your unconscious mind and alleviate the need to replay it through other marital incidents, bodily illness, or whatever. Inner child writing, as explained in the Edgework Exercises, is an additional tool available to assist in emotional wound healing. Once the emotions have subsided, then contemplate the issue, perhaps discuss it with your mate, and gain intellectual insight about yourself.

The technique sounds simple and it is. But it requires extraordinary self-honesty and courage. As Sigmund Freud wrote, "To be completely honest with oneself is the very best effort a human being can make." If, on the other hand, you blame the other person for your feelings, then you effectively disown the emotion, wrapping it in an excuse that prevents release. The emotion returns from your consciousness to the shadow, to be replayed again some time in the future.

The Edgework Exercises in the back of the book will give you detailed methods for owning the emotions that arise in relationships, or any other experience. For a more complete explanation of shadow projection in relationships, I recommend Harville Hendrix's book, *Getting the Love You Want, A Guide for Couples.*

There are also other common issues that contribute to relationship problems. Perhaps the two biggest are the passive/aggressive person, often the man, and the issue of boundaries. These topics are beyond the scope of this book, but Dr Hendrix's book will get you going in the right direction.

Your spouse may be your most constantly available mirror, but don't overlook other opportunities to use this invaluable tool in your life, starting with the opportunities your children provide. Carl Jung spoke to this when he wrote, "If there is anything we wish to change in the child, we should first examine and see whether it is not something that could be better changed in ourselves." By always looking first to what you can change in yourself rather than trying to change your family members, you become more generous and loving towards them because you are no longer jumping to conclusions about what they did to you or "the way they are."

We've been discussing mirroring as an approach to family therapy, but you can also carry the process much farther, making it your primary form of self-study. If you pay attention to the images and thoughts that pass through your mind as you're experiencing mirrored emotions, you'll notice that the feelings tied to your current issue can be traced back to childhood when they first took shape in your subconscious mind as a wounded inner child. Emotional self-awareness of this depth leads to true inner healing, and thus is the essence of all healing. Bottom line, everyone in your life is your mirror, so you will know just exactly how you're doing by looking around at what you have created.

# 12

# LAUGHTER, PASSION AND SPIRITUALITY

*From joy springs all creation.*
*By it is sustained*
*Towards joy it proceeds,*
*And to joy it returns.*

Mundaka Upanishad

*The moment one gives close attention to anything, even a*
*blade of grass, it becomes a mysterious, awesome, indescribably*
*magnificent world in itself.*

Henry Miller

The positive mental states and conditions of life—self-love, satisfying work, and close relationships—that we've been examining in previous chapters have two things in common: each constitutes a pillar of a fulfilled life, and it is very difficult to maintain vibrant health without any of them.

The same can be said for the qualities we'll be looking at in this chapter. Laughter and the ability to be in the moment both have tremendous capacity for reducing disease-causing stress. Having an avocation that you feel passionately about can go a long way toward producing the same benefits as satisfying work. And spirituality adds a dimension to life that no life can be complete without, for only spirituality—in its widest sense, as discussed below—provides a context big enough to contain life itself. Spirituality offers perhaps the deepest passion and has proved its health benefits over and over, not just in research but in virtually every healthcare provider's everyday practice, so that even the most dedicated non-believers among health professionals believe in its ability to heal.

All of this, of course, is also just good common sense. Add it up— a life filled with laughter, lived responsibly in the moment, where pain is turned into self-discovery and healing, full of joy and passion, and illuminated by a deeper meaning. If I were a disease looking for a host, I would look elsewhere to land.

**Laughing Your Way to Health**

Illness may not be funny, but the way out can certainly be. One of the most inspiring stories of someone recovering from serious illness through "laughter therapy" remains former *Saturday Review* editor Norman Cousins' remarkable reversal of ankylosing spondylitis, detailed in his best-selling book, *The Anatomy of an Illness.* Cousins came down with the illness, a painful and degenerative disease of the spine's connective tissue, in 1964 after an exhausting trip to Europe. His suffering started with fatigue, fever, and severe aching in his joints. Within a week, he was having trouble moving his neck, arms, hands, fingers, and legs. Medical tests revealed that his body was critically inflamed, and the specialists who reviewed his case confirmed the diagnosis of ankylosing spondylitis.

Cousins' future looked bleak. One doctor placed his chance of recovery at one in five hundred. Another told Cousins that he had never personally witnessed a recovery from the disease. He was placed on a course of pain-killing and anti-inflammatory medications that sometimes produced side effects as uncomfortable as the disease itself. Dismayed by his prospects, Cousins asked how he could have come down with such a thing but the doctors did not have any firm answers—perhaps heavy metal poisoning, perhaps the aftereffect of a streptococcal infection, among several other possibilities.

A highly intelligent and inquisitive man, Cousins wasn't satisfied with his doctors' explanations of his condition. Nor did he accept their expectations about his fate. He knew that his work-life had been intensely stressful prior to becoming ill, and remembered having read Hans Selye's classic, *The Stress of Life*. In particular, he recalled how Selye demonstrated that adrenal exhaustion could be caused by emotional tension—for instance, frustration or suppressed rage. He was also impressed with Selye's arguments about how negative emotions negatively affected body chemistry.

"The inevitable question arose in my mind, What about the positive emotions?" Cousins wrote in *The Anatomy of an Illness*. "If negative emotions produce negative chemical changes in the body, wouldn't the positive emotions produce positive chemical changes? Is it possible that love, hope, faith, laughter, confidence, and the will to live have therapeutic value? Do chemical changes occur only on the downside?"

These were excellent questions, the answers to which Cousins pursued in his own body. As is now well-known, he arranged to have a film projector brought into his hospital room so he could watch old Marx Brother films and "Candid Camera" episodes. His intuition proved spot-on. He discovered that just a few minutes of hearty laughter worked like an anesthetic, buying several hours of pain-free sleep. The laughter also measurably dropped his sedimentation test levels, an indicator that the inflammation was receding, too.

To be fair, Cousins didn't restrict his innovations to laugh therapy. Having read about the wonders of vitamin C and thinking it might help as well, he convinced his doctors to let him take it intravenously in enormously high dosages. The vitamin C dropped his sedimentation rate even more dramatically than did the laughter. But both made an unexpected and powerful impact. Cousins began a daily regimen that combined laughter sessions and vitamin C IVs; sure enough, his pain decreased so rapidly that he was completely off sleeping pills and drugs after one week.

Cousins continued to improve in the months following his discharge from the hospital. By one year's time, he was pain-free other than one shoulder and his knees, and he had regained full mobility in his neck, something his specialists told him would be impossible because his disease was degenerative.

Cousins' recovery sparked major changes in his life as well as his body. He left his editorship at the *Saturday Review,* a post he had held for more than a quarter century, to accept a faculty appointment at the School of Medicine at the University of California at Los Angeles. At UCLA, Cousins dedicated himself to proving to others what he had just proved to himself: that positive attitudes are biochemical entities that can vigorously promote health. His work culminated in the book, *Head First: The Biology of Hope*. In its predecessor, *Anatomy of an Illness*, Cousins summarized the essentials of his successful fight against ankylosing spondylitis:

> The answer is simple. Since I didn't accept the verdict, I wasn't trapped in the cycle of fear, depression, and panic that frequently accompanies a supposedly incurable illness. I must not make it seem, however, that I was unmindful of the seriousness of the problem or that I was in a festive mood throughout. Being unable to move my body was all the evidence I needed that the specialists were dealing with real concerns. But deep down, I knew I had a good chance and relished the idea of bucking the odds.

Cousins' inspiring and well-documented tale awakened interest in the therapeutic benefits of humor, especially by those already intrigued by the emotional aspects of illness. In his book, *Laugh After Laugh*, Dr. Raymond Moody argues that there is a link between a sense of humor and longevity. He goes on to say that "over the years I have encountered a surprising number of instances in which, to all appearances, patients have laughed themselves back to health, or at least have used their sense of humor as a very positive and adaptive response to their illnesses."

Breaking laughter down physiologically, we start to see the actual biology of how laughter could produce the benefits that both Moody and Cousins documented. A deep laugh gives your diaphragm, thorax, abdomen, and all the muscles of your body a brief workout, producing greater relaxation. It also oxygenates the blood through deep and fast breathing, quickens the heartbeat to carry more blood and oxygen, relaxes the arteries, and softens and moistens the eyes, among other benefits. On the biochemical level, laughter cues the hormonal system to release adrenaline, noradrenaline, and dopamine, thereby adding balance to the hormonal system. In addition, laughing causes the pituitary gland to stimulate the release of the body's own painkillers, the endorphins. We also know that, as you laugh, the right hemisphere of your brain, which governs emotions and creativity, becomes more active, both electrically and chemically.

Laughter appears to boost immunity, too. In research published in 1992 in the *Journal of Allergy and Clinical Immunology,* Dr. S. A. Salazar showed comedy videos to one group of healthy adults while a control group of healthy people studied a medical text. The control group showed a significant fall in natural killer cells (the immune cells that fight cancer) and T cell lymphocytes. The count of these important immune cells rose in the laughter group.

Not that we need to know all this scientific stuff about laughter to appreciate what it does for us. Intuitively, we can see how laughing pulls us into the moment, attuning us to our feelings and replacing for at least a short time the stress, depression, or physical pain that often marks our daily lives. Not surprisingly for something that transcends time and daily troubles, laughter also unites us momentarily with the lofty realms of spirit, as captured in this passage by Indian spiritual teacher, Bhagwan Shree Rajneesh:

> Laughter is tremendously healthy.
> Playfulness is as sacred as any prayer,
> or may be more sacred than any prayer,
> because playfulness, laughter, singing, dancing,
> will relax you.
> And the truth is only possible
> in a relaxed state of being.
> When you are totally relaxed, in a state of let-go,
> the impossible starts happening,
> the miracle starts happening.
> Let-go is the secret of meditation.

### Living in the Now

The world that we experience through the filter called personality, or ego, is locked into time. The pain of the past, held within the shadow, is projected into the future for the opportunity of ownership. Each moment then is an expression of the past and is therefore reduced from the totality that it offers. The result is the uniquely limited perception that each person experiences, and upon which an incomplete worldview is constructed. Each person perceives the world differently, based upon the individualized reducing valve called ego. William Blake once wrote: "If the doors of perception were cleansed, everything would appear to man as it is, infinite."

In order to see each moment as the infinite possibility that it is, we must be fully in the moment, or the Now. The Now is the moment of power because it moves us out of the endlessly reactive patterns of the ego and into freedom to make choices based on the issues of the moment. The joyful play of children is based on their innate tendency to live naturally in the moment. Indeed, the Now puts us on the edge of eternity. There is a Buddhist saying: "The absolute tranquillity is the present moment. Though it is at this moment, there is no limit to this moment, and herein is eternal delight."

Actually, according to the transcendent inner experience of the mystic, time does not really exist. The Buddhist scholar, D.T. Suzuki nicely spoke this truth when he wrote:

> In this spiritual world there are no time divisions such as the past, present and future; for they have contracted themselves into a single moment of the present where life quivers in its true sense. . . . The past and the future are both rolled up in this present moment of illumination, and this present moment is not something standing still with all its contents, for it ceaselessly moves on.

Our friend time apparently exists only within our thoughts, depending on the past, in order to create the future.

With his theory of General Relativity, Albert Einstein seems to agree with the spiritualist by concluding that there is no independent, or absolute, flow of time. Space and time are relative and are merely part of the language of a particular observer as he participates in the moving energies of the universe. Thomas Gold summarizes this issue:

> The flow of time is clearly an inappropriate concept for the description of the physical world that has no past, present and future. It just is.

Actually, since the holistic movement began in the late 1960s, hundreds of authors have commented on the benefits of living in present time instead of being caught up in your worries about the past and fears and fantasies about the future. We hear so much about this that there's a tendency to just take it in as excellent advice without actually doing anything about it in our own lives. But have you ever considered what living in the past or future might cost you in health?

Think about the usual condition of contemporary daily life. Most of us are addicted to time—not real time as understood by both physicists and mystics, but the illusory time marked by our watches, written on our to-do lists and calendars, and determined by our ambitions and responsibilities. If we love our work or our recreational activities, if we're under pressure to complete an important task, or if we've overbooked our days with loads of activities, time seems to race by. If we don't like our jobs and are bored with our outside lives, time moves at a crawl. In either case, we are completely out of touch with the actual experience of the moment, which is an experience of serene clarity, satisfaction, and infinity. It is quite literally an experience of being removed from time.

To get a sense of the price we pay for our "inappropriate concept," let's go back to the first example, which encompasses most of us. The average person in our society, whether she likes her job or not, has piled so many things on her plate that there never seem to be enough hours in the day to complete them. The ever-increasing demands of contemporary life—longer commutes on crowded roads, two-worker families, the mounds of paperwork just to maintain an ordinary household—make the very notion of relaxation and serenity seem like an unattainable goal.

This unending sense of urgency has created a new disease in human history: "hurry sickness." One form of it, so-called Type A behavior, has been implicated in heart disease, high blood pressure, immune system suppression, ulcers, and other all-too-common medical problems. Whether we are Type As or not, most of us have at least some time pressure as background noise in our lives, something that rarely troubled people in eras when the pace of life was slower.

Fortunately, though, the demands on us don't demand that we react to them as we do. It is entirely possible for even the busiest among us to find islands of tranquillity in our day. More than that, it is possible to achieve a state of near-constant calm in the middle of a light-speed life. Consider the example of an athlete—in particular, a team sport athlete such as a basketball or soccer player—who must relax his body in the midst of fast-flying action and big-game pressure just to perform well. An elite athlete realizes that trying to move faster than reality permits, or to be out of the moment at all, will make a winning performance impossible. He is forced by the nature of his sport to bridge the apparent paradox between stress and relaxation.

In fact, some of the greatest athletes hardly appear to be breaking a sweat while performing at their peak. It is not that success comes easily to them. It is that they understand that their success depends on relaxation. They have worked hard to develop the capacity of "centering" themselves, and thus can reach a state of serene alertness in the midst of stress that would paralyze the average person.

Not that one has to have special athletic abilities to find this place inside themselves. The athlete's situation is not different from, say, the person who finds herself in a fast-moving emergency and must think clearly and act quickly to avert disaster. Or the ambitious employee who must make a strong showing during an important presentation to get a promotion. The capacity is in all of us. We need only learn the keys to accessing it if we want to call on it in non-emergency circumstances.

For thousands of years, people have developed this ability in themselves through meditation. Ultimately, meditation is a spiritual exercise, a method of quieting the active mind into a profound stillness that opens into our transcendent and pure spiritual essence. But the process also involves focusing all our attention on the present moment. As such, it teaches us to operate outside the constraints of ordinary time and the worries, fears, and other thoughts that limit us. The classic meditation techniques also relax us physically through regular, rhythmic breathing, which releases tension trapped in our muscles. The medical benefits of classic meditation are well documented; essentially, meditation helps prevent all of the hurry sicknesses.

There are many other steps you can take to counteract the negative effects of a busy lifestyle. Obviously, you should schedule as much relaxation as you need—vacations, recreation, entertaining evenings and weekends, and so on. And make sure that you keep the purpose in sight, rather than creating more busy-ness by cramming too much activity into a small space. Don't forget, too, to take moments throughout the day just to plunge yourself into a pleasant experience—contemplating flowers growing outside your window, closing your eyes and paying attention to your inner experience, whatever. These mini-breaks can, and should, be fit into even the busiest of days, and give a lot of bang for the buck in terms of "serenity-per-second." Finally, time-management techniques may help you organize your days better so that stress is kept to a minimum.

The most lasting way to center yourself in present time, however, is through personal growth work such as Edgework. Your issues from the past that are stored in your unconscious and replaying in the present effectively trap you in the past. They can also be the source of worries about the future. For example, your self-esteem issues today that stem from times when your parents slighted you as a child reflect a time long past that never reflected who you are. They may also cause you to be anxious about your future prospects instead of calmly living and learning from life as it presents itself in the current moment.

When you begin clearing your unconscious of its storehouse of unexperienced emotions and erroneous thoughts, you will find yourself spontaneously centered in the present moment more frequently. Where normally you have been viewing life through a cloudy lens of thoughts and emotions rooted in the past, you begin to create clear spots in that lens and see life free of old beliefs, fears, and attitudes. You also open yourself to new, fresh experiences instead of the continuous replays of resisted ones. The effects on your health are multi-faceted. Being in the moment makes you less vulnerable to the sometimes unavoidable pressures of daily life. Even when you can't make the pressures themselves go away, you aren't adding your own internal pressures to them so it is easier to take things as they come. And all of this is just a bonus on top of the more general health benefits of Edgework, of not forcing your unconscious to grab your attention through bodily illness.

**Embracing Your Passion—The Story of Ginger**

In Chapter 10, we discussed the powerful health effects of having satisfying work. Again, satisfying work is important because work occupies such a major portion of our lives. But while work takes up much of our waking time, it doesn't take all of it. If work is your only passion, then you are still living a life that is far short of what it can be, and you may pay a price in health for what you lack, particularly if that lack is the source of depression or other unhealthy mental or emotional states.

One of my patients powerfully illustrated this point, and the health benefits of doing something about it. Ginger, 32 at the time, came to my office with multiple complaints. After moving to Oregon from Kansas, she frequently felt fatigued. She also felt acutely sensitive to cold weather and suffered from cold hands and feet. Far more seriously, she had been diagnosed with optic neuritis, a disease characterized by inflammation surrounding the large nerve that enters the back of the eyeball. She had first noticed the problem ten years earlier when objects began appearing to her as if "I was looking through a lace curtain." The effect would come and go, but seemed to worsen over time.

Ginger had undergone an MRI scan of her brain which proved normal. Her ophthalmologist told her that the cause of her illness was unknown, but that there was a 90 percent chance she would eventually develop multiple sclerosis, which obviously worried her terribly. She had been given Prednisone, an immune-suppressing drug, several times in the past, primarily when her vision deteriorated to the point that she could barely function. But she didn't like the drug's side-effects [fluid retention and fatigue] and often resisted taking it, much to the consternation of her doctor.

After reviewing Ginger's medical history, I queried her about her early and recent life circumstances to see if I could identify any disease-causing stresses. Raised in Kansas by Mennonite parents, Ginger loved to sing from a young age. Her interest in it continued to grow through her teen years and she moved to Los Angeles to study music in college. While in college, she married her high school sweetheart. Eventually, she was invited to join the Young Americans, a musical group that toured widely.

Although it didn't deter Ginger at first, her husband had stated that he didn't want to live with a famous person and that he felt a successful singing career could damage home and family life. Ginger didn't concur, but she and her husband decided to leave Los Angeles anyway and return to Kansas, which she did feel was a better environment for raising children. That meant quitting the Young Americans, a real sacrifice that deeply saddened her. Shortly after relocating, her first optic neuritis symptoms appeared. She also began to notice intermittent numbness and tingling in her arms. Several years later, Ginger and her family moved again, this time to Ashland, Oregon. Her neurological symptoms persisted.

Ginger's case confused me at first. I didn't see many obvious issues that might underlie her optic neuritis. Her childhood seemed devoid of abuse, abandonment, or other dramatic trauma. She also seemed to express her feelings fairly well. I was quite sure, however, that her Prednisone therapy was causing some physical imbalances: lowering her metabolism, weakening her immune system, and leading to food allergies. I told her that I felt it might be a good idea to follow a holistic, health-promoting regimen as an alternative to the medical approach she had been taking, advice she seemed to appreciate since she had had a tough time with her Prednisone anyway.

After thinking about it a bit more, I also suggested to Ginger that perhaps her optic neuritis was a response to having turned her back on her passion in life, singing. By giving it up, she was denying a deep and creative call from within. Could it possibly be that her body was telling her to heed that call?

As I offered this explanation, Ginger's eyes riveted on me and her face softened. I could tell I had hit home. She told me she had already seen a counselor who had told her that her eyes were a metaphor for deeper vision. The counselor added that she had "lost sight" of her dream as a performer, and perhaps this helped lead to her visual disturbance.

I took a blood sample from Ginger so I could design an appropriate dietary and supplement program for her to restore her internal balance and rebuild her health. I also recommended that she continue her personal growth, which seemed headed in a promising direction—specifically, toward restoring a vital part of her that was now missing in her life.

Ginger followed my advice with the same fervent commitment she had demonstrated in other areas of her life. She watched a video on the psychological characteristics of multiple sclerosis patients and started Hakomi therapy, a holistic system that looks for bodymind patterns associated with illness. She also undertook inner child therapy and discovered an inner child within who represented the little girl repressed by her strict Mennonite home environment. This inner child, whom Ginger called Ruthie, believed that performing on stage would lead to "worldliness" and conflict with the Mennonite tradition of modest, simple living. Her therapist asked her to imagine herself as an older woman and Ginger saw herself as an empty husk, cut off from her vital, creative, and sexual self. But perhaps the most important step Ginger took occurred out in the world, when she started singing seriously again. She began to rehearse with another local vocalist and was soon appearing at local coffeehouses and restaurants. She was elated to be performing once more.

During our follow-up office visits, Ginger noted that her episodes of optic neuritis were occurring less and less frequently. Her energy levels were increasing and she was feeling better overall. By the end of the third month, the visual disturbances and the numb sensations in her body had all disappeared.

I spoke to Ginger again shortly before completing this book, about five years after our first office visit. Her optic neuritis was 99 percent gone, she said, with only an occasional "flicker" in her vision. She had no numbness and said she had felt terrific for the past two years. Her breakthrough came, she felt, when she realized during her intensive personal growth phase that denying herself singing was costing her health. Her Mennonite upbringing and her husband's considerations about her career had caused her to snuff out something that meant the world to her, and her bodymind was trying to awaken her to that fact in the only way it could. She now felt that her illness was a "gift" that led her to restore her passion. She had also found a way to continue singing without destroying her family life. Most importantly, she now saw that recovering her passion and her physical recovery were inextricably linked.

I have seen many people like Ginger over the years who talk themselves into sacrificing the things that matter most to them for more transitory comforts—money, the approval of others, whatever. It is clear to me as I listen to patients that creativity, joy, and passion are aspects of the life force that flows from our very core. To deny them in ourselves is to deny our own essence and obstruct life itself. Is it any wonder that illness is often the result? And why should we consider it a medical revelation that "refilling" a hollowed-out life so often jump-starts our body's ability to heal? If there are better medicines than embracing what we most love doing, I would advocate them in a moment. But I have yet to see one, and can't imagine that even the wonders to come in the biotechnology age will approach the healing potency of this simple step.

## Spirituality and Health

Although traditional medicine likes to promote itself as a scientific health approach, I am hardly the only medical doctor who thinks that spirituality plays a vital role in healing. In a national survey of physicians attending the 1996 meeting of the American Academy of Family Physicians, nearly every doctor who participated said they believed that a patient's spiritual convictions could make a positive difference in the healing process.

This is not a surprising result. Almost everyone who practices medicine has seen patients who do much better than expected, apparently because of their spiritual beliefs. As one survey respondent put it, "many examples of mind/spirit healing occur in my practice on a week-in, week-out basis." We also saw in Chapter 7 that spiritual beliefs are one of the qualities that distinguish patients who spontaneously recover from cancer.

Researchers have long been interested in the connection between spirituality and healing. As a result, there is a wealth of information pointing to the positive effects of spiritual feelings on the bodymind. A study of 5,286 Californians found that church members have lower death rates than nonmembers, regardless of other risk factors such as smoking and drinking. Other studies show similar statistically significant associations between religious beliefs and various measures of health. Research also reveals significant differences in morbidity (that is, the measure of who gets sick) or mortality (the measure of who dies) with such diseases as cancer, stroke, heart disease, hypertension, and gastrointestinal disease among many others. Spiritual involvement has also been shown to positively affect how people describe their health as well as the types of symptoms experienced, how disabling a particular illness might be, and longevity.

The power of prayer to influence health outcomes has also been studied. Cardiologist Randolph Byrd did the most impressive research in this area. In 1988, Dr. Byrd randomly divided 393 heart patients entering San Francisco General Hospital into two groups. A group of Christians prayed for one of the groups while the other group received no prayer support. The patients in the two groups did not know which group was receiving the prayer support. After 10 months the medical experiences of the two groups was compared and surprising results emerged. The prayed for group were five times less likely to need antibiotics than the non-prayed for group. The prayed for patients were much less likely to go into congestive heart failure, had fewer cardiac arrests, and generally had fewer complications than the not prayed for patients.

Basically there are over 200 studies, which show that prayer, religion and faith improve our physical and mental health as well as our outlooks on life. People who attend church regularly have lower cancer rates, reduced blood pressure, less depression, fewer addictions and live longer.

Religious practice can also improve immunity, as shown by research done at Duke University. Blood tests of immune function were performed on 1,718 people. Those that attended church regularly had evidence of improved immunity.

### Religion—"Making Whole"

In a lovely little book titled, *Owning Your Own Shadow,* Robert Johnson speaks about religion with the following: "The religious process consists of restoring the wholeness to the personality. The word religion means to re-late, to put back together again, to heal the wounds of separation." Religion is more than good deeds and kind words. It is a process that transforms us from fragmented and alienated individuals driven by the wounded dictates of personal ego, into a whole person who recognizes his responsibility in the world outside, and can see himself in all people.

A spiritual teacher of mine expanded greatly my understanding of spiritual practice and growth when he said that for modern mankind releasing the pain of childhood through emotional expression was just as important as meditation. He explained to me that there was light within each of us, as well as darkness. The human personality, or ego, defends against the pain, or darkness, stored in our unconscious minds, and in doing so, it perpetuates denial about who we really are. Consequently, we live our lives controlled by the ego, which filters out the "undesirable" parts of consciousness, and presents to the world the façade of who we think we are.

He continued on, explaining that the essence of Self-realization was to accept all that we are in totality, in a sense of self-love. Love is the energy of healing, not only for those around us, but also for ourselves. The rejected parts of our psyche, stored in the shadow of the unconscious mind, are also a part of us, and they are a powerful part. The contents of the shadow can be accepted and released by feeling emotions as they arise within the challenges and difficulties of life. This healing process depends on accepting challenges, and the emotional pain they birth, as our own creation, instead of blaming them on others around us. In this manner the darkness within becomes a little lighter, and we know more of who we really are.

### Spirituality—The Ultimate Passion

It may be that seeking a higher understanding of life through religious practice of any kind can create the ultimate passion of all. History is full of examples of extraordinary accomplishments motivated by a personal experience of a higher power. For some a religious experience that has become mundane and routine can be re-kindled into a deeper passion for God and a higher understanding of the human condition.

I know one gifted natural healer who seems to agree. He is a simple farmer who developed two different cancers early in his life. His deep religious conviction guided his own healing journey into a complete remission of both episodes of cancer. His experience touched him profoundly and he began to receive calls from other people with cancer. Using simple healing methods combined with a powerful spiritual awareness, he has guided thousands of patients to recovery. His remission rate is close to an astonishing 95%. When I asked him about his approach with cancer patients, he told me that the first thing he asks people to do is replace their fear with a personal connection to God and a higher purpose in their lives.

Unfortunately, however, research answers few questions about the validity of spirituality itself, leaving it a matter of mystery and faith, which is probably just how it should be. But it does indicate some steps that all of us can take to take to be healthier or to help heal ourselves if we should fall ill:

- **Connect.** For many of us, our spiritual connection is something that stays in the background of our lives. It's not part of our daily thoughts or behavior. So spend a moment here and there to reconnect, whether through prayer, meditation, or simply recalling something positive about your relationship with spirit. Perhaps you'll want to remind yourself of a time that spirit seemed to intervene in your life—a "chance" occurrence that came right when you needed it, a passage in a book that seemed to be exactly what you needed to hear at that moment, a wise voice that spoke to you from inside your head.
- **Gather.** You may want to affiliate with a group, church, or organization that shares your beliefs or subscribe to a periodical that speaks to your faith. This approach doesn't work for everyone, especially those for whom spirituality is a private, individual matter, but it clearly has benefits for those who do affiliate in this way.
- **Use your intuition.** As Herbert Benson, M.D., author of the seminal *The Relaxation Response,* recommends, let yourself be guided at least in part by intuition the next time you are confronted with a medical or other major decision. Don't do this ignorantly. Put yourself in competent professional hands if appropriate and gather whatever research you can. But when it comes time to make the decision itself, let your feelings or instincts play a significant part along with the more logical factors.
- **Be positive.** Be aware of the flip side of the spiritual/health connection: bleak thoughts and emotions will hurt your health. I'm not suggesting that you be a Pollyanna about your condition because, as I've emphasized earlier, denial doesn't reverse or

disarm negative thoughts and emotions, it just sugar-coats them. But overly dark moods are just as divorced from reality as too sunny ones. Tell yourself the truth, in the most positive terms possible. The half-empty glass is also half-full.

No one should infer from the above that healing will somehow be denied to those who don't believe in spirit, or who aren't sure, or who are just plain uncomfortable talking about it. As I've emphasized throughout this book, health and healing are complex phenomena. The factors we have discussed play a big part in the health process but none of them dominates it. Spirituality clearly helps many people maintain or recover their health. I would go so far as to say it confers a real health advantage for anyone in touch with it. But that is not at all the same thing as saying that only the spiritually inclined can be healthy.

In the same vein, we should note that spirituality has no final form, despite the attempts of some religions to declare their version of spirituality the only true faith. And that means that even things that look like anti-spirituality can be spiritual in their essence. For instance, some scientists have a passion and sense of wonder for life, based on their scientific knowledge and insights, that shares many qualities with deep spirituality.

This means that when it comes to healing, what is probably most important is feeling a positive connection to the process of life, whether that takes the form of overt spirituality or not. If spirituality is not your cup of tea, maybe you draw inspiration from walking in nature, or reading poetry, or listening to powerful music. These experiences may well invoke in you similar emotions to what others draw from their spiritual encounters. To your body, it will all be the same. In other words, all of the steps recommended above can be taken in whatever secular version makes sense to you. They will make sense to your body, too.

# 13

# HEALING AS
# SELF-ACTUALIZATION

*We do not become enlightened by imagining figures of light*
*but by making the darkness conscious.*

Carl Jung

We have spent most of this book talking about how emotions and thoughts contribute to illness and how to use those same pathways to get well. But keep in mind that the "highest and best use" of this information is to use it for its own sake—that is, to pursue personal growth as a goal unto itself. This has the enormous side benefit of helping to prevent illnesses from forming in the first place because, through growth, we are emptying the unconscious mind of its disease-causing contents. But even this shouldn't be our ultimate aim in choosing to grow. For one thing, there is no sure-fire way to prevent all illness. A variety of factors can lead to sickness and while personal growth eliminates some of the most significant of those, it can't eliminate all of them.

But the most important reason for dedicating ourselves to our growth is the way it elevates our experience of life. It is, the sages say, why we are here—to learn and grow. The inner journey is also the most fascinating and richly rewarding journey we can undertake. There is no end to the dimensions and dynamics that make up our personalities and drive our perceptions and behavior. Studying them is like hiking in the Grand Canyon—at every place the trail goes around a bend, we find ourselves awed by a magnificent new vista. The real payoff on the growth path isn't the scenery, however— it's the life changes that occur as we apply what we learn about ourselves along the way. We often hear old-timers say, especially on birthdays, "I'm not older, just better." That's because they've learned so much in their years of living that hurdles that once seemed impossibly high now barely qualify as speed bumps.

If you stick around long enough, you too may reach a stage where things that once baffled or intimidated you no longer do. But why should you have to wait until the winter of your life for permission to start living? Wouldn't you rather have wisdom now so you can start applying it immediately? That's what a commitment to grow does for you – it front-loads the learning that takes most people a lifetime, if they accomplish it at all. And then it is available to enhance everything that you do.

## Abraham Maslow and His Self-Actualization Model of Health

Here in the West, the way we think about personal growth owes much to the pioneering ideas of psychologist Dr. Abraham Maslow (1908-1970). Born in Brooklyn, New York, Maslow received his professional training at a time when the physical sciences dominated psychology. But he wasn't convinced by his professors. He felt that the portrait of the person painted by psychology in those years was incomplete and deceiving. He was also frustrated with psychology's focus on sickness rather than health, which in his view only added to its limited view of people. He dedicated his career to reversing these trends and establishing a new psychology based on a more positive and expansive vision.

Maslow articulated his then-radical views in his book *Toward a Psychology of Being*, which would become a foundation work in the field of humanistic psychology. In it, he stated his belief that every human being possessed an essential, biologically based inner nature, which was "either neutral or positively good." He also argued that the impulse to grow and "actualize" one's full human potential was present in everyone even in infancy, regardless of the family and society into which they were born.

In Maslow's view, the drive to actualize ourselves competes with other more basic needs, such as the need to feed, clothe, and shelter ourselves and our need for affection and self-esteem. In most people, the basic drives win out and the person falls short of all he could be. But the potential is still there, waiting to be tapped at any time. Maslow hoped his psychology would inspire more people to seek their highest selves, in therapy and in their outside lives. He wrote, "it is best to bring [our inner nature] out and to encourage it rather than to suppress it. If it is permitted to guide our life, we grow healthy, fruitful and happy." Conversely, "if this essential core of the person is denied or suppressed, he gets sick sometimes in obvious ways, sometimes in subtle ways, sometimes immediately, sometimes later." These are not dramatic statements to make today, but in Maslow's time they were revolutionary, especially in a society that widely believed in "original sin."

Maslow came to his definition of psychological health in large part by studying the attributes of people whom he considered to be actualized. These models of exceptional health are characterized by the following qualities, Maslow wrote:

- Superior perception of reality.
- Increased acceptance of self, of others, and of nature.
- Increased spontaneity.
- Increase in problem-centering.
- Increased detachment and desire of privacy.
- Increased autonomy and resistance to enculturation.
- Greater freshness of appreciation and *richness of emotional reaction* [italics added].
- Higher frequency of peak experiences (see below).
- Increased identification with the human species.
- Changed (the clinician would say, improved) interpersonal relations, and the ability to love.
- More democratic character structure.
- Greatly increased creativeness.
- Certain changes in the value system.

Maslow's work coined two terms that go right to the heart of what I call Edgework: peak experiences and self-actualization. Maslow described peak experiences thusly:

> … an episode, or a spurt in which the powers of the person come together in a particularly efficient and intensely enjoyable way, and in which he (or she) is more integrated and less split, more open for experience, more idiosyncratic, more perfectly expressive or spontaneous, or fully functioning, more creative, more humorous, more ego-transcending, more independent of his lower needs, etc. He becomes in these episodes more truly himself, more perfectly actualizing his potentialities, closer to the core of his Being.

In short, peak experiences are our healthiest moments. We have all had them but they occur far more often in the lives of people in excellent psychological health. The healthiest among us are also self-actualizing, meaning that they actualize themselves in everything they do. They don't hide from or deny their problems; instead, they focus on resolving them, and they embrace challenges of all kinds. They have more peak experiences precisely because they are always choosing to "climb."

Maslow and other early humanistic psychologists set the stage for the human potential and personal growth movements of the 1960s and '70s. The excesses of these movements have invited derision and some savage (and often right-on!) satire from certain quarters, but no one contests the value of moving forward in life instead of staying stuck, of confronting our difficulties instead of pretending they don't exist, and of taking risks instead of always retreating to what is predictable and safe. The frontier issue now in personal growth is to prove that achieving psychological health will make a major impact on physical health. We are still some distance from satisfying science's strict criteria in that regard but I think you can see from the previous chapters that the evidence is already pretty strong and becoming more convincing all the time.

## Towards a New Model of Health

You've probably noticed that Maslow's description of actualized people, as well as his depiction of peak experiences, already alludes to several attributes we've discussed in previous chapters. These include:

- Self-love and forgiveness.
- An ability and willingness to experience emotions as they arise in consciousness.
- Meaningful relationships; the ability, and opportunity, to give and receive love.
- Living in the moment.
- A sense of humor about life.
- A feeling of spiritual connection.

We've also examined some human and lifestyle qualities that Maslow doesn't mention but that are just as critical to health, in my opinion. These are:

- Sensitivity to the messages your bodymind is sending you and willingness to accept those messages as challenges to grow, through Edgework or similar means.
- Discovering what your passion or creative purpose is in life and centering your life around it—in your work or your life outside work, and preferably in both.
- The awareness to recognize limiting thoughts or attitudes and the commitment to change them.
- The courage to take responsibility for the experiences in your life.
- Accepting the challenges in life as opportunities for shadow release and growth.

The sum total of all these items is a new model of mental and emotional health that I believe cannot fail to make a dramatic mark on a person's physical health as well. In fact, if you add to these mental, emotional, and lifestyle qualities a sensible diet, sufficient exercise, and proper rest, you become a virtual fortress of health that any disease will have tremendous difficulty penetrating.

But while prevention is an important goal, I would hope that you are aiming even higher when you choose to optimize your mental, emotional, and lifestyle fitness. I hope that whenever you are confronted with a personal limitation, you take it as an insult to who you really are and resolve to scale it; that few things excite you more than expanding awareness of your inner and outer worlds; and that for you, nothing less will do than a life filled with love, joy, and passion. Health is a marvelous thing, but more marvelous still is a life that is fully lived.

# 14

# EDGEWORK EXERCISES

*Know thyself.*

Plato

*Edges are important because they define a limitation in order to deliver us from it, . . . When we come to an edge, we come to a frontier that tells us that we are now about to become more than we have been before. As long as one operates in the middle of things, one can never really know the nature of the medium in which one moves. . . .*

William Irwin,
*The Time Falling Bodies Take to Light*

---

*There is an edge between what you know about yourself and what you don't know. Edgework is a process that explores the unknown territory within you. It will uncover aspects of consciousness that contribute to disease and, therefore, can be used for prevention, or, to assist in treatment. Edgework offers the greatest knowledge of all: self-knowledge.*

---

In Chapters 1 through 13, I presented to you important principles for self-healing as well as for the prevention of illness. I reviewed scientific research supporting these principles in order to create an understanding of their importance and validity. From your new knowledge and awareness you are ready to make these principles a reality in your life.

If you are ill, these exercises will constitute a self-help psychological regimen that will enhance whatever other treatments you are receiving and improve your chances of recovery. I believe that successful therapy for significant disease must entail elements of these processes. Often healing occurs when elements of these exercises are done naturally during the course of one's life.

Whether your interest is in prevention or healing, these exercises will help you explore your powerful and formative unconscious mind. They will also assist you in transforming dysfunctional beliefs and attitudes about yourself and the world around you. They will help you honor your emotions and live a fuller and happier life with fewer tendencies toward illness in the future.

Now comes the challenging part—translating principles and ideas into personal reality. It takes a significant commitment on your part to do the work necessary to make the exercises real for you. You may find yourself resisting doing the exercises due to the function of what psychologists call your ego. Your ego is constructed from the powerful, formative experiences of childhood, and one of its primary activities is to resist change and protect you from the pain of childhood. This resistance may present itself as lack of interest, skepticism, forgetfulness, and procrastination. But before giving into it, remember that your resistance represents the edge between your present self-knowledge and the depths of personal power and understanding waiting to be discovered. As Mary demonstrated in Chapter 1, it takes courage and will to venture into the unknown parts of you, but the rewards can be spectacular.

## Table of Contents—Edgework Exercises

## Guidelines for Doing the Exercises

1. Get a notebook to record your responses to the exercises.
2. Write your answers to the questions in the notebook. Don't just think of the answers in your mind. Psychologists have shown that writing has a powerful influence on the process of psychological healing. When you write about challenging events in your life, you are more likely to go deeper within yourself and produce new insights and understandings. Inner child writing is an excellent way to access your shadow and gradually discharge its contents. Writing the answers can produce profound physical and psychological changes.
3. Set aside one half-hour daily for the exercises at a regularly scheduled time. You may work longer, but at least the half-hour.
4. Select a quiet place to do the exercises where you won't be interrupted. Many of them are designed to bring up emotion, and you don't want to be disturbed during the process.

5. Try to have quiet time after completing each session. You will touch deep parts of yourself. You may leave a session feeling a lot of emotion and you will want to nurture yourself before returning to the rest of your day.

## Exercise 1: What Is Your Level of Commitment to Yourself?

Your commitment must always be to yourself. Most of us find it easier to commit to others, but without commitment to yourself you cannot grow to your full potential. In truth, your commitment to others will be compromised by the dysfunctional parts of self. Change occurs from the inside out. You are responsible for your life. No one else can take care of you. If you do not take responsibility to bring self-love to your wounds, you cannot break the vicious cycle of fear, guilt and blame. And you are worth it. You have the spark of divinity within you, and you deserve the happiness, fulfillment and healing that is your birthright.

This exercise is designed to measure your commitment to yourself. The following scale is from 0 to 10. Contemplate for a moment where your commitment lies on this scale.

| 0 | 1 | 2 | 3 | 4 | 5 | 6 | 7 | 8 | 9 | 10 |
|---|---|---|---|---|---|---|---|---|---|---|

none;                                                    total:
won't do the                                           will do
exercises                                              whatever
                                                       necessary
                                                     for personal
                                                        healing

Write down in your notebook your level of commitment to yourself.

If your commitment is high, congratulations. If it is not, consider what hidden parts of self are maintaining your fear, anxiety, anger, and dis-ease. If you have a serious illness, like cancer, and your commitment is low, please read Exercise 2 before you put this book down.

## Exercise 2: Becoming Friendly with Fear

I want to tell you about a remarkable man whose name is Mark Blakemore. Mark is a farmer who also has a unique ability—motivating "terminal" cancer patients to cure their cancer. He lives in a modest home, which he has transformed into a mini-medical clinic offering a range of natural therapies. Over the past four to five years, Mark has treated about 500 "terminal" cancer patients—patients who were told by their doctors that they had three to four months to live. *And of these 500 patients less than 10 have died!* He has helped thousands of other people with various medical problems, including less advanced cancer, HIV positive, AIDS, hepatitis C, lupus and more.

The key to Mark's incredible success is not his use of natural therapies, as similar techniques are used in many places around the country without such dramatic results. The key is Mark himself. First of all, he has cured himself of metastatic cancer twice. The first episode was lung cancer, and then years later, colon cancer. So Mark knows what he is talking about. But most importantly, his personal experience with cancer taught him to love God with such passion that every moment of his life is a reflection of his communion with the Divine. Mark is a humble, soft-spoken man who uses the word "we" when he talks about his healing work. He works in alignment with God moment to moment, letting Him make the decisions. People who come to Mark are transformed by his love and acceptance of them, and the vast majority choose life over death. His Christ-like energy helps people change fear into self-love, doubt into motivation, and helplessness into personal responsibility. And Mark does all of this without asking for a penny in return, so he is not practicing medicine without a license.

The first thing Mark tells those who come to him is that faith in God will get them through their dis-ease. He does not place a definition on their faith, as each person determines what God is for them. But he does tell them that faith in God will decrease their fear. This is essential, because, according to Mark, "the fear of cancer kills 20 times more people than cancer itself." His "terminal" patients have been told by their doctors that they have three to four months to live. This prophecy ignites fear in those that hear it. Perhaps these professional statistical proclamations are more of a death sentence than we realize. A more truthful statement from doctors would be: "We can't help you with what we do, and if you do nothing else, then statistically speaking, people like you die in three to four months. But we have seen remarkable cures and spontaneous remissions, and if you do exceptional things, you may beat the odds."

Mark then tells people that they must take responsibility for their disease and do whatever is necessary to get well. For Mark, it is "no big deal to get over cancer," and he communicates this with a strong and soothing conviction. Mark says that his 100% conviction in what he is doing with cancer patients helps them to heal. Most doctors don't have that level of conviction in what they do, and their patients become insecure and frightened.

Mark also tells his cancer patients that they must learn to love themselves instead of wanting to die. He says cancer patients have a death wish. If they were to use a gun, they would be called a coward, but with cancer you get sympathy, and you don't have to continue doing things in life, like relationships and work, that have burned you out over the years. Cancer is a socially acceptable way of stopping the relentless pain in life. A genuine faith in God combined with the power of self-love will transform the pain in life into a love of life.

Mark admits that it is easier for people to change when they experience the level of love he has for them. He also tells them that "there are a lot worse things than dying" and that "the worst day in heaven is better than the best day on earth," "so if dying is no big thing, then start living."

Mark's presence is a mission of love: the love of God, the love of mankind, and the love of self. That presence is in all of us. By connecting with that strength, you give yourself the power to heal yourself.

In the following exercises, you will identify the impact of fear in your life and consider ways to release it. This exercise is an essential first step for cancer patients. It will lead down a path with many important steps, including one of the later ones, forgiveness.

**Step 1:** Make a list in your notebook of your major fears in life. They could be illness, losing your loved one, or fears at work, or performing something. They could be rejection, success, failure, or being alone. Take your time and think carefully. Make your list as long as you can.

Fear is like a magnet, it attracts the very thing that you fear. Your list represents the things that you are drawing toward you. For example, if I am afraid of speaking in public, I will worry about the next time I am called upon, then my fear will escalate, and sure enough, when I step to the front of the audience, I will stammer and stutter with my heart pounding in my chest. If I fear failure, it is more likely that, when I try something, my worries will interfere and I will fail. If I fear my illness, I will increase the illness by activating the stress system, which will eventually break down my body's resistance to the disease.

It is as if your Soul, or Higher Self, wants you to go through your fear so you can learn more about yourself and realize how powerful you are. Perhaps this is what Friedrich Nietzsche, the great German philosopher, meant when he wrote his famous words: "That which does not kill me makes me stronger."

**Step 2:** The list you made in Step 1 is just the tip of the iceberg. You and I live in a society that is based on fear. We buy insurance because we fear something bad will happen to us. We fasten our seat belts in the car because we are afraid of having an accident. We have a Department of Defense because we are afraid someone will attack us. We attack others because we are afraid they will hurt us.

If you think about it for a moment, all negativity is based on fear. The very idea that someone or something is "bad" is based on fear. All our judgments about anything are based on fear.

Look around as you go through the days to come and see how many examples of society-based fears you can identify.

Also, look within yourself and watch your thinking for signs of fear. Observe your thoughts as you go through your day and see how many times you can identify fear within yourself. Jot them down and write them in your journal later on. The first step in handling fear is to recognize it.

**Step 3:** Fear is also our friend. When you walk to the edge of a cliff, it is your fear that keeps you back a safe distance. Some people say that the fear of heights is the only fear built into us as standard equipment. Our fearful parents who live in a fearful society hand over all the rest of our fears to us.

As you go through the next few days, look for times when you have fear, which helps you in some way. Then write your observations in your journal later in the day.

**Step 4:** The only antidote for fear is love. We live in a world of polar opposites: hot and cold, up and down, happy and unhappy, fear and love. The only way to release the fear is to move towards love. Love is acceptance and as we accept our fears they become our teachers.

If you accept your illness as your teacher, you will allow it to be what it is. You stop resisting it, and you will listen to what it tells you. You will consider that your body is calling for change in your life and you will seek out the changes that are needed.

If you accept your fear of public speaking as a teacher, you will consider ways you can begin to speak in small groups and gradually build your confidence.

If you accept a fear as a teacher, you will stop making it into a potential disaster. Your exaggerated fearful thoughts are replaced by a conscious awareness of the situation as it is, because you are listening to your teacher.

Look back at your list in Step 1 and consider each item as your teacher. Write a short paragraph or two about how the fear could become your teacher.

**Step 5:** Converting your fear into your teacher may sound risky, but risk is an essential part of life. Actually, you cannot grow without risk. Consider a child. Perhaps a child is the greatest risk-taker of all, for at the moment of birth he or she is inherently an explorer. The prime directive for the child is to explore and make the unknown, known. Imagine what it is like for the newborn infant to open her eyes for the first time and to touch, feel, hear and gaze into a world that is unknown? The lights, colors, sounds, forms, and people are imprinting on a consciousness that has known only the warmth, darkness, and safety of the womb. From the moment of birth the child is an instant explorer embarking on a dangerous journey to live, learn and grow.

As the child grows, her curiosity about the unknown world outside is a guiding force in her life. The infant wants to touch, taste, and feel everything around her, for this is the only way that she will learn what the world is all about. Pain becomes a reliable teacher as some things she touches are sharp and some are hot. She stumbles and falls, sometimes crying as she retreats to the safety of her mother, only to do it all over again. Occasionally she triumphantly announces, "I did it—I did it all by myself!"

As the child gets older, she continues to explore and dangers become greater, for the world is a vast and complicated place indeed. Scuffed knees, scratches, sprains, and occasionally broken bones are signals of the need to try new things, to understand more, and continuously explore. This is Edgework in its primal form and it is built into all of us.

Unfortunately, the need to take risks is often lost as children grow up and become adults. The adult personality all too often succumbs to the socially engendered influence of playing it safe. Risk taking atrophies, as does the "need to know." The inquisitive liveliness of childhood so often becomes the burdened, protected and defensive ego structure of the adult.

In your childhood, what were you taught about fear and risk taking? Complete the following sentences about your childhood in your notebook. You may need to complete a sentence more than once.

When I was afraid, my mother _____

When I was afraid, my father _____

I was afraid_____

I felt protected _____

I did not feel protected when _____

It was risky for me to _____

If other people knew I was afraid _____

Imagine for a moment a frightened small child huddled in a dark corner with her arms around herself trying to hide from something that has terrified her. You would want to go to that child and hold out your arms to her and invite her to come onto your lap where you could comfort and reassure her. You would want to make her feel safe. You would ask her about her fear and explain to her that you will protect her and she will be okay. Well, that frightened child exists in your unconscious mind and he/she is calling for the same comfort and reassurance. We all have a fearful inner child and the only way he/she can get our attention is to project into our lives, creating scary situations for us to deal with.

Inner child writing is the tool that will help you listen to, comfort and reassure the fearful child within your shadow. You will learn this powerful method in Exercise 7. For now, just consider what the fearful inner child within you went through in your childhood years.

**Step 6:** *Feel the Fear and Do It Anyway* is the title of a wonderful little book written by Susan Jeffers, Ph.D. On page 30, she writes "The Five Truths about Fear":

1. The fear will never go away as long as I continue to grow. *(I would add that as you grow, fear changes from a paralyzing emotion to an adrenaline based excitement that prepares you for the task at hand.)*
2. The only way to get rid of the fear of doing something is to go out . . . and do it.
3. The only way to feel better about myself is to go out . . . and do it.
4. Not only am I going to experience fear whenever I'm on unfamiliar territory, but so is everyone else.
5. Pushing through fear is less frightening than living with the underlying fear that comes from a feeling of helplessness."

Dr. Jeffers has taught courses on handling fears for many years and she summarizes her work in her book. She offers a step-by-step approach that has helped millions of people.

**Step 7:** Worry is fear that is held in the mind over time. Worry is such a common part of everyday mental life that it is hard for some people to conceive of life without it.

What do you worry about? In your notebook, make a list of as many worries as you can think of. When you have completed your list, then write next to each issue the number of days, months or years that you have worried about it.

Has worry helped you to solve these problems? I doubt it, because worry does not solve problems—planning and preparation do that. But worry does accomplish two things. It serves to attract the fearful issue to you. It also activates the stress system to wear you down physically. It weakens your immune system, makes you tired, and contributes to a host of medical problems, including headache, upset stomach, back pain, high blood pressure, depression, and many more.

In her book, *Feel the Fear and Do It Anyway,* Susan Jeffers demonstrates the power of positive and negative thinking on the body with the following exercise. She calls for a volunteer from the audience to come forward. She asks the volunteer to make a fist and extend his arm out to the side. She tells the person to resist with all his strength while Dr. Jeffers stands in front of him and tries to pull the arm down with her outstretched hand. Not once did she succeed in pulling down the volunteer's arm.

She then asks the volunteer to close his eyes and repeat ten times the negative statement, "I am a weak and unworthy person." She then repeats the exercise with the outstretched arm as before, and immediately Jeffers is able to bring the arm down. "It is as though all strength had left him." They do the exercise again and again for the astonished audience with the same results.

According to Dr Jeffers, "this is a stunning demonstration of the power of the words we speak. Positive words make us physically strong; negative words make us physically weak." I would add that positive and negative thoughts have the same effect.

Worry is a bad habit that has a host of negative influences on your mind and body. Like any habit, it can be changed. Now go back over your list of worries and write down what planning and preparation you can make to deal with each issue. For some of them there may be nothing you can do, because you are not responsible for other people, unless they are your young children. We will discuss responsibility later on in Exercise 4.

**Step 8:** A wonderful teacher of mine once said, "When fear arises in you, remember, it is a possibility, not a probability. And you can release it back to the Father." When we accept our fears and use them to guide us in becoming more powerful, we no longer fuel them with more and more fear. Your awareness will guide you in learning about yourself and what you can do about your fear. If fear arises again and again, simply know that you are much greater than your fear and send it back to God.

As Mark Blakemore suggested in the opening of this exercise, you can put your faith in God to get you through illness. Your faith in God can be rekindled into the highest passion of all—the love of God. Perhaps you can come to believe in your Higher Self as a source of wisdom, love and guidance.

Franklin Delano Roosevelt summed it up nicely when he said, "The only thing we have to fear is fear itself."

## Exercise 3: Feeling Emotions

*Being in touch with your feelings is the only way you can ever become your highest self, the only way you can become open and free, the only way you can become your own person.*
David Viscott, M.D., *The Language of Feelings*

Many people have problems feeling and expressing their emotions. Women tend to be more expressive than men, but even many women avoid it. We live in a society that favors the rational over the emotional, and it has been that way for centuries. We are often taught in childhood to suppress our emotions. Little girls are told it is not nice to be angry. Little boys are told that "big boys don't cry." Parents usually do the best they can, but they teach their children many of the same things they learned in childhood. Repressive traits are passed from generation to generation.

The abuse of a child is another reason that emotions are denied. The intense emotions that occur for a child who is emotionally, physically, or sexually abused are overwhelming and too much for a child to fully feel and release. Therefore the child avoids the pain by both repressing and suppressing the emotions, and this avoidance may last for the remainder of her life. Repression is an unconscious, automatic mechanism to avoid feelings, while suppression is a conscious choice to deny them. When abused children grow up, they often live in the "safety" of their intellect and can always find good reasons to suppress emotions later in life.

When emotions are denied for long periods of time, the effects can be devastating. First of all the natural self-healing mechanism of the unconscious mind (shadow projection) is thwarted, sometimes for a lifetime. Medical research has shown us that suppressing emotions makes us prone to illness as the emotions denied in shadow projection have nowhere to go. They eventually percolate into the body, thereby contributing to disease. In other words, if you don't express your emotions, your body will. *The hallmark of the majority of cancer patients is the denial of emotion.*

The denial of emotion not only puts our physical health at risk, it also impairs our ability to relate to other people. The nationally known psychologists, Dr. Gay Hendricks and his wife Kathlyn, write in their book *Conscious Loving*: "In our therapy practice we have come to see that the act of hiding feelings is perhaps the most crippling component of relationship difficulties."

In addition to putting our health and relationships at risk, Dr. David Viscott, believes that by denying emotions, we compromise our ability to be fully alive. He writes in *The Language of Feelings,* "feelings are the way we perceive ourselves," and "they are the way we sense being alive." Depression is a common form of lowered vitality which occurs when people deny emotions, especially anger.

Emotions come from the heart, so to speak, and offer a balance to the intellect. They can guide us during decision-making in many aspects of our lives. It is important to recognize whether an issue simply feels good, regardless of the reasons pro and con around it, and give weight to that feeling. Conversely, if something feels bad, take heed of this feeling as you consider other aspects of the issue.

Being able to feel, identify and express your emotions will offer you healing in many areas of your life. When you know your feelings, you are more able to be truthful to yourself and others. Communicating your feelings to others will improve your relationships and lead to greater intimacy. It will make you more alive and present in the moment. The deepest feeling is love which is considered by many to be the most powerful healing force of all. It has been said that God is love.

There is one important point that needs to be made before we go any further. You can feel your feelings without acting upon them. I have heard many patients say that they cannot express their anger because they might lose control and kill someone. The unfortunate irony is that people who persistently hold in anger and other emotions may slowly kill themselves. These people need to learn that anger can be felt and simply released. I have advised people to rant and rave in the privacy of their bedroom, or on a walk in the woods, or while driving alone in the car. In so doing, they learn that it is a relief to let go of this powerful emotion, and then, no one gets hurt.

So now, take a look at where you stand on the continuum of emotional expression. Rate yourself on the scale below. The zero end of the scale is rarely found as almost everyone will scream in rage if the aggravation is intense enough. Those at the lower end of the scale hold in all emotion on a day-to-day basis and give themselves "good" reasons for doing so. The ten side of the scale represents the person who honors what he or she feels and who expresses emotion freely and in a socially appropriate manner.

| 0 | 1 | 2 | 3 | 4 | 5 | 6 | 7 | 8 | 9 | 10 |
|---|---|---|---|---|---|---|---|---|---|---|

no                                                                                      complete
emotional                                                                           & natural
expression;                                                                         emotional
numb                                                                                  expression

If you scored on the upper end of the scale, good for you. You may move to the next exercise. Remember to be increasingly attentive to the nuances of feeling that arise within you during the day. This will help you explore your shadow as well as learn a lot about what is going on around you. Emotional IQ is just as important as intellectual IQ.

If you scored on the lower end of the scale, you need some help in developing emotional skills. There is no quick fix here. You will need to retrain yourself gradually. But you will succeed. You have a shadow that has been projecting into your life since childhood, but you have never been taught to take advantage of this self-healing mechanism. The shadow is fully dedicated to its work, and you will have ample opportunity to practice your new skills in the future.

So, let us begin.

**Step 1:** Sensing your body.

Your mindbody allows you to think and feel. Unfortunately, however, most people spend so much time thinking that they forget about feeling. Your mindbody has intricate sensing mechanisms that let you know what is going on in your body as well as what is going on outside your body. This information is continuously sent to your emotional brain (limbic system) and your thinking brain (cerebral cortex). Some of this internal information is beneath your level of awareness, but a lot of it is available to you and can provide important guidance in your life.

Your mind lives in the past. In order for you to think, you must remember the past and then project the past into the future. Your body, however, lives only in the moment and tells you about what is going on now. Therefore, you can only experience the present moment, or now, if you take your awareness away from your thoughts and focus it in your body in order to sense the feelings in your body. Your feelings tell you what is real and happening right now. They allow you to make sense of the world. Your feelings tell you if the world is safe or scary. They tell you if the moment is painful, happy or exciting. Your feelings connect you to other people with much greater persuasion than your thoughts do. Emotions provide the rich tapestry of life as they connect you to all of humanity. They are to be valued for the guidance they give you as well as the inner healing they offer.

Find a comfortable place to sit or lie down where you won't be disturbed. Focus your awareness into your body and away from your thoughts. If you have pain in some part of your body, simply be aware of it without any thought. (We will get to an exercise for pain later on.) Now focus your awareness in your left leg and foot. Notice any sensations you find and simply be aware of them. Do the same for your right leg and foot. If there are tense muscles, relax them. Now move your awareness to your pelvic area and abdomen. Notice any sensations like a curious child who is exploring the world. If you find yourself thinking, simply refocus on your body. Can you feel the distance between the left side of your abdomen and the right side. How many inches do you feel? Remember, no thoughts or judgments. Now focus your attention into your chest. Feel your heart beat for a moment. Is the time between each beat exactly the same, or does it vary? Next become aware of your breathing. Follow a breath in and then follow one out as you exhale. Notice the pause between breaths. How long is that pause? Stay aware of your breathing for a minute or two. Then move your awareness to your arms and shoulders. What do you feel in your hands? Now focus on your head, scanning your face and scalp. Feel these areas as if you are searching for subtle nuances of sensation. Now return your awareness to the room around you and the exercises.

You have just scanned your body with simple awareness. There is no special technique other than curious awareness without any interference from thought. By moving your awareness from the thoughts in your head to your body, you listen to your body as though it is a messenger offering you information about the world inside of you as well as the world outside of you. Pain and illness are the body's desperate attempt to get through to us the message that something is dramatically out of balance in our lives. But before the pain and disease, there is a lot of information available. Your feelings and emotions can not only guide you to a richer experience of the world and the people in it, but they can also offer you valuable guidance in preventing pain and disease, as well as healing them.

While there may not seem to be much going on in your body when you are sitting still, a lot more information will be available to you as you periodically sense your body during your daily activities.

Pain Awareness Exercise: Focus your attention on the pain in your body. Give the pain a rating on a scale of one to ten (1 is no pain and 10 is maximum pain). Now sense your body as described above. Become aware of your pain as if you are examining it in detail like a curious child. Visualize the shape of the pain. Is it round, oblong or in some other shape? How far is it from the back of your body? How many inches? How many inches is it from the front of your body? Now that you have it located and know the shape, how much volume of fluid would the shape hold? Could you pour a cup of water into the pain? Perhaps two or three? Simply be aware of the pain in this manner. You are curiously aware without any thought or judgment. Sometimes the pain will change with a few moments of pure awareness. What is the shape and volume now? After you have sensed your pain for a few minutes, measure its intensity on the scale of 0 to 10 once again.

If this exercise is done properly, the second rating will be less than the first. You will have reduced your pain significantly based on simple non-judgmental awareness. Most of the time we resist our pain by thinking about it and wishing it would go away. We judge the pain as bad and, since our judgments are based on fear, the pain increases, as fear attracts that which we fear. This resistance from the mind will make the pain more intense rather like holding a hot coal tightly in the fist. But if we open the fist and look at the pain with simple awareness without resistance, the pain will decrease. Remember, what you resist will persist.

**Step 2:** The following is a short list of feelings and emotions. Actually there are hundreds of them, but this list will do for this exercise.

| | | | | |
|---|---|---|---|---|
| fear | anger | hate | worried | hurt |
| shame | guilt | sadness | frustration | discouragement |
| love | sympathy | happiness | caring | shyness |
| resentment | anxiety | helpless | hopeless | bored |
| vulnerable | confusion | degraded | cranky | criticized |
| disgust | jealous | cheerful | depression | abandoned |
| abused | hostile | lazy | sexual | neglected |
| rebellious | proud | ridiculed | stressed | tired |

Go to a comfortable place where you will not be disturbed. Pick one of the feelings listed above and think back in your life to a time when you felt this feeling. Visualize the scene that brought on the feeling and do so in as much detail as you can. Think about the episode and talk to yourself if you need to. You want to recreate the experience in your mind's eye so you can evoke the feeling that you have chosen.

Once you have the feeling, then locate it in your body. Look for tightness in your chest or throat, a heavy feeling on your shoulders, or a jittery feeling in your belly. Sense your body carefully like you did in Step 1. Describe the feeling in your body. Feelings are always located somewhere in the body. Initially these body sensations may be subtle, but with practice you will identify them quickly.

Try the exercise with other feelings from the list.

The value of this exercise is that you move the awareness of a feeling from your mind to your body. The mind remembers the past and can paint a huge, scary picture for you, while the body simply tells you what is going on right now. For example, for a person with an abusive childhood, the thought of anger could bring up images of an angry parent, punishment, violence and possibly years of turmoil. No wonder people want to suppress such a painful emotion with so much negativity attached to it. On the other hand, anger in the body has no attachments and is just a hot, tense, and trembling feeling located in the head or chest. We will deal with the conscious and unconscious memories of emotions later on in the exercises, but for now simply locating feelings and emotions in the body takes the drama and fear out of them and makes the experience a useful part of living life.

**Step 3:** E-motions are energy in motion. They arise within the body and then they flow until their flow is completed, and they pass out of the body. But when the flow of an emotion or feeling is interrupted and not allowed to complete, you can develop an uneasy, disturbed feeling. In other words, a person needs to cry until he or she doesn't feel like crying any more. Many well-intended people try to comfort the tearful person by telling him/her things like, "don't cry, it will be okay."

Emotions are like streams that flow out of the mountains. As they take their natural course down the mountainside, they create a beautiful scene. However, if you damn up the stream, it will overflow and destroy the terrain.

Think back to your childhood and recall what your parents told you about emotions, especially about showing anger, sadness and crying. Write these down in your notebook.

Then recall what you have told your family and yourself about anger and crying. Write these recollections down in your notebook.

**Step 4:** Anger is a powerful emotion that people often get stuck in. For example, one of the well-documented features of the coronary prone person is hostility or perpetual, aggressive anger. Rheumatoid arthritis and lupus are other examples of common diseases that occur in people who hold onto anger and resentment for long periods of time.

Anger is a protective emotion. It allows you to set boundaries. It can be felt and then released. However, you need to understand that anger is a cover for hurt feelings. People don't get angry unless their feelings are hurt in some way. Anger is like the lid on the garbage can, and you must look deeper within for the hurt that precipitated the anger in order to achieve a complete emotional release.

We get angry at inconsiderate freeway drivers because they don't respect us, and our feelings are hurt, just a little. Think back a moment to the last time you were angry, and see if you can determine the underlying hurt feeling. Write your answer in your notebook.

When you uncover a hurt feeling, somehow you were invalidated or not respected. Stay with the feeling for a moment and try to expand it—feel more of it. See if you can locate the feeling in your body—maybe your chest or abdomen. Just stay with the feeling and perhaps some tears will arise. Celebrate the tears. They are very healing.

During your days to come, notice each time you become angry, or even aggravated or frustrated just a little, and find how your feelings were hurt. Write your experiences with anger in your notebook.

**Step 5:** Take every opportunity your day offers to cultivate your ability to feel emotions. Instead of thinking so much about what you see or experience in your day, stay in your body and feel as deeply as you can about what your days offer. Feel your way through the day. Again, there are plenty of opportunities for bringing up emotions. Take a moment to feel for the innocent deer or squirrel that lies dead at the side of the road on your way to work. Turn on the evening news on your television and watch the emotional display that occurs every night at the same time. Consider the abused child, the wounded child, the dying families in famine-plagued areas of Africa, the abused wife, the list goes on and on, night after night. See how deeply you can feel for the people you see—people just like you. Imagine what would happen in this country if every person fully felt the pain and suffering of those displayed on the nightly news. It would change complacency into heartfelt action that could transform society.

**Step 6:** Dr. Claude Steiner opens the second chapter of his book, *Achieving Emotional Literacy,* with the following paragraph:

> Nearly everyone feels emotional distress when approached by a homeless beggar. Many of us immediately try to shut off our feelings, preferring to pretend that he doesn't exist or somehow deserves his fate. Others feel guilt, and may think that they should be giving more money to charity rather than buying luxury items like CDs or perhaps even this book. Still others will actually feel indignant and hostile toward this person, treating him as if he is an unwelcome intruder into their lives.

What is your reaction to the homeless person? The next time you are in an area where they are, carefully check out your emotions and the thoughts behind them. What did you learn about yourself?

**Step 7:** The movies are a rich source for vicarious emotional experience, and this may be a big reason people like them so much. Go to the video store and rent a few real tearjerkers. As you watch a film, identify with one or more of the actors as they move through emotional experiences. Become that person and feel what they feel. Men who have trouble crying can especially benefit from this exercise.

**Step 8**: I recommend Dr Steiner's book, *Achieving Emotional Literacy,* for anyone who wants to increase and refine his or her emotional skills. Remember, emotional IQ is just as important as mental IQ. One without the other is an imbalance that will limit your potential. Some people believe that genius arises more often when the two are balanced in a person.

Remember the techniques and experiences of this exercise as you move through the days of your life. Emotional sensitivity to yourself and others is one of the most important skills you can have in order to maintain your health, both physically and psychologically. If you have illness, emotional release will help you in the healing process. You are opening your heart and, as the noted French philosopher, Pascal, simply stated, "the heart has reasons the mind knows not of." As you progress in your emotional awareness, be gentle with yourself and have compassion for your journey.

## Exercise 4: Taking Responsibility for the Experiences in Your Life

The single most important thing you can do to begin the healing process is to take responsibility for the experiences you have created in your life. You have created all the experiences in your life in co-creation with other people around you. Taking responsibility shifts you from a helpless and powerless victim who blames those around him or her for problems, into an active person seeking to understand and transform problems. In doing so, you take back the power that you have given to others and you can use it to heal your own wounds, tell the truth to yourself, and start the path to greater self-knowledge, happiness and fulfillment in your life. Our society teaches victim consciousness, so your path may be a lonely one at first. The rewards are immense, because you will be starting the process that can lead to solving the problems and challenges in your life.

You have created your life experience through two basic methods. The first is through your conscious choices in life (or sometimes non-choices) which are based on your thoughts and attitudes about life in general and certain issues specifically. The second method is more challenging and consists of unconscious choices and directives that spring from your unconscious mind, or shadow. Your shadow contains the emotions you did not express fully at the time of some difficult experience, such as rejection, abandonment, abuse of any kind, neglect, and a host of other invalidating experiences starting at birth and continuing every day of your life. It is a storehouse of unowned fear, pain, anger, resentment, tears, and rage. If you express your emotions at the time of a difficult event, they are released and nothing is added to the shadow. That is why emotional expression is such an essential part of the healthy personality. Because no one has a perfect childhood, the shadow is filled with unfinished business in all of us. The shadow also contains beliefs and attitudes that you made about yourself and others in the immature years of your childhood.

The reason it is important to explore your shadow is that it is dedicated to one purpose—discharging its contents, which is also called shadow projection. It wants you to express the emotions it contains, thereby owning and completing them. This process is also called **emotional wound healing**, and it is just as important as physical wound healing, which happens, for example, when you cut your finger. Emotional wound healing occurs when your shadow influences your choices in life without you knowing about it, in order to set up circumstances that would let the previously denied emotion to come forth. This is the reason a child who is abandoned will likely create relationships later in life that lead to abandonment. It is also the reason that the children of alcoholics marry alcoholics so often later in life. Powerful emotions are often too much for the child to express, so they are suppressed (conscious choice) or repressed (unconscious choice) into the shadow. However, later on in life as we mature, we are more able to express them, unless we have decided to avoid emotions altogether. We will get to this issue later on.

I am asking you to not only become responsible for the experiences in your life but also for the thoughts that created them. For example, the thought that "nobody loves me" is usually based on childhood experiences that deprive a child of parental love. Examples could include parents who do not know how to show love, or loss of a parent. If you accept responsibility for this thought and feel the pain and sadness of not being loved, without blame on others, you begin to release these emotions from your shadow. You will probably need to do inner child writing (Exercise 7) to complete the release. As the buried emotions are released and owned, then there is no need to draw to you experiences that prove that "nobody loves me." You can then let go of that dysfunctional belief, and you have made an important start in the process of becoming aware of your negative thinking and the emotional states that bring suffering to your life. You will also see how your negativity becomes a self-fulfilling prophecy.

Indeed, shadow projection is a self-healing mechanism built into you that often creates suffering, but can lead to personal healing and the resolution of problems. You are more powerful than you think, and now is the time to take that power back from where you have placed it with blame of others.

One word of caution, however—do not judge yourself as you uncover your hidden motivations. If you judge yourself, you will prevent release of the shadow issue. This process is based on self-love and self-acceptance, not self-judgment.

So let us begin.

**Step 1**: Make a list of all the good things you have created in your life. Perhaps your family, spouse, your work (or some aspect of it), your church, social club, or whatever. List things you are proud of or feel good about. These things did not arise from luck. It is not so hard to take responsibility for these things, right?

**Step 2**: Now make another list of all the problem areas in your life— the things that bother and challenge you. Examples include diseases, marital conflict, job dissatisfaction, and family problems. Take time to contemplate these issues so your list can be as complete as possible. You may include social, or global, problems, like environmental pollution, but you are co-creating these issues with millions of people, so their resolution is more challenging than close personal problems.

**Step 3**: Now for each item listed above, write down who or what you have blamed for the problem in the past. Possibly you blamed your boss at work, or your spouse or child, etc. If you have already taken responsibility for an issue, good for you. But if you haven't, take time to make your list carefully and accurately. You have given your power away to these people or things. You erroneously thought that they held the keys to resolution of the problem, not you.

**Step 4:** Now take each item on the list and consider it as your creation (or co-creation with another). Take your time and feel the feelings that arise within you. Now next to each item, write down the emotion that could have surfaced or is surfacing in relation to the problem. The emotion holds the key for transformation. If you release an emotion underlying a problem, you may no longer need that problem in your life. But the process also takes time and the underlying issues may be complex and overlapping, so be patient with yourself. But you have taken the first steps on a path toward self-healing, self-love and the reclamation of your personal power. If you have trouble finding the emotion beneath a problem, imagine one of your more emotional friends and consider what emotion they would feel. If you still cannot find the feeling, go back and review Exercise 3 once again.

**Step 5:** The next step is just as important as the previous one, so take your time to do a thorough job. For each item on your list from Step 2, write two or three paragraphs (or more if you need to) that describe how the problem developed and how it has been sustained over time, all based on your perspective. Also write the reasons, as you understand them, for the problem. For example, if you have a problem with your spouse, write down possible reasons, such as, "he doesn't listen to me," or "he is too busy for me," etc. If the problem is a medical illness, also write down the reasons that you can think of. An example would be, "I don't eat the right foods," or "my work is too stressful." Take your time with each issue. You want to uncover your thoughts, beliefs and attitudes about the problem.

**Step 6:** Now take each paragraph from Step 5 and pull out any thought or belief that may have contributed to the problem. For example, "people don't meet my needs," or, "people don't listen to me," etc. You want to find the thoughts that create your problem. Each of us maintains negative thoughts and attitudes about ourselves and others and these become a self-fulfilling prophecy based on the power of thought to create experience. If I believe it is hard for people to get to know me, I will always create circumstances that fit my belief. So take your time and contemplate each problem carefully. Each problem you create for yourself usually has a combination of unfelt emotion and dysfunctional beliefs behind it. It is important to identify these formative aspects of consciousness. By identifying these dysfunctional beliefs you can then change them. Most of them took root in your childhood and the source of each of them will come later in the exercise. But for now just list as many thoughts and beliefs as you can.

For now, just be aware of the emotions, thoughts and beliefs that underlie your problems in life. It is not so important now to change them. Awareness alone will bring change to some extent. You have moved some of these contributing factors from your unconscious mind to the light of your awareness and you have begun the healing process. Many of them are limitations to the kind of experiences you want in your life. Stay aware of them and watch yourself during the days to come to see what other beliefs about yourself are beneath the experiences in your life.

Congratulations. You have taken the first steps toward self-mastery by identifying emotions, thoughts and beliefs that in the past have limited you and shaped your experience in dysfunctional ways.

## Exercise 5: Taking a Close Look at Your Thoughts, Beliefs and Attitudes

If you want to find out about your thoughts, beliefs and attitudes, take a look around you. They create the world you live in. Take a look at your body, your family, your employment, your home, your relationships, and you will see the results of what you think. If you live in a world filled with happiness and fulfillment, one with loving and passionate relationships, one with stimulating and creative employment, one in which your body serves you with good health, then congratulations. If, on the other hand, there is something about your health, relationships, employment, or whatever, that you would like to change, you must first see why you created it the way you did.

The formative power of thought is an ancient topic. The Greek philosopher Epictetus told us 2000 years ago, "Men are not worried by things, but by their ideas about things." William Shakespeare tells us, "There is nothing good or bad, but thinking makes it so." More recently, John Williams wrote in his book, *The Wisdom of Your Subconscious Mind,* "You are now just what, and only what, you desire to be. By every thought and feeling growing out of your mind, you have built the house in which you now live." And the great physician Albert Schweitzer gave us hope when he said, "The greatest discovery of any generation is that human beings can alter their lives by altering their attitudes of mind."

No one is responsible for the house you live in except you. You can blame others, as that is what our society often encourages, but it won't get you anywhere, as only you can change your experience. There is no point in looking for someone else to do it for you.

You may say, "How can my thoughts create my reality? I have a million of them popping in my mind." That is true. Most of us have so many thoughts throughout the day, often conflicting with one another, so that not much comes of it. As we continue to think the same thoughts, they coalesce into beliefs and beliefs become attitudes. Attitudes are focused forms of thought which do not change so much. In order to take responsibility in our lives, we need to assess the beliefs and attitudes that shape our experiences. That is what this exercise is all about.

In the exercises below, you want to get a list of your thoughts and beliefs for each topic listed. In order to do so, think carefully about each topic and review your childhood, as well as your adult life, looking for beliefs that have recurred for you. Remember the beliefs your parents told you that you held onto, as well as the beliefs you developed after childhood. Take your time and make your lists as complete as possible.

**Step 1:** My thoughts and beliefs about my body.

Use the phrase, I believe my body is _____ and fill in the blank. An example would be, I believe my body is basically healthy, or, I believe my body isn't shaped right. Write as many beliefs as you can think of. Then complete the following sentence: I think my body is _____, and again fill in the sentence as many times as you need to.

**Step 2:** My thoughts and beliefs about my health.
Use the phrases, I believe my health is _____ and I think my health is _____. List as many as possible for each phrase.

**Step 3:** My thoughts and beliefs about my illness.
If you have an illness, use the phrases, I believe my illness is _____. And, I think my illness is _____ List as many as possible for each phrase.

**Step 4:** My thoughts and beliefs about my doctor.
Use the phrases, I believe my doctor is_____ and, I think my doctor is_____

**Step 5:** My thoughts and beliefs about my immune system.
Use the phrases, I believe my immune system is _____ and, I think my immune system is _____.

**Step 6:** My thoughts and beliefs about my chances for recovery.
If you have an illness, use the phrases, I believe my chances for recovery are_____ and, I think my chances for recovery are _____.

**Step 7:** My thoughts and beliefs about my life.
Use the phrases, I believe my life has been _____ and, I think my life has been _____.

**Step 8:** My thoughts and beliefs about my family.
Use the phrases, I believe my family has been _____ and, I think my family has been_____.

**Step 9:** My thoughts and beliefs about my spouse.
Use the phrases, I believe my spouse is _____ and, I think my spouse is _____ .

If you are not married in your relationship, you can use the word "mate."

**Step 10:** My thoughts and beliefs about my marriage.
Use the phrases, I believe my marriage has been _____ and, I think my marriage has been _____ .
Long-term relationships without marriage are okay here too.

**Step 11:** My thoughts and beliefs about my work.
Use the phrases, I believe my work has been _____ and, I think my work has been _____ .

**Step 12:** My thoughts and beliefs about money.
Use the phrases, I believe money is _____ and, I think money is _____ .

**Step 13:** My thoughts and beliefs about my ability to succeed in life.
Use the phrases, I believe my ability to succeed in life is _____, and, I think my ability to succeed in life is_____ .

**Step 14:** You are now going to determine if each belief and thought listed for each topic above has been positive, or supportive to you, or negative and counterproductive for you. Contemplate each thought and belief in each topic and write *pos* if that belief has been helpful or supportive to you, and write *neg* if that belief has been an interference or distraction to your success in that area. If you are unsure of the effect of a belief on you, then write *unsure.*

**Step 15:** Now list all the positives from your writings and make another list of all the negatives. Do the same for the unsures. Count the number of positives, the number of negatives, and the number of unsures. For each topic consider how well your beliefs and thoughts have served you over the years. Have they helped you succeed in the area, or have they hindered you and become self-fulfilling prophecies? Now burn the negative list in the fireplace or outside and release them from your life.

You have assessed your thoughts and beliefs in important areas of your life. Your lists may not be complete, and you may uncover other beliefs as days go by. Stay aware of your thoughts as you go through each day. Be vigilant and watch for negative thoughts and beliefs because they may reappear out of habit. If you notice a negative thought pop into your mind, say "I release this thought as it no longer serves me," or simply say "cancel."

Scientists are beginning to consider thought as a subtle energy in the universe, which may be measured at sometime in the future. Regardless of our understanding of thought, it is a formative energy that works to create your reality. Your beliefs can empower you and bring to you what you want, or they can be the prison bars and limit your ability to succeed. The choice is yours.

## Exercise 6: Healing Emotional Wounds

Healing the emotional wounds contained in your shadow is the most important skill that you can develop in order to prevent illness, assist in the treatment of illness, and make your life work better in general. You have learned how thoughts and beliefs shape your reality. Now you are going to learn a method to heal the emotional wounds that are also shaping your reality. First, let us briefly review the principles of shadow projection and emotional wound healing.

Your personality, or persona, is your psychological clothing. It is how you present yourself to the world around you. Beneath the persona is the shadow, the psychic storehouse, or dumping ground, for all the parts of yourself that you have rejected. It contains all the experiences in your life that were considered "unacceptable" to your conscious mind. It contains the pain, rejection, abandonment, anger, and abuse that seemed too great to simply feel and allow. The child that cries in the night and receives no attention experiences pain that registers in the shadow. The toddler that is told he or she is "bad" for knocking an intriguing knick-knack off of the coffee table seeds the shadow. The emotionally, physically or sexually abused child who cannot express all the pain and anger and recoils into submission pushes these disowned emotions into the shadow.

Fortunately, the shadow is under pressure to release its contents. If you cut your finger, it will heal automatically through the wonderful inflammatory systems in the body. You don't have to think about "how to heal a wound," it just happens naturally. In like manner, the emotional wounds within the shadow have a natural healing mechanism. The contents of the shadow will project into your reality by unconsciously influencing your conscious choices in life in order to set up experiences for you to feel, accept, and own the stored emotions, thereby releasing and healing these psychic wounds. This is the reason that a sexually abused little girl is likely to have an abusive sexual experience later in life. If the tears and anger flow, then she has accepted a previously rejected part of herself and healed a deep inner wound. If she denies the feeling again, then the pain stays in the shadow only to be projected again at some time in the future.

Shadow release, or projection, accounts for many of the so-called unfortunate experiences in life. Broken relationships, employment problems, financial worries, marital conflict, and the vast array of life's difficulties and challenges are all the result of shadow release. By allowing ourselves to feel the painful emotions and thoughts associated with these events, we accept the shadow content, grow wiser and expand knowledge of self. We see the problems in life as gifts and opportunities for healing that arise from our shadow. We are making the unconscious parts of ourselves conscious. In this manner we can understand the wisdom of Carl Jung when he said, "We do not become enlightened by imagining figures of light but by making the darkness conscious."

The intensity of shadow release is not confined to the "unfortunate" adversities, or dis-eases, in life. If we do not learn from the painful experiences in life and thereby own the shadow, then the shadow turns up the volume, so to speak, and seeks to get our attention in a more persuasive manner—physical disease. Disease then becomes the messenger of shadow issues, and, symptoms become our teachers. This is an essential key to understanding the higher dimensions of healing. Every symptom is an aspect of the shadow that has precipitated itself into the body. The source of much disease is in our consciousness and the body is simply letting us know what is there.

You can categorize all the wounds that you received in childhood into broad categories based on various emotions or characteristics, such as fear and anger. The little girl that is told by her parents that it is not okay to be angry, will stuff her anger into her shadow each time she is rightfully angry. The little boy whose feelings are hurt by a controlling and strict mother will push his wounds into the shadow if he is taught not to cry. The assortment of denied emotions coalesce, so to speak, into categories of emotion, and we are going to call each category an inner child. In other words, an inner child is a sub-personality of yours and contains a certain type of emotional experience. We all have an angry inner child, a fearful inner child, and perhaps a wounded inner child or timid one. Whatever the recurrent themes were for you in childhood, they each can become an inner child, who lives in your unconscious mind.

These inner children make decisions about themselves and the world that are faulty or misinterpretations of reality. For example, if a child is abused in some way, the child thinks, "I must be bad," or, "no one can love me." In inner child writing, you listen to everything the child has to say, and then you re-educate him or her, forgive the judgment of "badness," and tell the child how loved he or she really is. Each inner child is projecting into your reality to create circumstances that would allow its contents to be felt, understood, and released. So emotional healing depends on healing the inner children. Think of them as small children with no logic. Inner child therapy allows you to learn from them and to reeducate, or re-parent, them in a way they didn't receive when you were little. In doing so you are loving all of you, including the parts you have rejected in the past.

So let us begin.

**Step 1:** Think for a moment about a stressful experience that is going on for you now in your life. Find an experience that brings up a particular emotion in you, like fear or anger. If you have an illness, do not use it at this time, but rather some other stressful experience. Write a brief paragraph in your notebook about the experience you have chosen.

**Step 2:** Select the dominant feeling from your story. Let us use fear for example. Now you have created an experience that brings up fear for you, so you want to talk to the fearful inner child to find out more about what is going on for him or her.

**Step 3:** Using your dominant hand: right one if you are right-handed and left if you are left-handed, write in your notebook as if you are talking to a child. For example, Dear Fearful Child, How are you? Would you please tell me what you are feeling in relation to _____ (the stress you described in Step 1).

**Step 4:** Use your non-dominant hand to let the inner child answer you. Your non-dominant hand may not write so well, but it will access your unconscious mind as it is less controlled by your ego. It will look like a child's writing. Using your non-dominant hand will be awkward at first, but you will get used to it. Now let the child answer by writing down whatever comes to your mind. Do not analyze or think about your answers. Just write what comes to you easily and freely. Trust the process. The information is coming from the child in your shadow. Write for as long as you want and get as much information as you can. Often the source experience of the child's fear or sadness will come forth, sooner or later.

For example, let us say you are afraid of going to a new job. The fearful inner child could tell you how she is afraid people won't like her, how it is hard to talk to new people, perhaps some painful rejection that occurred, etc, etc. Let it flow—all from the child's immature and non-logical perspective. Let go of your doubts about the process; they are coming from your ego.

**Step 5:** Now you will respond to the inner child by writing back with your dominant hand. You thank the child for the information, tell him/her you understand the fear or pain, and then re-parent the child by explaining the situation in mature, adult terms. For example, "I am sorry it was scary for you, but taking risks is how we grow" etc, etc. Perhaps remind the child of a time when you did take a risk and it worked out. Also thank the child for sharing these feelings and tell her she is helping you heal by resolving these fears and building more confidence for the challenges in life. The inner child wants to know what you think. You are his/her parent, and you are raising the child in a loving and responsible manner.

**Step 6:** If the inner child is angry, let her rant and rave as long as she wants. Let her give all the reasons she is so upset. Perhaps she will tell you about experiences in your/her childhood that made her angry too. Remember she doesn't have logic yet. When she is done, you write back with your dominant hand that you are looking deeper into the problem that you both created in order to learn and gain wisdom. You are letting the contents of your shadow out in a controlled manner instead of having it come out only through shadow projection.

**Step 7:** Do the above exercises again with another stressful event in your life.

As you progress with your inner child writing, you will become familiar with each inner child. For example, you will learn more about your fears in various situations.

Congratulations. You are learning a powerful method for self-healing. It is based on the psychological truth—**what is revealed is healed**, or, what was unconscious is now conscious. The wounded part of you that has been stored in your shadow since childhood is now recognized, acknowledged and loved. You have many inner children within you, each containing a suppressed or denied pattern of emotion. There are fearful, angry, critical, abandoned, shy, inadequate inner children, just to mention a few. You know of them when an emotion comes up for you in any situation. Each of them needs to be parented by you. You can help them to release their emotional pain and help them to grow up. In this manner they will stop their endless efforts at healing through shadow projection and creating negative experiences in your life.

Inner child writing allows you to transform any stressful episode into a healing experience. **It is the most important tool for you to take away from these exercises.** So practice this method and become proficient in it because it will help you transform the difficulties in your life into opportunities for self-understanding and personal growth. If something stressful occurs during your day, jot it down so you can do inner child writing later in the evening.

For a more comprehensive look at this powerful healing tool, I suggest you find an inner child therapist in your area, and/or, follow the guidance of one of the books listed below:

*Your Inner Child of the Past,* Hugh Missildine
*The Inner Child Workbook: What to Do with Your Past When It Just Won't Go Away,* Cathryn L. Taylor
*Healing the Child Within,* Charles L. Whitfield, MD
*Recovery of Your Inner Child,* Lucia Capacchione, Ph.D.

### A Word of Warning

Initially, it is very common to resist doing inner child writing. You may come up with doubts about its effectiveness, or how it is done, or if you are really accessing your unconscious mind. You may find yourself procrastinating doing the writing, or resisting in other ways. The reason for your doubts and hesitation is your ego. The purpose of the ego is to keep the painful parts of your life hidden in your shadow, so you can continue the façade of who you think you are, regardless of how accurate the façade really is. The ego defends against growth and change, even amidst the most painful life circumstances.

Practice inner child writing and you will quickly develop confidence in this powerful healing tool.

Robert Johnson, the acclaimed Jungian analyst and best-selling author, writes about the importance of shadow discharge with these words taken from his book, *Owning Your Own Shadow:*

> To honor and accept one's shadow is a profound spiritual discipline. It is whole-making and thus holy and the most important experience of a lifetime

## Exercise 7: Exploring the Emotional Wounds Behind an Illness

Unfortunately, there is no simple formula that we can use to find the cause of every disease. We live in a complex world filled with potential challenges to our health—pollution, environmental toxins, many opportunities for poor nutrition, heredity, stress at every turn, bad health habits, to name a few. While the majority of medical research is focused on external cause of illness, there is a clear and growing body of research that reveals the causes of illness that come from within us. It is certainly wise to eat a good diet, avoid toxins, drink pure water, get plenty of rest and take care of ourselves physically, but our greatest resource for healthy living is to understand how we draw illness to ourselves and don't even know we are doing it. I believe that conscious and unconscious factors are the most important factors in the development of illness. Dr. Carl Simonton, a pioneer of psychological healing in cancer patients, said it another way: "Some patients find no way to solve their problems except through illness."

The exercises in this section are for people who have disease. They are designed to help you track backwards from the time your illness began and into the stressful experiences that coalesced over months, years, or even decades, to make you susceptible to physical disease. In this process you will become an explorer of your own mind, entering the darkness of your shadow, discovering dysfunctional beliefs and crying tears that are long overdue. It will be a great adventure of self-discovery, for as Norman Cousins so simply told us, "your body has been trying to tell you something and you haven't been listening."

The majority of illness arises when shadow projection is repeatedly denied over time. We deny shadow projection when we fail to accept responsibility for our experiences and refuse to allow the stored emotional traumas in the shadow to be felt fully and thereby "owned." In other words, we play victim and stuff our emotions. The shadow keeps discharging and we keep denying the emotions with all kinds of good reasons as we blame others for our problems. The tension keeps building and eventually we "find no way to solve our problems except through illness." The shadow is going to dump its contents somewhere—if not into your life for healing, then into your body for disease. Now the urgency is greater and the message louder.

In tribal societies, the shaman would intuitively guide patients toward resolution of their emotional wounds. But in our society we take pills to get rid of symptoms, and no one points us to the inner healing that is beckoning.

These exercises are especially useful for people with serious illness, like cancer, heart disease, ulcerative colitis, rheumatoid arthritis, and lupus, but they can be used for any illness. Please remember what you read in Chapter 7, the inner healing that is prompted by your illness may or may not cure your physical disease. Often it will, sometimes it does not.

So, let us begin.

**Step 1:** In your notebook, write down the month and year that you were first diagnosed with your medical problem. You may have had symptoms earlier, but use the time of diagnosis. Now list all of the major stressful experiences that occurred before the diagnosis and number them one, two, three, etc. Sit quietly and think back to get as much detail as possible. Examples might be—marital conflict, job stress, family problems, etc. You want to go as far back into time as you can. Cancer, for example, can take many years and sometimes decades to slowly grow prior to diagnosis. Try and take your list of stressful experiences all the way back to childhood. If you have trouble remembering, ask family members or friends to help you make your list.

**Step 2:** Next, write down the number of months or years that each of the numbered stress lasted for. Some of them can last for decades, even a lifetime.

**Step 3:** Next, consider which of the stresses on your list is still going on. In other words, the stressful issue is still unresolved. Write "still current" next to these stresses.

**Step 4:** Take each item on your list, starting with the most recent, and write a *description* of what happened in the stressful episode, as well as an *explanation* as to why it happened as you see it. Don't worry about your prose, just let the information flow out of you. Take your time and write for as long as you can, putting in as much detail as possible. Write at least a few paragraphs and preferably a few pages. You may want to contemplate the stressful episodes for a day or so and add to your original writing.

**Step 5:** Using the written story for the most recent stress, write down the person or thing that you thought was responsible for the problem. In other words, who or what did you blame at the time the stress occurred. Then do the same thing for each stressful episode on your list.

 These are the people you gave your power to, as you avoided responsibility for the episode.

**Step 6:** Go over each story on your list, starting with the most recent, and write down the emotions you were feeling at that time. Start with the most intense or predominant feeling and then list the others you felt as well. Use this list of feelings to be as complete as you can:

| | | | | |
|---|---|---|---|---|
| fear | anger | hate | worry | hurt |
| shame | guilt | sadness | frustration | discouragement |
| love | sympathy | happiness | caring | shyness |

**Step 7:** Rate the intensity of each feeling you have listed for each story on a scale of 1 to 10, 1 being the weakest and 10 being maximally strong, or overwhelming.

**Step 8:** Take each feeling on your lists and contemplate for a moment how much you expressed the feeling to others versus holding the feeling in. Write EXPRESSED next to the ones you expressed and HELD IN next to the others.

 As you know, when you hold in a feeling you prevent the shadow from discharging its emotional content and the problem is less likely to resolve. Often you will find the same kind of emotional event replayed later on, again and again.

 Expressed feelings can also recur if you don't take responsibility for the episode and blame someone else. Expressed emotions are released to some extent, but for complete shadow discharge it is best to take full personal responsibility.

**Step 9:** Now review each of the stories on your list and see if there was a time when the stress was so overwhelming or recurrent that you felt like giving up. Did you feel helpless or hopeless? Did you think to yourself, "This is too much, I can't take it anymore." (I am not talking about suicide here, although that is certainly one result of such feelings.)

If you felt this way, how long did these despairing feelings last? Days, weeks, months, perhaps years?

As you know, your body is strongly influenced by what goes on in your mind. The immune system is very sensitive to mental stress especially if it is sustained over long periods of time. Remember that one feature of many people with cancer is this hopeless, helpless feeling. It is as if the immune system hears "this is too much, I can't take it anymore" long enough, and eventually offers you a way out of your dilemma through death.

**Step 10:** Let's look for passion in your life. Go over your stories for each stressful episode one more time and think of the months or years between the challenging episodes. How often were you involved in some activity that you were passionate about? Try to remember times when you were really excited and enthusiastic about something and you couldn't wait to do more of it. Possibly there was a job or special project, maybe a hobby or community activity of some kind, a new lover or relationship, perhaps a time of learning in school. How long did the episode last? How many of them did you have? Compare the length of time under stress versus the length of time involved in a passionate excitement. How well did you accomplish the important things in your life?

Every cell in your body has a purpose that it follows with unswerving dedication. If you, the person living in those 100 trillion cells, has no sense of fulfilling accomplishment, nothing to get turned on about, it affects your body too. Research has shown that passionate, fulfilling activities help the body to work better in many ways.

Ralph Waldo Emerson said the same thing with greater eloquence when he wrote:

> Enthusiasm is one of the most powerful engines of success. When you do a thing, do it with all your might. Put your whole soul into it. Stamp

it with your personality. Be active, be energetic, be enthusiastic and faithful, and you will accomplish your object. Nothing great was ever achieved without enthusiasm.

If these words do not describe your life in the past, perhaps they can describe your healing process.

**Step 11:** Now look back on your life and consider one of the highest passions of all—spirituality. If you are a religious person, how deeply do the spiritual truths touch you? Was your religion a routine, or a powerful force that affected every aspect of your life? How important were prayer, meditation, and the company of spiritual people to the daily functioning of your life? If you do not consider yourself a religious person, how strongly do you believe in yourself?

**Step 12:** Now go back to Step 6 in this exercise and take each of the emotions you experienced during the difficult times in your life and do inner child writing, as described in Exercise 6. Write to the angry child, the hurt or wounded child, the fearful child, or the abused child. These wounded parts of you have been in your shadow since childhood and they are calling for attention. They are the rejected parts of you that need loving attention and acceptance. Let each of them write his or her story.

Remember, what is revealed is healed. Inner child writing helps you reveal deep wounds and is an essential tool for healing. It can be used for every challenging occurrence in the past and for those yet to come. And, do not judge yourself, or others, for what has happened in the past. We will talk about forgiveness in Exercise 12.

Congratulations. This exercise is a long and challenging one. But the rewards are immense. You can resolve these stressful issues even though they may have been around for years. You make big changes in your life by using this exercise.

Such personal transformation becomes the exception to what the English poet, W.H. Auden meant when he wrote:

We would rather be ruined than changed; we would rather die in our dread than climb the cross of the moment and let our illusions die.

## Exercise 8: Mirroring—Discharging Your Shadow Every Day

A teacher of mine once told me that "people live in their unconscious mind." It took me a while to understand what she meant and it goes something like this. We create our experiences in life by making conscious choices about what we want to do. As everyone knows, things don't always turn out the way we want them to. Unexpected turns in the road occur frequently, in spite of our best efforts to "control" the events in our lives. Accidents, misfortunes, surprises, and challenges occur quite often and with painful, frustrating, disappointing, heart-breaking, and frightening effects on the course of our lives. These unfortunate experiences can occur again and again, making us wonder if there is any sense to life. The answer lies in the unconscious mind, or shadow. The shadow is constantly trying to discharge its storehouse of disowned emotions. If we take responsibility for the experience and feel, or own, all the emotions that arise within us, we have healed an emotional wound carried in the shadow. In this manner, the painful experiences in life offer inner healing. If we stuff our feelings, or play victim and blame others for our problems, shadow discharge does not occur and we are destined to repeat the process again and again.

Shadow projection is a relentless process that happens every day all day, hence, "living in the unconscious mind." It occurs with the little events of the day as well as the big catastrophes. The key to successful shadow discharge is expressing your feelings and owning the experience as your creation, or co-creation with others around you.

Mirroring is a term for the observation of yourself as reflected in the mirror of your daily experience. It is an invitation to self-exploration, self-understanding and is a key to personal growth and responsible living. It is especially useful in your relationships with others in your life and at work where you spend so much of your time. For example, if a fellow employee at work makes an uncalled for derogatory remark about you and you feel embarrassed and hurt, a standard victim response would be to blame the person as a jerk, perhaps get angry, maybe retaliate, and simply try to forget about the whole thing as soon as possible. The responsible approach would be to know that everything that happens to you is "called forth" from the conscious or unconscious mind. If it brings up a feeling, express and own the emotion as fully as possible. Everyone has issues of self-worth, so that part of self is calling for healing. After the feeling is gone, think about the issue to see what more can be learned. Perhaps you have a belief about yourself that you are not good enough in some way.

In this manner, you transform the problems and challenges in your home and work life into opportunities for greater self-knowledge as you discharge your shadow and look for dysfunctional beliefs you have about yourself. I believe that such vigilant self-observation and personal responsibility releases the disowned contents of the shadow slowly and steadily, and therefore will reduce the likelihood for illness in the future.

**Step 1:** Your marriage, or primary relationship, offers the most frequent opportunities for mirroring, because your unconscious mind even decides whom you will marry. Harville Hendrix, Ph.D., a psychologist and founder/director of the Institute for Relationship Therapy, writes in his wonderful book, *Getting the Love You Want, A Guide for Couples,* "You fell in love because your old brain (part of the unconscious mind) had your partner confused with your parents! Your old brain believed that it had finally found the ideal candidate to make up for the psychological and emotional damage you experienced in childhood."

During the initial romantic phase of a relationship, we see only the good in our partner mixed with our fantasies of the ideal mate, but as this phase inevitably winds down, the road gets rougher as the mirroring begins. Hendrix writes: "As the illusion of romantic love slowly erodes, husbands and wives begin to:

1. Stir up each other's repressed behaviors and feelings.
2. Reinjure each other's childhood wounds.
3. Project their own negative traits onto each other."

Mirroring and responsibility for your experience then become the essential tools to complete the healing designed by your shadow. Without these tools, husbands and wives become victims, blaming each other for their problems. Then they risk becoming one of the

50% of marriages in this country that end in divorce, or, they settle into a dead and withdrawn marriage that offers no hope for real happiness, much less inner healing.

**Step 2:** Make a list in your notebook of all the problem areas you perceive in your marriage. If you are not married, you may use your lover, good friend, or any significant relationship.

Now consider each issue on your list as something you have called forth from the shadow in order to gain greater self-knowledge. Be grateful for the opportunity for healing with each issue, and take your time as you contemplate them. By taking full responsibility in this manner you begin the healing process offered to you by yourself, as reflected by your mate or friend.

**Step 3:** If the issue brings up a strong emotion in you, then by feeling it as much as you can without blame, you own it, thereby releasing it from your shadow. It has left the shadow and become conscious. What is revealed is healed. Repeat this process for each issue on your list that is emotional for you. Take your time. You are beginning to heal yourself as well as your relationship.

**Step 4:** Sometimes the issue on your list may be a "disown," which means your mate is acting out for you some part of you that you have rejected years ago. A common example is the person who was taught in childhood to not be angry. Your mate will be angry a lot, acting out your anger, until you own it. Review your list for disowns.

**Step 5:** Review your list once again and determine the inner child that is at the core of each issue—perhaps the angry child, wounded child, fearful child, or abandoned child. Do inner child writing for each of them.

**Step 6:** Now let us take a look at the thoughts and beliefs that shape your relationship. Complete each of the following sentences. You may repeat them if you wish.

I need my relationship to _____

I need my spouse to _____

I want my spouse to _____

I expect my spouse to _____
Relationships are meant to _____
To be happy in my relationship, I _____
When we argue, I_____
My parents taught me that relationships are_____

Talk these issues over with your mate, or friend.

**Step 7:** A successful relationship will use the principles of mirroring on a daily basis. For more detail, I recommend Dr. Hendrix's book, *Getting the Love You Want, A Guide for Couples.* For difficult problems, find a marriage counselor who believes in this type of approach to therapy.

**Step 8:** Your employment or work life provides the other fertile ground for self-exploration, because you spend a lot of hours there. The following is a summary of the approach used above for relationships, as it applies to the work environment.
   1. List the problem areas at work.
   2. Consider the problems as your creation (in co-creation with others).
   3. Own the emotion underlying each problem by feeling it without blame.
   4. Consider disowns for each problem area.
   5. Do inner child writing for each problem on your list.

**Step 9:** Complete the following sentences about your work or employment.
   To me work has always been _____
   My parents taught me that work was _____
   My co-workers consider me _____
   The purpose of my job is _____
   I was taught that money is _____
   (I suggest repeating the money sentence as many times as possible.)
   What I like least about work is _____
   What I love about work is _____

**Step 10**: These exercises will assist you in finding the thoughts and beliefs that determine your work experience. Change the ones that are dysfunctional into ones that support you. They will also help you to complete emotional healing thereby transforming the problem areas into greater self-knowledge. Your work experience will change as a result of such personal self-empowerment. You may find that your work is not right for you any longer. The next exercise will help you find the gift you have as you seek work that makes you feel excited and passionate.

## Exercise 9: Loving Yourself and Finding Your Passion

Love of self is the essential ingredient for good health, as well as success in life. It is also required for healing because it provides the motivation and determination to do whatever is necessary to get the job done. Self-love comes easily if your parents loved you unconditionally throughout your childhood, nurtured you whenever your feelings were hurt, praised your creativity and taught you to express your emotions. But for most of us love, the ultimate nutrient, wasn't available as much as we would like. Instead it was replaced with inattention, neglect, loss, smothering attention, excessive discipline, judgment and abuse by parents who did the best they could, but didn't know how to love fully. For these children self-love does not develop, and in its place shame is birthed. "I am bad," "I am not worthy," "I can't do it," "I am not lovable," "I don't deserve it," and the like, become the self-defining beliefs for a lifetime.

In this exercise you will learn about your current levels of self-love and self-esteem. You will also identify the inner children that perpetuate your self-concept, but are also waiting to be loved, healed and re-educated by you. You will look at obstacles to self-love, like criticism and judgment, and, you will explore ways you can express your self-esteem. Your dis-ease has gotten your attention and now offers you healing. The choices are yours.

**Step 1:** Write to complete the statements listed below **in reference to your childhood**. Consider each statement carefully and then write in your notebook what first comes to you. Write as much as you can, but at least a few sentences or a paragraph. If you are not sure about one of the statements, then guess.

I think of my mother as _____
I think of my father as _____
I think of my brother(s) as _____
I think of my sister(s) as _____
My mother treated me _____
My father treated me _____
My siblings treated me _____
My mother thought of me as _____
My father thought of me as _____
My mother's love for me could be described as _____
My father's love for me could be described as _____
My mother criticized me _____
My father criticized me _____
My mother loved me _____
My father loved me _____
My parents were angry when _____
My childhood was _____

**Step 2:** Complete the following phrases based on what you think about yourself now. Again write your answers in your notebook.

The main thing about me is _____
What I like most about myself is _____
What I like least about myself is _____
My body is _____
My health is _____
My illness is _____
When challenged with a big task, I _____
My self-esteem is _____
In life, I deserve _____
I am ashamed of _____
In relationships, I _____
If you really knew me, you would _____
I give the impression to others that _____

I pretend to be _____
I am afraid of _____
I resent_____
I hate _____
I give up_____
My work is_____
My spouse is _____
My life is _____
I find joy in _____

**Step 3:** Review your answers in Step 1 and identify inner children that need your love and attention. For example, if a parent abandoned you, you would have an abandoned or wounded inner child in your shadow that contained pain, lack of self-worth, and doubt. You would also have an angry inner child.

Using the inner child writing skills you learned in Exercise 7, write to each child. You want to learn what he/she thinks and feels about the world. You want to listen with compassion and comfort the child. Remember, **what is revealed is healed.**

**Step 4:** Review your responses in Step 2. They should give you a pretty good idea about your outlook on life and how much self-love you have. These are the beliefs that shape your world. What have you been drawing to yourself in the areas of health, relationship, employment, in general?

No one is as hard on you as you are. Your self-worth and self-esteem are the conditions of your life, and your purpose in life is to change them by changing your way of thinking. You have accepted the judgments and criticisms of others, but that is not the real you. The real you is inherently good, capable of giving and receiving love, and knows that you can do anything if you believe in yourself.

By taking responsibility for your wounds, you stop blaming others, and you start the healing process. Regardless of the experiences in your childhood, you are a child of God and you deserve success in your life. You deserve happiness, good health, and the respect and love of others in your life.

**Step 5:** Criticism can be damaging to your self-esteem. Keep in mind the truth about criticism: what others criticize in you is what they dislike in themselves. You can listen to them, but they are telling you about themselves in reality. Likewise, what you criticize in others is what you dislike about yourself. Make a list in your notebook of people you have criticized in the recent past and consider what this tells you about you. Make another list of people who have criticized you and contemplate what this tells you about them.

**Step 6:** Judgment is opposite to the acceptance birthed by love. It is your shame, or, "I am bad," that brings forth your judgment and blame of others. You have never been bad. You have only had experiences that will teach you and lead you to greater self-love. What we judge in others is what we judge in ourselves. Make a list in your notebook of people that you have judged by thinking they were wrong or bad in some way. Make another list of people who have judged you in some way. What do these lists tell you about yourself and others?

**Step 7:** An essential part of your healing process is to find your passion in life. Passion is based on self-love and harmonizes the functioning of the body like nothing else.

Paul Ferrini has written a wonderful series of books called *Reflections of the Christ Mind.* In Part II, *Silence of the Heart,* Christ speaks about your gift with the following words:

> The gifts you have been given in this life do not belong to you alone. They belong to everyone. Do not be selfish and withhold them. Do not be selfish and imprison yourself in a lifestyle that holds your spirit hostage and provides no spontaneity or grace in your life.
>
> Do not withhold your gift from others. Do not make the mistake of thinking that you have no gift to give. Everyone has a gift. But don't compare your gift to the gifts of others, or you may not value it sufficiently.
>
> Your gift brings joy to yourself and joy to others. If there is no joy in your life, it is because you are withholding your gift. You are not

trusting it. You are not actively bringing the gift forward into manifestation in your life.

What brings you joy? What is your gift from God? Write your answers to these questions in your journal. Consider these questions in the days to come and add to your writings. Your health, and possibly your life, depends on it.

**Step 8:** Your self-esteem will improve if you are around people who have it already. Consider joining a group of people who are involved in something that brings you joy or excitement. Find a church group, club, or some organization with people who are nurturing and supportive. They can help you build your self-love.

**Step 9:** If you feel you need more work to increase your self-esteem, I suggest reading one or more of the following books:
* *How to Raise Your Self-Esteem,* by Nathaniel Branden
* *Breaking the Chain of Low Self-Esteem,* by Marilyn J. Sorensen, Ph.D.

You can also find a counselor or therapist to help you, but ask the person about their experience with low self-esteem. Low self-esteem is not included in the diagnostic manuals for psychological problems, so many therapists do not consider it as a primary problem for therapy.

In summary, your thoughts about yourself shape your experience. You can change your thoughts. Your shadow projects experiences into your life based on your childhood issues. You can heal and transform your shadow. Be gentle, compassionate and patient with yourself. Your self-love and self-acceptance will grow. The important thing is that you started a wonderful journey of self-discovery.

## Exercise 10: Releasing Resentment

The difficulties and challenges in life can be overwhelming. In my medical practice over the years, I have listened to thousands of intensely painful stories as patients recounted the dramas that preceded the onset of their illness. Years of abusive marital conflict, child abuse and neglect, abandonment, relentlessly stressful employment, and violent family conflict are just a few examples of the chronic discord that entangles a lot of people in our society. It is easy to become addicted to the pain and build an identity around our wounds. Some people tell their painful stories over and over again, while others recoil into isolation and depression, escaping their prisons only to go to the doctor.

Doctors offer an endless assortment of pills to ease the suffering for a moment. Pain pills, tranquilizers, anti-depressants and other medications are offered to these "victims" of dis-ease.

It is easy to see how anger at an abusive spouse can become resentment and last for years, perhaps decades. Occasionally the resentment births thoughts of revenge. But resentment, or chronic anger, is debilitating to the mindbody, just like anxiety and depression. Anger is a powerful emotion that allows you to protect yourself, set boundaries and take action to solve problems with authority. It activates the stress system, preparing you for action, in case you need it to make your point. The recurrent anger of the resentful person is much like the hostility of the cardiac patient. In both, the fight or flight system is activated repetitively day in and day out which is damaging to the body, producing common symptoms, like headache and eventually contributing to disease.

Pain and suffering are inevitable for us all. They are the greatest teachers in this world. Pain is the messenger that gets our attention and motivates us to make changes in our life. But a messenger should leave once the message is heard. If pain and suffering move in and become our constant companion, we are resisting the message and refusing to change. Prolonged pain and suffering are due to our resistance to the lessons of life. These are lessons we ourselves have authored from our beliefs and shadow projection. Instead of looking within for answers, we blame someone else, give our power away, and invite the messenger to move in.

In this exercise you will identify areas in your life where you hold resentment. You will look at how it may be affecting your body. You will also have the opportunity to accept the message and look within yourself for answers. In doing all this you will transform your resentment into self-understanding and greater personal power.

This exercise is especially important for people who have the following medical diagnoses: rheumatoid arthritis, cancer, lupus, and asthma.

**Step 1:** In your notebook, write down all the people, organizations, or anything that you have repeatedly resented in the past. Do not include short-term resentments that last for a short time and then go away completely. The significant resentments are the ones that keep popping into your mind, say, whenever you see the person, and recur over months and years. Think carefully—it could be the IRS or some politician, or some activity that you dislike. Write down as many as you can.

**Step 2:** Take each person, or item, on your list and write a narrative about the situation. How it started. What are the reasons for the problem? Why it kept recurring. Write as long as you like, but at least one page. Repeat the process for each person or item on your list of resentments.

**Step 3:** Now write down what happened to your body during the time of each recurrent resentment. Think back over the years and remember if you had any health problems during the time of each resentment. Headaches, high blood pressure, arthritis, etc, etc.

The original pain and suffering was the first message calling you to reevaluate your life and make changes that would improve your life. The changes could be inside you and reflect a need for a new way of communication, establishing clear boundaries, forgiveness, and the like. The changes could also be outside you in your life circumstances. Possibly you could have left the person or taken some action that would have resolved the problem.

Since you didn't resolve the problem, your body began to give you messages as well. These were reminders to make changes in your life. Usually the body speaks softly at first: headaches, fatigue, upset stomach. But if the messages go unheeded, then the volume is turned up, eventually leading to all types of diseases. Your body is your friend, and symptoms are messages the body uses to heal itself. How well have you been listening?

**Step 4:** Now write down the person or thing you blamed for each resentment on your list. Who was responsible for the problem?

This is the person(s) that you gave your power to as you played victim to them. It was difficult for you to do anything to resolve the issue because you erroneously thought that this person(s) was at fault.

**Step 5:** Now reread each narrative from Step 2 and write down the beliefs you held that sustained the resentful situation. For example, resentment towards a spouse might have a belief like, "He never listens to me." For each resentment, list as many beliefs as you can. Consider how each belief contributed to the resentment over time. Your beliefs help to create your reality, and you need to release those that sustain your pain. No matter how long you have held a dysfunctional belief, it can be released. You are in charge of your consciousness. You can take back the power to make the changes needed.

**Step 6:** Now take each belief from Step 5 and change it into a belief that can help you resolve the problem that created the resentment. For example, "he never listens to me" can become, "he will listen if I communicate clearly," or, "if he doesn't listen, I will find someone who will."

**Step 7:** Now review each narrative from Step 2 once again and identify your inner children involved in the scenario. Resentment is anger, so there definitely will be an angry inner child. Perhaps there is a fearful one as well or possibly a wounded child. Use the inner child writing skills you learned in Exercise 7 and write to each child. Let the child get all her anger out. Allow the child to give her reasons for the situation. Take your time and write as long as you can. Once the child has had her say, then thank the child, re-educate her based on how you see the situation now. Repeat the process for each resentment on your list. There is no rush. It may take a while to complete the inner child writing for this exercise.

Congratulations! You have taken steps toward releasing resentment in your life. Resentment is sustained anger and it is okay to express your anger. Anger is a useful emotion designed to protect you and then to be released. If you received the belief from your parents that anger is bad and you shouldn't express it, simply acknowledge another dysfunctional belief that was handed down to you and let it go. The challenges in life are to help you grow. Letting go of dysfunctional beliefs is an essential part of the process. You have also pulled from your shadow some of the anger and pain held by your inner children. What was previously unconscious is now conscious and will be released from you. As you release the shadow contents that created your problem, the problem too will change. You have taken back power you gave to others and you understand more about why you drew the problem to you. Now it will change. You will see.

## Exercise 11: Transforming Anger and Hostility

Hostility is a feature of the heart disease personality as well as other illnesses, such as rheumatoid arthritis. Hostility includes cynicism, persistent mistrust of others, and aggression. At the core of each aspect of hostility lies anger. Anger has become a way of life. It is a theme that is echoed throughout the day, and in our complex society there is no shortage of things to be angry about. The hostile person has plenty of good reasons for sustaining his anger and may not even recognize the degree of his hostility.

Hostility, like resentment, carries a heavy price tag. It produces a chronic activation of the fight/flight system which, in turn, wears down the bodymind, eventually leading to disease. High blood pressure, heart disease, headaches, stomach upset, gastritis, arthritis, are a few of the signs that may be due to chronic anger.

So what are hostile people so angry about? That is what you will explore in this exercise.

**Step 1:** Are you chronically angry, even hostile at times? Since you are reading this, you are probably considering the issue. You may have coronary artery disease and have read about hostility in that regard. Persistently angry people often don't categorize themselves that way. After all, they believe that they have a lot of good reasons to be angry: endless challenges at work, a dysfunctional society, etc, etc. And the ego does a good job of convincing us that we are right as it strives to make sense of the world and keep the pain of childhood out of conscious experience. If you are not sure, ask other people in your life whether you seem angry a lot, aggressive or competitive, cynical and perhaps hostile at times.

**Step 2:** Writing in your notebook, complete each of the following sentences as many times as you can. Think carefully and repeat the sentence again and again.

I am angry about _____
I am cynical about _____
I do not trust _____
I can be aggressive about _____
I get hostile about _____
I do not believe _____
I feel rushed _____

How long have these issues angered or bothered you? Write the number of months or years next to each sentence listed above.

There is nothing wrong with anger. It is a strong emotion that everyone experiences. The appropriate expression of anger is an essential part of a healthy personality. However, when anger is acted upon, violence can occur. It is important to know that you can feel your feelings without acting upon them. Anger, like all emotions, is to be felt and released without blame. However, it is dangerous to get stuck in anger.

**Step 3:** What has your body been telling you over the years? If you have heart disease, think back as to what was going on in your life in the few years prior to the first heart attack or first episode of angina. Were you the Type A personality with "hurry sickness"—too much to do in too little time? What other symptoms did you notice over the years? Headache, gastritis, fatigue, depression, etc. These are the messages from your body, perhaps telling you to slow down a bit.

Write in your notebook the body signals that you recall prior to the onset of your heart disease.

**Step 4:** Now complete each sentence below as many times as you can, again writing your responses in your notebook.

When I was a teenager, I was angry about _____

When I was a teenager, I was cynical about _____

When I was a teenager, I was aggressive when _____

When I was a teenager, I did not trust _____

When I was a teenager, I did not trust because_____

When I was a teenager, it hurt me when _____

When I was a teenager, I was sad when _____

When I was a teenager, I was afraid _____

Do you recall any health problems in your teen years?

**Step 5:** Now complete the following sentence as many times as possible, again writing your responses in your notebook.

In my childhood, I was angry about_____

In my childhood, I did not trust _____

In my childhood, I did not trust because _____

In my childhood, I was aggressive when_____

In my childhood, I was sad when_____

In my childhood, I was really hurt when _____

In my childhood, I was afraid of _____

In my childhood, anger was _____

In my childhood, crying was _____

Do you recall any recurrent health problems in your childhood?

**Step 6:** In order to transform anger you must have the courage to look beneath it and find the hurt, sadness, or fear. It takes courage to step out of long-established ego-based identity and look for an underlying truth. It takes courage to set aside a familiar, tough and aggressive attitude and become vulnerable. It takes courage to let go of the façade, tell the truth about oneself, thereby becoming authentic.

People get angry because their feelings are hurt in some way. We get angry while driving when another driver does not respect us. It hurts to be disrespected and disregarded. We get angry at the government because they do not treat us the way we want to be treated. We get angry at work when our plans are thwarted and we fear we may not do as well as expected.

Review your sentences in Step 2 and write down next to each sentence the hurt, pain, sadness or fear that was beneath your anger, cynicism, and aggression. Do the same for Step 4 and Step 5. If you are not sure about an answer, give it your best guess.

**Step 7:** Now think back to your childhood, and complete the following sentences, again writing your responses in your notebook. Write the first thing that comes to your mind. Your answers can be as long as you like and you can repeat the sentence if you wish. If your parents were divorced, consider your stepparent, if appropriate.

My mother was _____

My relationship with my mother was _____

The way my mother took care of me was _____

My father was _____

My relationship with my father was _____

The way my father took care of me was _____

When I cried, my parents _____

**Step 8:** Medical research shows that heart disease patients have a tremendous amount of emotional pain in childhood. Their heart is wounded in these early years by abandonment, neglect, abuse, excessive control, cold and distant parents, and myriad other invalidating experiences. The shadow is seeded early on with pain, sadness, fear and anger. The intensity of these feelings can be overwhelming. Often the child unconsciously decides to avoid emotions in the future and to stay in the relative safety of the intellect where issues can be reasoned through. In doing so, emotional wound healing is thwarted, often for a lifetime.

Lacking for parental love, the wounded child seeks love through achievement. By doing more and more, perhaps he can find the love that he needs. His sense of self-worth is low, providing another reason for endless hard work for recognition and achievement.

Using the inner child writing skills you learned in Exercise 7, write to the angry child, fearful child, wounded or abused child, abandoned child, or any other that seems appropriate for you. Let the angry child rant and rave as long as he wants about the current issue and then let him recount the conditions of his childhood, if he wants. Let each child express his feelings as long as possible. Then thank the child and express your understanding at his problems. Re-parent the child by telling him about healthy relationships, how it should have been, and finally, how you will take care of him and protect him because you love him.

**Step 9:** If you, like a lot of people in our society, suffer from "hurry sickness" or Type A behavior, it is a good idea to learn to meditate. Setting aside 20 minutes daily to quiet your mind will have innumerable benefits on your mental and physical health. There are many books on meditation of various types. I recommend *Full Catastrophe Living—Using the Wisdom of Your Body and Mind to Face Stress, Pain and Illness,* written by Jon Kabat-Zinn, a psychologist working at the University of Massachusetts Medical Center and *The Power of Now,* written by Eckhart Tolle.

By using the principles in these exercises, you can transform your anger into the underlying emotion of pain, fear, or sadness. By expressing these feelings you expand your emotional IQ and re-ignite emotional wound healing in your life. Inner child writing will help you to heal your wounds from childhood. Remember that emotional blockage precedes coronary artery blockage. You have opened your heart, both figuratively and literally.

### Exercise 12: The Healing Power of Forgiveness

*The weak can never forgive. Forgiveness is the attribute of the strong.*

Mohandas Gandhi

Paul Ferrini writes in his wonderful book, *Love Without Conditions, Reflections of the Christ Mind:* "The willingness to forgive yourself and release others from your judgment is the greatest power you can know while you live in this embodiment." In the world we live in, it is so easy to feel victimized and to judge and blame others for our problems. It is even easier to blame ourselves for the "wrongs" we have done and to add to our burden of guilt and shame. But as we have seen, blaming others, or ourselves, reflects our resistance to learning the lessons of life. These are lessons that we ourselves have unknowingly authored from our shadow and the beliefs handed to us by our parents. Indeed, the pain and suffering in life are not meant to torment us endlessly, but rather to help us heal and gain wisdom and self-understanding. Forgiveness of others and ourselves is the essence of healing.

People who hold resentment and hostility toward others lock themselves into a cycle of judgment, blame, pain and suffering. People who blame themselves for mistakes in life lock themselves into guilt, shame, pain and suffering. In both cases, the only way out is to take responsibility for the problem, honor the feelings that arise, learn from the experience and then, through forgiveness, let it go. No wonder Christ, in Ferrini's book, calls forgiveness the greatest power you can know.

The well-known author Caroline Myss refers to forgiveness with similar awe, when she wrote in *Anatomy of the Spirit:*

> . . . forgiveness is a complex act of consciousness, one that liberates the psyche and soul from the need for personal vengeance and the perception of oneself as a victim. More than releasing from blame the people who caused our wounds, forgiveness means releasing the control that the perception of victim-hood has over our psyches. The liberation that forgiveness generates comes in the transition to a higher state of consciousness—not just in theory, but energetically and biologically. In fact, the consequence of a genuine act of forgiveness borders on the miraculous. It may, in my view, contain the energy that generates miracles themselves.

To forgive yourself is an expression of your love and acceptance of yourself. To forgive others is also an expression of your love and acceptance of what you have created in your life. Forgiveness is the power of love that changes guilt into self-love, blame into responsibility, and suffering into wisdom.

In this exercise you will consider what the power of forgiveness can do for you in your healing process.

**Step 1:** Make a list of all the people that have caused significant pain for you at any time in your life. Go back to childhood and consider those that hurt you and you still feel the pain. You may have carried your wounds for years, perhaps a lifetime. They may have become part of your identity. You may refer back to Exercise 4, or the Resentment exercise if you wish.

**Step 2:** Now take each person on your list and consider the painful situation in light of your understanding of shadow projection and personal responsibility for experience. In reality, you called the painful event to yourself. Unconsciously, you wrote the script and you asked the person to play the role. When he/she did, you freaked out. Perhaps you have blamed him/her all these years.

Through inner child writing you have already owned a lot of the emotional pain contained in the people and events on your list. Now is the time to forgive yourself. You called forth your lessons in life in order to grow, to gain wisdom and become whole by making the dark parts of self come into the light of consciousness. Take a moment to forgive yourself for these painful episodes.

**Step 3:** Now go over your list once again and contemplate each person and the events that caused you pain. Consider the viewpoint of each person who hurt you. When you are ready, write a letter of forgiveness for each person on your list. Be careful not to write words of blame. Make your letter as genuine and complete as you can. You may want to revise your letter over a few days. When it is done, *burn* it as you release the wound completely.

You may want to talk to the people on your list and share your forgiveness with them, but be careful as you may produce strong feelings in people. Also, not everyone shares your new vision of personal responsibility for experience. It is up to you.

**Step 4:** When children feel they have done something wrong, they feel guilty. Often young children feel they are responsible for the problems of their parents or other family members, even though there is nothing they can do at such an early age. Consequently, children feel they have failed to help mom or dad and they feel guilty about it. In dysfunctional families people blame others for their problems, adding more to the burden of guilt.

Take a moment to recall your childhood. Consider mom, dad, brothers and sisters. Did you feel responsible for someone and then felt guilty about it? An example would be: "I felt responsible for my sister's accident. I could have helped." Or, "I feel bad that I couldn't make my mother happier." Make a list of the things you felt guilty about in your childhood.

Now consider your adult life and look for guilt you feel about the people in your life. Make another list of the things you felt guilty about since childhood.

**Step 5:** Now consider the truth that you have never done anything bad in your entire life. As a child, how can you be responsible for anyone else's problems? We each create our own problems—no one else does it for us.

And in your adult life, you have not done anything bad. The unfortunate experiences in life are created for learning, not for judgment. We all make mistakes, for that is how we learn.

Take your lists of things you feel guilt about from Step 4 above and burn them, forgiving yourself for your misunderstanding.

Stay aware of the patterns in your life that are based on guilt and shame. Watch your thoughts and interactions with others in your life. Remember that everything you think or say about someone in your life reflects what you think about yourself. What you judge in another is what you judge in yourself. And, what you criticize in another is what you criticize in yourself.

Congratulations! You have taken powerful and essential steps in the self-healing process by forgiving yourself and those around you. You have transformed resistance into acceptance and pain into love.

## Exercise 13: How to Transform Your Stress into Personal Signals for Self-knowledge

As you know, your stress system is designed to protect you from *physical* danger. That is why it is called the fight or flight system. If you are not convinced of how powerful your stress system is, rent the movie *Quest for Fire* and watch it. The cavemen in the movie are using their stress physiology for its designated purpose—taking physical action in order to survive. Do the stresses in your life require fighting and running? Society has certainly changed, but you have the exact same stress system as your ancient ancestors.

**Step 1:** Make a list of the areas in your body where you commonly feel stress. Start listening to what your body is telling you during your normal daily activities. As you notice stress reactions, make a note and grade them on a scale of 1 to 10, with one being the least intense and ten being the most intense you can imagine. Listen closely to see if you can pick up stress before it reaches its usual levels.

**Step 2:** For each stress experience there is an underlying emotion that has triggered your body's reaction. Anger, fear, resentment, anxiety, shame and guilt are a few common emotions that activate the body for action. For each stress experience, jot down on a piece of paper the corresponding emotion and review them at the end of your day.

**Step 3:** Using your list of emotions and bodily reactions to them, contemplate each one to see why you react in the way you do. For example, if you feel anger at slow freeway drivers, consider if the reactive emotion is helpful to your day or not. Sometimes our emotional reactions are not so clear. For example, you may feel anxiety at work and not really understand why you feel the way you do. Make a list of these 'not so clear' reactions. They represent areas of yourself that you need to understand better. They are markers at the edge and can be used to explore yourself in the exercises later on.

**Step 4:** Using your list of stresses and emotions, consider what thoughts, if any, preceded the stress reaction. What do these thoughts say about you? Are they necessary or can they be dropped in the days to come? Do you understand why you have these thoughts?

**Step 5:** Make a list of the diseases or problems you have in your life that are, or may be, stress related. Common examples include headaches, fatigue, high blood pressure, upset stomach, heart palpitations, depression, anxiety, and drug or alcohol use. Consider how long your body has been calling your attention to the problem you are experiencing. All symptoms and diseases are messages from your bodymind. How well have you listened to yourself in the past? How well do you understand the messages now?

**Step 6:** Make a list of the things you currently do to reduce stress in your life. Examples include alcohol, tranquilizers, anti-depressants, shopping, eating, exercise and communication with others. How well do these methods work for you? Have they led to greater self-understanding, or are they ways to ignore what your body is trying to tell you? How well have you honored your bodymind as you make your way through your day?

Listening to the messages coming from your bodymind is an essential part of self-healing. By doing the exercise outlined above day to day, you will transform a bothersome stress reaction into a signal to "look within." You will shift your stress system from a liability, which produces symptoms and diseases, to an asset which can guide you in your process of transformation and self-understanding.

## Exercise 14: Visualizing the Healing Power of Your Bodymind

"As long as one's knowledge of, and confidence in, the Power are greater than his fear of the condition with which he is faced, he can bring healing." These are the remarkable words of Frederick Bailes writing in his 1941 classic, *Your Mind Can Heal You.* Bailes documents many cases of serious illnesses being cured with what he calls Mental-Spiritual Treatments. These treatments are based on the healer and the patient believing fully in the "Universal Mind" as it expresses itself in perfect health in the body, and releasing the "pattern of sickness" (thoughts and emotions) that created the illness.

Now, I am not recommending mental healing, although I do believe that it is possible, but I am recommending the confidence and faith in the healing "power" that is built into everyone.

For Bailes, the "Power" was "Universal Mind," or God, which blended into, and was part of, the organizing intelligence of the human body. Bailes believed that the creative intelligence that orchestrates life in the body was the same universal intelligence that governed all life on earth, as well as the movement of the stars and planets that make up our universe. He believed that having faith in this universal intelligence within, and without, was the key to maintaining, and restoring, health. And for him, maintaining that faith was easy—all you had to do to enhance your faith was to observe the marvelous human body. When you consider for a moment all the incomprehensibly complex activities of the body, it is easy to be struck by the powerful intelligence that exists within us all, much beneath the level of conscious awareness. There are many examples, such as a single fertilized egg differentiating into the trillions of highly specialized cells that make up a baby, the maturation of a child, the healing of a cut on your finger, the workings of the immune system, hormones, vision, hearing, the ability to think, and memory are just a few of the wonders that we take for granted, but surely reflect the creative intelligence that binds us to the Divine.

In our world it is easy to lose confidence in yourself. It is even easier to lose confidence in your own body wisdom and its ability to heal. We go to doctors who tell us more about the disease than they tell us about our bodies' ability to heal it. We don't hear about the power of the body wisdom that kept us healthy until the onset of illness. Nor do we hear about how that wisdom can be restored. We live in a society where we are warned about the chances of being afflicted with this disease or that one, and many require screening tests for early detection. It is no wonder that when an illness does occur we feel victimized and helpless. We spend more time worrying about the problem than having faith in a greater power, whether we consider that greater power our body wisdom, God, or both.

So this exercise is about visualizing the healing power of your body. If you have an illness, it is your body wisdom that kept you healthy prior to your illness, and that same intelligence will help you to restore it. The exercises that you have already completed are meant to show you how you have interfered with the healing power of your body's intelligence.

Dr. Carl Simonton and Stephanie Simonton were the first to bring national attention to the power of visualization in treating serious disease. In their 1978 book, *Getting Well Again,* they document several dramatic cases of cancer remission based on a combination of traditional cancer therapy (surgery, chemotherapy and radiation) and relaxation followed by mental imagery. Dr. Simonton instructed his patients to enter a deeply relaxed state by releasing tension in all the muscles of the body from head to toe. He then asked them to visualize the radiation as "millions of tiny bullets" that would hit the cancer cells and kill them. Then they were to picture in their mind the white blood cells of the immune system coming in and carrying off the dead cancer cells so they could be flushed out of the body through the liver or kidney. And finally, they were to visualize the cancer shrinking in size as their health returned to normal. They were then instructed to do this relaxation/imagery exercise for ten to fifteen minutes three times daily for the duration of their cancer therapy.

The first patient who used this method was a 61-year-old man who was very weak with advanced throat cancer. However, he practiced avidly and began to improve and, much to Dr. Simonton's astonishment, his cancer was gone in two months. Other patients had similar results and the Simontons refined their mind/body program and offered it to thousands of cancer patients as an adjunct to traditional cancer therapy.

Not all of the Simonton's patients did as well as the first few, but many improved and lived longer than expected. As with any therapy, there are many variables from patient to patient. Some people are powerful visualizers and practice avidly, while others have problems with the technique and don't practice as intently for a variety of reasons.

I believe that visualization is an important technique to be used as a component of the mind/body treatment for illness, but it is not strong enough to stand alone. However, when it is added to emotional wound healing and the other Edgework methods, visualization will strengthen one's chances for recovery.

Perhaps the biggest reason for using visualization is to refine and focus this powerful tool in a positive and healing direction. You have been using visualization and imagery your entire life. We all use our imaginations to create pictures in our minds about how we would like our life to be. A mental picture precedes almost everything that we obtain and achieve in life. We hold these mental images in our mind's eye day after day, changing and refining them, and one day most of them appear. This is how you prepare to go to college, plan a wedding, buy a new car, go shopping at the grocery store, or go to the refrigerator for a glass of juice.

Not everything we visualize happens. We disturb our mental pictures with worries and doubts about our goals and ourselves. We think contradictory thoughts and cloud our images with pictures of failure, inadequacy and bad outcomes. Sometimes we use visualization negatively and see pictures of pain, suffering and the disease winning out in the long run. Therefore, the power of visualization is often weakened or misdirected and may contribute to disease. I am not asking you to stop all doubt and worry, but I am asking you to take charge of your visualizations and focus them positively as much as you can. The creative power of your mind can be used to help create health, or, to contribute to illness.

The following exercises will give you a mental picture of the awesome healing power of your bodymind. Use this visualization in your healing process and try to replace negative images about your health with pictures that represent this natural healing power. In doing so, you will follow Baile's advice and have more faith in your body's ability to heal than you have fear about your illness.

Shakti Gawain is an expert on successful visualization and has written several books on the topic. She writes in her popular first book, *Creative Visualization,* that the following three elements are required for successful visualization:

1. DESIRE
   You must have a strong clear desire and purpose for the visualization. Ms. Gawain recommends asking yourself, "Do I truly in my heart, desire this goal to be realized?"

2. BELIEF
If you strongly believe in your goal and the possibility of attaining it, you are more likely to succeed.
3. ACCEPTANCE
You must be fully willing to accept and have your goal.
So let us begin.

**Step 1:** In order to visualize effectively, you need to quiet your mind and relax your body. You also need a quiet location to do these exercises so telephones or other people won't disturb you. Use the following relaxation guidelines before each of the visualization exercises.

1. Sit in a comfortable chair with your feet flat on the floor and close your eyes.
2. For a few moments place your attention on your breath. Follow each breath in as you inhale and follow it out as you exhale. As you exhale, feel the tension leaving your body, as you become more and more relaxed.
3. Now focus your attention on your feet and see how they feel. If there is any tension in the muscles of your feet, release it.
4. Next move your awareness to both of your legs from the ankles to the hips and feel the muscles in your legs. You may tense your leg muscles and then feel them relax, as your body feels heavy and deeply relaxed.
5. Next focus your awareness on your pelvis and abdomen. Look for any tension and release it as your body is becoming more and more relaxed.
6. Next focus on your chest and release any tension that you notice. Feel your heart beating slowly as you sink deeper toward complete relaxation.
7. Next move your awareness to your arms and relax any muscle tension that you notice.
8. Now focus on your face. Tighten the muscles around your mouth and then your eyes and then fully relax these muscles as your whole body sinks into full relaxation.
9. Stay in this relaxed state for a few minutes and keep your attention in your body and away from your thoughts. Scan your

body from head to toe and again relax any tension that may have developed.

10. Thoughts may come and go during your relaxation exercise. If you find yourself thinking about something, simply refocus your awareness on your relaxed body.

This relaxed state is necessary for all the visualization exercises that follow. You may do this relaxation process quickly in preparation for each visualization below and for practice in the future.

**Step 2:** Immune system visualization.

Your immune system is as sophisticated as your brain and has protected you from infections, helped to heal your physical wounds and destroyed cancerous cells during every day of your life. If you have an immune-related illness, your immune system worked well until the onset of your problem. It will likely do so again if the disturbances to its function are removed. The majority of immune related medical problems arise after months and sometimes years of stress, worry, denied emotions and dysfunctional thoughts and beliefs. It will assist your healing process for you to visualize this intricate system functioning powerfully once again.

FOR CANCER PATIENTS:

1. Relax your body and mind like you did in Step 1.

2. Mentally see a staircase with ten steps. Starting at the top, count down from 10 to 1 and, as you take each step, feel yourself getting more and more relaxed, so by the time you are at the bottom you are deeply relaxed.

3. See your natural killer cells (NK cells) patrolling the inner recesses of your body, looking diligently for cancer cells. See them as powerful and persistent, using whatever image works for you. One of the NK cells finds a cancer cell and approaches. The cancer cell looks disoriented. After all, this is not a normal environment for the cancer cell and it does not always know what to do. It looks tattered and weak as if trying to hide and survive. The natural killer cell corners the cancer cell and slowly approaches. When the killer cell is next to the cancer cell, it releases a bolt of light, or electricity, which penetrates the cancer cell like

a bullet. The cancer cell breaks apart, spilling its cellular contents, and dies. The NK cell calls for a macrophage (big eater) which alters its previous course and heads straight for the dead cancer cell. The macrophage reaches the dead cancer cell and voraciously engulfs all the remains. Excited by their success, the two cells then resume their patrol of your body with greater energy, looking in every corner and recess for other cancer cells and repeating the process again and again. The two cells find a large primary cancer and signal other immune cells which arrive quickly. The NK cells attack the cancer and one by one all the cancer cells are killed.

4. Picture your cancer shrinking as the NK cells and macrophages do their dedicated work to heal you. The cellular debris left after the cancer cells' death is eaten by macrophages or sent to the liver for elimination from the body.

5. Picture yourself getting stronger and more excited as you prepare to return to a new life, which will be much different from the one you knew prior to your illness.

6. Picture yourself free of cancer, filled with energy and joyous to be alive.

7. See yourself reaching the goals (Exercise 9) that bring you passion, creativity and fulfillment in your life.

8. Now walk back up the staircase to the top and, as you reach the tenth step, open your eyes.

## SPECIAL NOTES FOR CANCER PATIENTS

1. If you are receiving chemotherapy, then add the following to the above exercise. Imagine the drug entering your bloodstream and circulating in your body. See the weaker cancer cells taking in the drug, becoming sick and dying. The immune cells are smarter and avoid the drug, but rush in to finish off the cancer cells.

2. If you are receiving radiation therapy, then add the following to the above exercise. Picture the radiation streaming through your body like tiny bullets and see them penetrating the weaker cancer cells and destroying them. The immune cells are not bothered by the radiation and they rush in to finish off the injured cancer cells.

## FOR PEOPLE WITH WEAK IMMUNE SYSTEM

Chronic fatigue syndrome, various forms of hepatitis, and chronic or recurrent infections indicate a weak immune system. Read the visualization for cancer patients and modify the exercise to show an aggressive, strong immune system circulating in your body and killing viruses instead of cancer cells. Otherwise, complete the visualization as written.

## FOR PEOPLE WITH AUTOIMMUNE DISORDERS

Rheumatoid arthritis, lupus and Graves disease are some of the illnesses that result from an overactive and aggressive immune system that begins to attack parts of your body. Read the visualization for cancer patients and modify the exercise to show a gentle, loving immune system removing the inflammation and soreness from the painful areas of your body, thus restoring normal function to those parts. See yourself moving gracefully and complete the rest of the visualization as written.

**Step 3:** Healthy heart visualization

As with the other imagery exercises, visualization is not meant to stand alone as the only approach to healing. I place it last in the exercises for good reason. The emotional and thought healing must come first. Visualization then allows you to imagine the creative intelligence of your body as it was prior to the onset of illness. Your heart worked well until it was disturbed by the things you did to yourself. It is important to replace diseased images of the body with those that represent its ability to heal and function with power like it was originally designed to do.

## FOR HEART PATIENTS

1. Relax your body and mind according to the guidelines in Step 1 noted above.
2. Mentally see a staircase with ten steps. Starting at the top, count down from 10 to 1 and, as you take each step, feel yourself getting more and more relaxed, so by the time you are at the bottom you are deeply relaxed.

3. Picture your heart in the center of your chest. It is about the size of a grapefruit, and you can see it pumping as it moves life-giving blood to every cell of your body.

4. Imagine the little cluster of cells in your heart that have the mysterious and tireless ability to spark a heartbeat every moment of every day throughout your life.

5. Imagine the power and dedication of your heart as it pumps your blood, which carries oxygen and nutrients throughout your body and then carries wastes to your kidney for elimination. This is the way your heart unconditionally loves every part of you—every cell in your body.

6. Picture the cells of your immune system carried in your blood to every part of your body in order to protect you from infection and cancer.

7. If the arteries to your heart have been narrowed, imagine them opening up widely so your heart, too, can receive more oxygen and nutrients. See the heart beat stronger as it receives more blood.

8. If your heart muscle has been damaged by a heart attack, picture the injured area shrinking and the surrounding muscle becoming stronger and easily compensating for the damaged area.

9. See your body getting stronger as it receives more oxygen, nutrition and love from your heart. Picture yourself active and doing what you enjoy in life.

10. Imagine how you can send love to the important people in your life.

11. Now walk back up the staircase and, as you reach the top, open your eyes.

**Step 4:** Visualizing the creative intelligence of your body.

This visualization is for everyone. It is designed to remind you of the magnificent and wondrous universe that exists within your body. Scientists who gaze at the complex movement of electrons, molecules, cells, hormones, enzymes, and antibodies, to mention a few, are as awestruck as the astronomer who gazes at the universe on a clear and starry night. This enchanted internal intelligence allows you to live your life day after day without consideration of what enzyme does what and which antibody should be created now. Regardless of how incredible this organizing intelligence really is, we take our bodies for granted. As the years go by we worry about what is wrong with them and rarely consider the creative intelligence that is still keeping us alive. Healing depends on restoring balance to the body's intricate systems. So this exercise will help you build confidence in the power of your bodymind for health and healing. Use any image that works for you, and don't worry about anatomical accuracy.

1. Relax your body and mind as you did in Step 1 noted above.
2. Mentally see a staircase with ten steps. Starting at the top, count down from 10 to 1 and, as you take each step, feel yourself getting more and more relaxed, so by the time you are at the bottom you are deeply relaxed.
3. See your heart pumping in your chest—weighing less than a pound, yet capable of pumping almost 2000 gallons of blood every day of your life with never a moment to rest.
4. Picture your lungs—each containing about 350 million alveoli, or little sacs, that allow your blood to pick up life-sustaining oxygen and release carbon dioxide.
5. See the inside of your bones where the marrow produces red blood cells at the astonishing rate of 2 million per second.
6. Imagine each red blood cell which contains 280 million molecules of hemoglobin, a marvelous molecule structured out of 10,000 separate atoms and designed to carry oxygen from your lungs to every cell in your body. The mapping of the complex hemoglobin molecule led to several Nobel prizes.
7. Picture the 30-foot long tube called your intestinal tract which takes the food you eat, breaks it down, and assimilates the good parts and rejects the undesirable parts.
8. Imagine your two kidneys, each weighing about 5 ounces, yet containing 50 miles of nephrons, or kidney cells, which filter your blood, retaining some molecules and releasing others, all so your blood and body fluids can maintain a precise life-giving mixture.
9. Imagine your immune system, which is made up of about one trillion cells that patrol every recess of your body in order to keep

you from getting infections. The coordination of this marvelous system is thought to be as sophisticated and complex as your brain.

10. Picture the natural killer cells (NK cells) of your immune system approaching a cell in your body that has gone awry and become cancerous. See the NK cell shoot a beam of light into the cancer cell, which breaks apart and dies. This has occurred every day of your life.

11. Imagine your brain, a three-pound organ, containing 12 billion brain cells. It is believed that your brain has the ability to store more information than all the libraries in the world.

12. Picture your brain as it monitors thousands of functions inside your body, such as breathing, blood circulation, and digestion, while integrating this with the constant flow of information coming through the senses from the world around you. And, this is all done without you having to think about it at all.

13. Imagine the 1/8th inch thick outer layer of your cerebral cortex, a folded sheet of gray matter that provides you with awareness and the ability to think.

14. Imagine the force that unzips one of your DNA molecules, permitting it to form two new strands. This mysterious process allows you to create new cells and tissues in your body throughout your lifetime, as well as to pass your "immortal" genes onto your children.

15. Imagine the 100 trillion cells in your body, each following a specific purpose, and the sum of this mysterious intelligence is for one reason only—your life.

16. Now walk back up the staircase and, as you reach the top, open your eyes.

This visualization could be ten pages long and still there would be more wondrous micro-events for you to imagine in your body. The point is easily made that you can have confidence in the healing power of your bodymind.

Congratulations! You have just completed a powerful set of exercises that offer you healing in many areas of your life. Sometimes the healing occurs emotionally or mentally. Sometimes it occurs in our relationships with others. Sometimes it is spiritual. Sometimes the body heals and sometimes it does not. When it does not, then illness has served to motivate us to heal on other levels.

You have seen that it is from the edge that life can be known. You have become friendly with fear and know that fear is a marker of the edge where the opportunity for growth exists. You have transformed resistance into acceptance, for it is a law of the universe that what you resist persists. You have taken back your personal power from those that you gave it to when you blamed them for your problems. You have recognized the power of thought and emotion to create personal experience. You have reclaimed your body wisdom as a messenger to guide you in your life. You have considered the healing power of emotional expression. You have considered your gift to the world and the healing power of passion. You have taken responsibility for the experiences in your life.

In short, you have taken steps toward Mastery. A Master has gratitude for all that life offers, for the Master knows that he or she called it forth. You can now understood what one Master, Confucius, meant when he said: "Everything has beauty, but not everybody sees it."

God bless you in your journey.

# INDEX

# About the Author

### Ronald L. Peters, M.D., M.P.H.

Since graduation from UCLA School of Medicine in 1970, Dr. Peters has practiced family medicine, emergency medicine, and returned to UCLA for a Masters in Public Health. He has practiced holistic family medicine for the past 20 years, paying careful attention to origins of disease within the mind. He has attended many psychological seminars and workshops and engaged in extensive spiritual training and practice around the world. He has taught the material presented in *Edgework* in seminars in Los Angeles, CA and Ashland, OR.

2675249R00151

Made in the USA
San Bernardino, CA
21 May 2013